W9-CLG-153

The Learning Curve

IE Business Publishing

IE Business Publishing and Palgrave Macmillan have launched a collection of high-quality books in the areas of Business and Management, Economics and Finance. This important series is characterized by innovative ideas and theories, entrepreneurial perspectives, academic rigor and practical approaches which will make these books invaluable to the business professional, scholar and student alike.

IE Business School is one of the world's leading institutions dedicated to educating business leaders. Palgrave Macmillan, part of Macmillan Group, has been serving the learning and professional sector for more than 160 years.

The series, put together by these eminent international partners, will enable executives, students, management scholars and professionals worldwide to have access to the most valuable information and critical new arguments and theories in the fields of Business and Management, Economics and Finance from the leading experts at IE Business School.

The Learning Curve

How Business Schools Are Re-inventing Education

Santiago Iñiguez de Onzoño
Dean of IE Business School
President of IE University

palgrave
macmillan

First published 2011 by
PALGRAVE MACMILLAN

Palgrave Macmillan in the UK is an imprint of Macmillan Publishers Limited,
registered in England, company number 785998, of Houndmills, Basingstoke,
Hampshire RG21 6XS.

Palgrave Macmillan in the US is a division of St Martin's Press LLC,
175 Fifth Avenue, New York, NY 10010.

Palgrave Macmillan is the global academic imprint of the above companies
and has companies and representatives throughout the world.

Palgrave® and Macmillan® are registered trademarks in the United States,
the United Kingdom, Europe and other countries.

ISBN: 978–0–230–28023–6

This book is printed on paper suitable for recycling and made from fully
managed and sustained forest sources. Logging, pulping and manufacturing
processes are expected to conform to the environmental regulations of the
country of origin.

A catalogue record for this book is available from the British Library.

A catalog record for this book is available from the Library of Congress.

10 9 8 7 6 5 4 3 2 1
20 19 18 17 16 15 14 13 12 11

Printed and bound in Great Britain by
CPI Antony Rowe, Chippenham and Eastbourne

To *Diego del Alcazar Silvela*
Marquis of la Romana
Founder of IE Business School

Contents

LIST OF TABLES

List of Figures

Acknowledgments

Given the short span of human lives for learning, for achievement, and for joy, many people would like to live at least two lives. Those of us who work in education can say that we live twice: we live our own lives; and we live out the dreams of the students with whom we have worked and whom we have known, and whose development we have contributed to.

I consider myself enormously fortunate to have been able to dedicate my life to teaching, a vocation I identified with while still very young, when I would give classes to my uncomplaining younger siblings; it's a passion that has only increased over the years.

Academic life is tremendously satisfying, but also demanding, as well as highly competitive. After completing my MBA at the IE Business School some 20 years ago, I was lucky enough to receive an offer to work there. My circle of good fortune was completed when I began working alongside Diego del Alcázar Silvela, the Founder and President of IE Business School. He has been my teacher, mentor, and personal and professional reference for the past 17 years. It is to him that I would like to offer my thanks first: he is the intellectual and spiritual source of inspiration for this book. His strategic vision and energy have made the IE Business School what it is today: a business school known and respected around the world for its achievements in business research and teaching. Diego has shown us new ways to dream.

As head of external relations, and then as Dean of the IE Business School, I have been privileged to work with the impressive team of professionals who comprise the board of directors at IE. I would like to thank Javier Solano, whose work as Financial Vice-President of IE allows me to sleep at nights. I would also like to thank Alfonso Martínez de Irujo, Gonzalo Garland, Rafael Puyol, Margarita Alonso, Celia de Anca, Miguel Sagüés, and Salvador Aragón. I owe a debt of gratitude for their support, their ideas, and for putting up with me during our weekly meetings. In memory of absent friends, I would like to remember José Mario Álvarez de Novales, who was also a member of the board, and the stamp of whose intellect and energy remains both on the institution and on those of us who worked with him.

As Dean, I have been privileged to walk on the shoulders of giants, specifically those of my close collaborators. I can count on the support of an unparalleled talented team, whose job is to implement our mission in education. I learn something new from them every day, and have discussed with them many of the ideas and proposals outlined in this book: Salvador Carmona; David Bach; Joaquín Garralda; José María de Areilza; Manuel Fernández de Villalta; Arantza de Areilza; Adriana Angel; Isabel Armada; Luis Solís; Marco Trombetta; Samuel Martín Barbero; Martha Thorne; Javier Quiintana; Antonio de Castro; and Antonio Montes. I am very proud to work with them, and cannot thank them enough for their professionalism and friendship.

Over the years, I have taken part in myriad initiatives and projects aimed at developing management education and business schools around the world. I have benefitted from the exchange of ideas in conferences and meetings with other deans, teachers, business leaders, opinion makers, and the heads of a wide range of institutions, but I would particularly like to thank, in alphabetical order, Gabriela Alvarado, Paz Alvarez, Kofi Appenteng, Richard Barker, Fernando Barnuevo, Fernando Bartolomé, Jerónimo Betegón, George Bickerstaffe, Xiang Bing, Frank Brown, John A. Byrne, Jordi Canals, Federico Castellanos, Bernadette Conraths, Eric Cornuel, Sue Cox, Rolf Cremer, Carlos Cruz, Enrique Dans, Fernando D'Alessio, Emerson de Almeida, Teppo Felin, John Fernandes, Ernesto Gore, Mauro Guillén, Maria Lorena Gutiérrez, William Haseltine, Louis Lavelle, Dan Le Clair, Peter Lorange, Xiongwen Lu, Colin Mayer, Carmelo Mazza, Francesco Mazzuca, Arnoud de Meyer, David Parcerisas, Kai Peters, Jeanette Purcell, Nunzio Quacquarelli, Paolo Quattrone, Michael Osbaldeston, Robert Owen, Bernard Ramanantsoa, Carlos Ramos, Quique Rodríguez, Juan Santaló, Alfons Sauquet, Gordon Shenton, Blair Sheppard, Cristina Simón, Jonathan Slack, Ted Snyder, Matt Symonds, Pierre Tapie, Howard Thomas, Marianne Toldalagi, Margaret Touborg, Jerry Trapnell, Julio Urgel, Arpad Von Lazar, Zhong-Ming Wang, Blake Winschell, Matthew Wood, Zhihong Yi, and Lin Zhou.

Six years ago, Paul Danos, Della Bradshaw, and myself created Deanstalk, a management education blog, which has turned out to be an important forum for discussing ideas about business education. I am grateful to both of them for participating in an experience that was then disruptive and uncertain. Many of the ideas outlined in this book have been developed and tested in the blog, and I have benefitted enormously from the exchange with those who read and commented on it. I have also been lucky enough to continue working with Paul Danos through the countless Dean's Roundtables he has organized around the world with the goal of sharing best practices in business schools. These roundtables have given me a deeper, wider vision of management education, as well as allowing me to form a lasting friendship with Paul, with whom I shall continue to organize workshops in the future.

During the past years, I have counted on the continuous support of Bryan O'Loughlin, an invaluable administrative and academic collaborator, and I would like to thank him for going the "extra-mile" on many occasions and helping in molding and shaping my ideas, including with this book.

I feel particularly indebted to the members of the Communication team at IE, led by Jose Félix Valdivieso. They have assisted me over the years in identifying and refining the ideas and messages conveyed in my public addresses. Many thanks to Maite Brualla, Igor Galo, Geoffroy Gerard, Yolanda Regodón, Juncal Sánchez Mendieta, Kerry Parke, and Verónica Urbiola. Let me also mention Maripé Menéndez, Ulla Karpinnen, and Michael Aldous, who preceded them in said department.

I would also like to offer a special thanks to Des Dearlove and Stuart Crainer for their support in editing this book, as well as their proposals for ways to make the ideas outlined in the book more accessible to a wider public. I would also like to thank Palgrave Macmillan's Stephen Rutt for his support in bringing to fruition the original idea of this book, and for his constant encouragement. Let me also thank Eleanor Davey-Corrigan, Cynthia Fernandez, and Vidhya Jayaprakash for their assistance during the editorial process.

Finally, Nick Lyne, Juan Ramón Zamorano, and Igone Jayo have been an inestimable help in organizing the content of the book, providing much needed encouragement on a daily basis to complete the task at hand.

The desire to ignite the flame of learning has inspired this book; it is a desire I share with the many people I have been fortunate enough to meet in business schools around the world, and in particular my colleagues at the IE Business School. And with them our students, who, when all is said and done, will inherit and carry the flame that will transform our global society.

PREFACE

Higher education is one of the most fascinating and fastest growing industries in the world. Today, it is experiencing change on a scale unprecedented since the founding of the first universities. Leading the way in higher education is a new type of educational provider – the business school. Since their inception in the US in the early part of the twentieth century, business schools have blazed a new educational trail.

More recent – and even more pioneering – are the European business schools. These emerged after World War II with their one-year MBA model and their emphasis on practical vocational learning rather than on academic theory. On the basis of the experience of business schools, and his unique experiences at one of Europe's leading players, Santiago Iñiguez de Onzoño addresses some of the major challenges that higher education faces today.

These include: selecting successful strategies to compete in a global context; defining the role of universities in the modern knowledge value chain; designing the ideal structure and profile of faculty bodies; and developing multiple forms of intelligence and interpersonal skills in students.

The Learning Curve describes how educational institutions can act as effective bridges between the *Academia* – in Greek, the place where knowledge was generated and delivered – and the *Agora* – the professional world where knowledge is applied. Here, business schools provide a compelling case and an important reference point for all in higher education, given their successful development in recent decades.

The purpose of this book is not only to describe the experience of business schools to date but also to anticipate the shape of things to come – both in terms of business education and of higher education in general. The author shares both his in-depth knowledge of what it takes to build a world-class educational provider and his vision of higher education for the future.

Illustrated with fascinating examples drawn from interviews with some of the most influential figures in business education around the world, Iñiguez's book delivers a unique perspective and valuable insights on what it takes to create an organization capable of delivering a world-class higher education. It offers a compelling route map for leaders in education and beyond in the twenty-first century.

FOREWORD

Dean Santiago Iñiguez and I have partnered on a series of Dean's round-tables in many regions of the world, touching on many of the topics he covers in depth in this book. Being long-time deans of very different schools (his is urban and with a whole array of programs and locations and mine is smaller, rural, and highly focused on the full-time MBA), we often diverge in opinions about the way forward for management education, but I have come to admire his knowledge of the worldwide management education industry and, above all, his sincere concern for his students and of the role higher education plays in advancing all societies.

In this book, Dean Iñiguez offers a sweeping and comprehensive view of management education, its history, its present, and its future. He traces the historical milestones that have led to today's complex, worldwide management education industry and gives the reader the benefit of his extraordinary insights that form his vision for the future.

This is not a dispassionate history or a purely demographic or economic analysis, but a delineation of a deeply felt philosophy based on a keen interest and long experience. With an eye on key fundamental factors, he analyzes many of the most important forces such as the importance of management itself, the massive influences of technology and globalization, the crucial roles of research and teaching, among many others. He weaves all these factors into a comprehensive and consistent view.

The organization of this book is based on a deep understanding of management education and indeed of higher education in general that is rooted in Dean Iñiguez's vast knowledge of the history and philosophical base of academia. He blends this classic understanding of education with the lessons he has learned from his intense practical experience in the development of his school, IE, which he has led through unprecedented change and growth. He believes that a school such as his gets stronger as it responds to the challenges of the marketplace and the practical demands of students. The necessity to be responsive to demand, without the cushion of the huge endowments and alumni giving with which some of the other great Western schools are blessed, has in his view led to much innovation and efficiency in many of the European and Asia schools.

One of the major themes of this book is the interplay between academia and the professional world. While honoring the concept of the researcher-teacher, which is the hallmark of many of the top USA-based programs, Dean Iñiguez delves deeply into the more blended approach which he espouses and which is becoming prevalent in many parts of the world where business education is seen to be the nexus of ideas from practice and research, without a clear dominance by either. His is a world where the professor is a teacher first, and the weight of research and practical experience in that teaching depends on each situation. That contrast with the classic USA model where research professors are seen as the prime teaching asset, and research itself fosters expertise about the world of practice.

Dean Iñiguez has a global and forward-looking view, and he gives the reader the benefit of his extensive experience in all parts of the world where he has interacted with innumerable people who are involved in higher education. He predicts the future movements of the tectonic plates of business education, and gives how such changes relate to the ultimate goal of educating the virtuous manager. He predicts that the best business education will be more and more multidisciplinary, with the most successful practitioners coming from schools that help mold students into well-rounded and more virtuous human beings.

This book is a must read for those who want a succinct analysis of what created the vast current world of management education and who want views and opinions from a key global participant in that world who does not march to the conventional drummer.

PAUL DANOS
Dean
The Laurence F. Whittemore Professor
Tuck School of Business at Dartmouth

About the Author

Santiago Iñiguez de Onzoño studied at Madrid's Complutense University and Oxford University. He is a Doctor of Law and holds an MBA from IE Business School, where he has been Dean since 2004. He is also President of IE University since 2010.

Iñiguez has spent 20 years working in higher education. He has worked as a management consultant and has played an active role in the field of quality control and the development of management education in Europe. He is a member of the boards of the EFMD (European Foundation for Management Development); the International Advisory Board of AMBA (Association of MBAs, UK); the European Advisory Council of AACSB International (Association to Advance Collegiate Schools of Business); and the Awarding Body of EQUIS (European Quality System). He is the Chairman of GFME (Global Foundation for Management Education), and he serves on the boards of CENTRUM (Universidad Católica, Perú); Antai Business School (Jiao Tong University, China); and Renmin University Business School (China). He has been described by the *Financial Times* as: "One of the most significant figures in promoting European business schools internationally." Iñiguez is also President of the IE Fund in the United States.

Iñiguez is co-editor of a blog focused on management education (www. deanstalk.net). He has published a number of articles and case studies on business management and is the author and co-author of articles on moral philosophy and management education. As a professor of strategic management and expert in management education, Iñiguez regularly speaks at international conferences and frequently contributes to journals and media worldwide.

INTRODUCTION

Around the world, the need to compete in a global economy is transforming higher education. The challenge facing every nation is to improve access to universities that use modern learning tools and technologies without compromising quality and to improve relevance without losing rigor. In short, the challenge is to move from a system geared to educating a small elite to creating an entire population of knowledge workers.

There are two clear implications of this change. The first is that education itself has become a key source of individual economic value (this was always implicit but is now explicit in a global economy). The second is that this fosters more competition among educational institutions to deliver competitive advantages at a global scale.

What a growing number of higher education providers – from stand-alone business schools to traditional universities – are grappling with is a challenge that is central to economic and social progress in the twenty-first century: How do you create world-class educational institutions that are academically rigorous *and* vocationally relevant? How do you combine the best of the traditional *Academy* with the speed and technological sophistication of the modern *Market* – to meet the needs of both?

I believe one possible answer is provided by the experience of the world's leading business schools. Over the past century, business schools have come from nowhere to establish themselves. Business education is now a truly global enterprise and one that, I firmly and passionately believe, offers important lessons and inspirations for higher education as a whole. Business schools are not perfect, but they have encountered and often overcome many of the challenges now facing organizations and leaders in higher education.

Yet, despite the huge success of business schools in the twentieth century, the financial crisis led some observers to question their credentials. Many social analysts and opinion makers blame business schools and MBAs for the global economic crisis. Indeed, management is questioned as never before.

I would counter that management can be one of the noblest professions that young students can embrace. Management and entrepreneurship create growth, wealth, and development in society, provide jobs, catalyze innovation, and improve living conditions. Furthermore, good management is one of the best antidotes to bad international politics, since it promotes convergence and understanding among civilizations.

The next learning curve

My journey has been fascinating and, truth be told, often frustrating in equal measure. Common with other business schools, my institution, IE Business School, has been a trailblazer. Despite – or perhaps because of – the regular questioning of why they exist and how they deliver education, business schools have made a big impact on higher education in recent decades and have contributed hugely to the convergence of university studies. This book considers the growing influence of business schools as an educational model. It also examines how other convergence initiatives, such as the Bologna Process – which seeks to harmonize higher education systems across Europe – are shaping a flatter world of knowledge.

It is important to put this in a historical context. In ancient Greece, *Agora* and *Academia* meant, respectively, the place for doing business and the place for educational activities. Interestingly, in ancient Athens, the Agora and the Academia were located close to each other on the slopes of the Acropolis. This proximity facilitated interaction between academics and business people, as evidenced in many intellectual contributions of that time, such as Plato's *Dialogues*. For the ancient Greeks, there was no separation between thinkers and managers; rather they belonged to the same genre: educators believed that their scholarly work should deal with the problems of political and social life.

But that changed in the Middle Ages. At that time, monasteries became the exclusive loci for developing and transmitting knowledge – and were reservoirs of all existing knowledge. Monasteries, though, were closed places, separated from the rest of the community, and monks socialized only occasionally with their fellow citizens. This influenced the way knowledge was then conceived and developed, normally as a diverse activity from mundane practices and, at most, only linked to the reduced number of activities developed at the monastery's pharmacy or garden. This resulted in a progressive separation between the generation and the application of knowledge.

Monasteries were the predecessors of modern universities, and many aspects of the former traditions, practices, and culture are still embedded in today's higher education institutions. In fact, one of the common criticisms addressed at universities is that they are detached from the real world, that they focus mainly on academic rigor but show disdain towards professional relevance. Is it time to bring the Agora and the Academia closer? I believe it is, and business schools provide thought-provoking lessons on how this gap might be bridged.

The changing nature of knowledge

Business schools are fundamentally practical places. Since the activities of business schools focus not on a speculative but on a clinical subject – i.e., management – a substantial proportion of academic research should deal with real business problems, jointly with top managers. This does not appear, to me at least, an especially contentious statement. In practice, however, some academics in business schools and elsewhere have sometimes neglected the practical relevance of their research.

This has to change. And it will change. The educational world is changing, and the rate of change will continue. Driving the new educational agenda are three trends: new technology; globalization; and changing demands on graduates.

The first and perhaps most obvious trend is the advent of new technologies. Today, no one can seriously dispute the impact of ICT (Information and Communications Technology) on the learning process. Surveys show that distance learning is thriving. Many business schools – over 80 per cent – that used to offer only face-to-face programs now run online courses.

Traditionally, distance learning was the domain of big education providers that played on scale, had a high volume of students, and based most of their offerings on self-learning modules. The development of new technologies and the entrance of schools that have a leading role in conventional classroom-based learning are not only altering the boundaries of this educational segment but also the very nature of the learning process.

Many people believe that online programs cannot entirely match the human experience and vividness of face-to-face education. In addition, online education is often associated with cheap, low-quality, and massive programs. Those intuitions are wrong. Indeed, good online programs are the closest experience to how many multinationals manage communication and decision making nowadays, and they may provide experiences as intense as in face-to-face offerings.

A plethora of new learning methodologies is also now coming of age, supported by new technologies ranging from the Internet to the latest video conferencing technologies. Today, for example, it is possible to replicate the classroom experience for people on different continents using the latest telepresence technologies. And this is just the start.

The second trend shaping education is globalization. Higher education has become a global industry and very few institutions have the resources to run their activities on an international scale without establishing alliances with foreign institutions. International partnerships have evolved from simple student exchange agreements to joint degree programs and sophisticated collaboration. Some business schools have gone a step further and opened greenhouse or satellite campuses abroad, following the model of related industries like consultancies and other professional services companies.

The evolution of international partnerships among business schools is already underway. A number of different strategies are available to cope with the challenge of globalization – ranging from traditional joint ventures to new multidimensional strategic alliances, which are more open and indefinite in time, with competitors joining forces in collaborative initiatives. There are also new species emerging in higher education, such as for-profit universities, multi-branch campuses, and online institutions.

The third trend driving the learning curve of the future is the changing demands placed on graduates. These new demands mirror the changing requirements of the working environment, but they also reflect broader changes in society. Today, young people have their own agenda for learning, which is equally demanding as their future employers. Young people expect more from their education than to simply have their heads filled with traditional knowledge. Increasingly, they want it to include new learning experiences, such as treks to new and exciting locations, as well as opportunities to be involved in hands-on work on life-enriching projects in the developing world and beyond.

In short, the students of tomorrow and their future employers expect a more rounded education than ever before. I believe this includes a more integrated approach that includes the humanities, such as art and history, in business degrees.

The Learning Curve describes this new world of education.

Part I examines the journey that business schools have been on, including their rise to prominence in the twentieth century. In Chapter 1, we consider the reasons for this, especially the growing recognition of the importance of management to all human affairs. But if Chapter 1 is a celebration of the arrival of business schools, Chapter 2 addresses their shortcomings – and especially the criticisms that have been leveled at them in the wake of the global financial crisis. Some of these criticisms are justified, while others are merely sniping. The question of whether management is – or should be – regarded as a profession akin to law or medicine is also dealt with here. Chapter 3 concludes Part I of the book with some practical suggestions for how we can develop better managers in the future.

Part II looks at the three major trends that are driving the changes in higher education – new technology, globalization, and changing demands of students. Chapter 4 examines the impact these trends are already having on the educational landscape in which business schools now operate. It includes a taxonomy of the different types of business education providers that are now competing – from traditional university business schools to corporate universities. Chapter 5 describes some of the exciting new learning technologies that are revolutionizing business schools and other parts of higher education, and looks forward to what those technologies might mean in the future. Chapter 6 looks at how globalization and the ease with which people now cross national borders are creating an international set of stakeholders for business schools and other educational institutions, and the implications in terms of international alliances and satellite campuses. Chapter 7 considers how the spread of business education around the world is leading to new demands – for both internationally recognized standards and local knowledge generation. New educational hubs in places such as India, and China as well as the Middle East, for example, are evidence not only of the globalization of business education, but also of the need for locally generated knowledge to provide the context for learning in these places.

Part III looks to the future and the challenges of teaching tomorrow's students. Chapter 8 examines the purpose of business schools in the coming years and argues that they must reinvent themselves to remain relevant. Chapter 9 celebrates the changing nature and increasing diversity of the student population – and their rising aspirations. As the expectation of students increase, so does the need to provide the very best teachers. Understanding the aspirations of the students of tomorrow also means reassessing the qualifications and experience of those who teach them. Chapter 10, then, examines who should be the faculty of tomorrow. Finally, in the Epilogue, the threads of the book are pulled together to argue that business schools need to embrace new ways of learning – especially the teaching of the humanities and the classical notion of virtues.

The Learning Curve describes the world in which business schools currently operate and tries to make sense of this changing educational landscape. It is not a manifesto – though I believe passionately in many of the issues. Nor is it a lament about the lost glories of the past. Instead, it is, I hope, filled with hope and excitement. Learning has never been more central or important to our lives. This means that the stakes for all involved in education are commensurately higher. We cannot afford to fail.

PART I

The trailblazers

CHAPTER 1

Why management matters

One of the most compelling and relevant business protagonists in the world of fiction is Monroe Stahr from F. Scott Fitzgerald's *The Love of the Last Tycoon* published in 1941.[1] Stahr is a character that was in my mind as I wrote this book. Unlike the complacent characters portrayed in most CEO autobiographies, Monroe Stahr feels like the genuine article – flaws and all. A successful movie producer, and still relatively young, Stahr is an exemplary boss. Utterly devoted to his job and caring towards his subordinates, he is in total control of his company – despite the many conspiracies he faces – and an expert in his business.

When the novel was written, business schools were still in their infancy. Stahr's business education was "founded on nothing more than a night-school course in stenography."[2]

Stahr is portrayed as a paternalistic manager who won't let down anybody working for him. He encourages innovation and boosts the careers not only of ambitious, bright youngsters but also of seniors who show their commitment to the company. When Ridingwood, an aging movie director, goes off the rails in the middle of shooting, Stahr quietly sends him off for therapy and pays for his treatment. When Stahr's best cameraman begins to lose his sight, he sends him to an ophthalmologist, suppresses the rumors about his eyesight, and then invites him back to work.

Stahr is certainly a boss who looks after his team. The novel also reveals that he "looked spiritual, but at times he was a fighter."[3] On one occasion, he commissions parallel teams of screenwriters to work on the same story to see which team can come up with the best result, even mixing the different contributions. Few conscientious writers would put up with this, but what is wrong with Stahr's approach if it drives writers to produce their best work, thereby boosting morale? In reality, many companies do set up parallel teams to figure out new ideas; in the same way, managers often try to get the best price by asking for offers from different suppliers.

Another of Stahr's characteristics, common to other great managers, is his enthusiasm and selfless dedication to work: "He was born sleep-less without a talent for rest or the desire for it,"[4] says a fellow character. But, despite his many managerial skills and his intuition for good business opportunities, Stahr seems unable to manage a healthy balance between his professional and personal lives. At one point, when asked whether he is going to stay in the studio after a long day at work, he replies: "Yes ... I've got no place to go in the evenings so I just work."[5] He has a property in the Malibu hills that remains little more than a wooden structure on stilts years after it was begun. Aware that he should have dedicated more time to finding the love of his life, Stahr eventually decides to marry Cecile, the daughter of another producer: a marriage of convenience rather than true love.

Stahr is a literary compendium of the qualities required by a successful manager: strategic vision coupled with an instinct for business opportunities; a voracious appetite for work; leadership qualities; a profound knowledge of their sector; and the ability to try out new ideas, while retaining day-to-day control. The fact that Scott Fitzgerald was not an expert in management is, in this case, an advantage, freeing his protagonist of the usual clichés that characterize the biographies of business leaders. Instead, we are face-to-face with a human being with all his virtues and defects, who is neither an angel nor a demon, somebody who gets things right, but also makes mistakes: an accessible character from whom we can learn.

The Stahrs of the future

The character of Monroe Stahr stuck in my mind. He is an exemplar of the power of management and the need for management. He also led me to wonder about the role of education in creating the Stahrs of today and tomorrow.

This was not simply idle contemplation. The need to consider what managers and business leaders do and how they contribute to society as individuals and as members of organizations is acute. From this, it follows that the need to think about how best to develop managers and business leaders is also of paramount importance. Developing future leaders does not just involve a decorous debate; it is vital to the future of economies, societies, and civilizations.

Why? Well, most pressingly, the financial crisis that started in 2007 continues to reverberate around the globe. Its effects will be felt for many years to come. An ocean of ink has already been devoted to examining the factors that caused it. That is as it should be. But, in addition to learning from the mistakes of the past, we need to move forward. Business schools have their share of lessons to learn. They also have an important part to play in rebuilding the reputation and efficacy of business.

What the world needs now is good entrepreneurs, good managers, and good business leaders. I believe that the best remedy for the world's ills, the best antidote to intolerance or the clash of cultures or poor foreign policies, is to develop good managers, create new businesses, innovate, and generate value and wealth at all levels of society.

The rise of management

First, let us consider the evolution of management. Management is timeless and universal. People have always managed. But it was only during the past 100 years or so that management gained recognition.

Management has changed from an unspoken, informal, *ad hoc* activity into one that is routinely analyzed and commented on from every angle possible. Management has emerged from the shadows to be recognized as one of the driving forces of economic and personal life. No organization, no activity now appears beyond the scope or ambition of management.

While management came of age during the twentieth century, it would be foolish to suggest that it did not exist prior to 1900. Management has been practiced since the very dawn of civilization. But only during the past one hundred years has it been recognized, analyzed, monitored, taught, and formalized.

Over this period, management has often been narrowly defined as relating to business. As the great management thinker Peter Drucker pointed out, this does management a disservice. Management applies to more than the world of business. Indeed, Drucker argues that the creation of "city managers" in the early 1900s was one of the first occasions when management, as it is now understood, was applied to a particular job. Management is as appropriate in local government as it is in a corporation. Management is as at home in politics and government as it is in healthcare and hospitals. It is as useful in sports – coaching is just one aspect of management – as it is on the factory floor.

Management is all-pervasive. "There are, of course, differences in management between different organizations – mission defines strategy, after all, and strategy defines structure. But the differences between managing a chain of retail stores and managing a Roman Catholic diocese are amazingly fewer than either retail executives or bishops realize," Drucker observed.

The differences are mainly in application rather than in principles. The executives of all these organizations spend, for instance, about the same amount of their time on people problems – and the people problems are almost always the same.

So whether you are managing a software company, a hospital, a bank or a Boy Scout organization, the differences apply to only about 10 per cent of your work. This 10 per cent is determined by the organization's specific mission, its specific culture, its specific history and its specific vocabulary. The rest is pretty much interchangeable.[6]

The recognition of management as a distinctive discipline has been hard earned. Despite the executive superstars with their superstar salaries, the power and influence clearly enjoyed by managers, and the fact that a huge percentage of the working population work in managerial jobs, management is rarely regarded as the noblest of callings – or a calling at all. Management is something people fall into: a job in the customer service department leads to marketing and, before you know it, you are vice-president and people are asking you the meaning of management.

"Corporations and managers suffer from a profound social ambivalence," leading theorists Sumantra Ghoshal, Christopher Bartlett, and Peter Moran have observed. "Hero-worshipped by the few, they are deeply distrusted by the many. In popular mythology, the corporate manager is Gordon Gecko, the financier who preaches the gospel of greed in Hollywood's *Wall Street*. Corporations are 'job killers'."[7]

Management has had a bad press. The attraction – and the trouble – is that management is multi-faceted. Pinning it down is problematic. It is marketing. It is strategy. It is inspiring people. It is budgeting. It is organizing projects and commitments. It is a complex, highly personal, and now truly global, calling. It also has a huge impact on people's lives.

The age of business

In a 1993 article about the search for the next CEO of IBM, the *Financial Times* invented a job advertisement that read: "Executive willing to take on the most challenging management job in the World. Must be a natural leader, able to make tough decisions, boost the morale of 300,000 employees and win the confidence of millions of shareholders and customers worldwide. Knowledge of 'computer-speak' helpful. Salary high and negotiable. Benefits include worldwide instant recognition. Wearers of white shirts need not apply."[8]

I often use this fictitious advertisement in my course on strategic management to explain that the ideal profile of the CEO of an international corporation has more to do with their political skills than with their technical ability. To inspire the confidence of millions of shareholders, or to run an organization with hundreds of thousands of employees with a budget exceeding that of many nations, is comparable to or indeed more difficult than the work of many senior politicians. As the advertisement suggests, a CEO is as visible as many world leaders, and in the same way, his or her decisions and actions are subject to the same public scrutiny.

In October 2010, a newspaper in Mexico City ran a story on the creation of a museum dedicated to business leaders in the capital. This unique institution intends to house photographs, films, and other documentary material, along with interactive exhibits that will tell the story of Mexico's most illustrious entrepreneurs, among them Carlos Slim Helú (one of the world's richest men) and Eugenio Garza Sada (the man who set up the Tec de Monterrey, Mexico's most prestigious university).[9] The aim of the museum is to encourage a new generation of entrepreneurs through example.

Museums are the temples that society erects to celebrate the arts, the sciences, technology, or the knowledge of earlier cultures and civilizations. There are museums dedicated to just about every human or natural activity, yet until the Mexicans came along, there wasn't one dedicated to business leaders. Neither are there any Nobel-style prizes for business leaders recognizing their work in creating wealth or running organizations. There may be prizes rewarding their philanthropy and commitment to the arts, but not for their contribution to business and management. How come?

The phenomenon of the business magnate, as we understand it, is relatively new. But, more broadly, the concept of management, in terms of organizing resources and people towards carrying out a productive activity, can be applied to many projects over the course of history. The very universality of management may count against it being taken seriously.

Entrepreneurs are similarly neglected. Research into their function and economic impact as individuals is relatively recent. Joseph Schumpeter was probably the first economist to put entrepreneurs under the microscope. His theory of creative destruction highlighted the entrepreneur's role in stimulating investment and innovation.

Professionalizing management

The development of management and the elevation of business as a discipline led to the creation and development of organizations to train and develop managers and business leaders: business schools. It is when business schools appeared in the first half of the twentieth century that widespread study of the entrepreneur as an individual, as the driver of economic change, first emerged. Business schools began to combine the study of economic theory and management with an analysis of the function of management and the relations between managers and the rest of a company's stakeholders.

The first business schools were set up to meet the needs of large corporations, particularly those of the railroad industry. *A Delicate Experiment: The Harvard Business School, 1908–1945* identifies two antecedents that directly influenced the decision to set up Harvard Business School (HBS): The first is former student George Leighton's proposal, published in *Harvard Graduate's Magazine*, that railroad management should be recognized as a science, and that those at the highest level of railroad management required a very varied range of skills. Leighton wrote that the profession of manager "is one of the most versatile of all professions."[10]

The second prosaic antecedent that led to the creation of HBS comes from Charles Eliot, the then president of Harvard University. Writing in *Atlantic Monthly*, he poignantly asked: "What can I do with my boy? I want to give him a practical education that will prepare him better than I was prepared to follow my business or any other active callings."[11]

In the case of Wharton Business School, several anecdotes about Joseph Wharton, the main founding donor to the school that bears his name, illustrate that among his fundamental objectives were "to teach economic protection of American interests' globally, the same issues he had labored for in Washington over protective tariffs."[12]

The objective of business schools remains a topic of justifiable and useful debate. Likewise, the objectives of management are similarly and endlessly debated. However, some respected scholars, led by Rakesh Khurana, a professor at Harvard Business School, ask whether management should be regarded as a profession in a collegial sense, that is, whether management studies should lead to getting a license to operate as a manager that should be revalidated periodically, in a similar way to what happens in some other regulated professions. Would this professionalization help managers to be better prepared to face crises and to behave ethically?

I think that management as a profession could be considered synonymous to a job, but not in the strict, regulated, and collegial way proposed by Khurana. Let's look at some of the arguments in favor and against.

Khurana argues that university-based business schools, and in particular, HBS, were set up with the objective of institutionalizing the profession of manager, and he defines the concept of a profession as, "comprised, among other things, of a social contract between occupations deemed 'professions', and society at large, as well as a certain set of relations among professional schools, the occupational groups for which they serve as authoritative communities, and society."[13] Business schools were thus intended not just to prepare students for careers in management but also to serve as major vehicles of an effort to transform management from an incipient occupation in search of legitimacy to a bona fide profession.

Khurana charts the different stages of the evolution of business schools, principally in the US, along with the accompanying challenges and changes in direction. He concludes that all professionalism has been lost, and with it managers' legitimacy. In Khurana's opinion, the university-based business school, "an institution created to legitimate management, has become, through the abandonment of the professionalization project that provided its initial direction and impetus, a vehicle for the delegitimizing of management."[14]

Khurana argues that we have moved from the early stages of "managerial capitalism" to "investor capitalism." In this latest stage, the guiding principle is to maximize shareholder value to the detriment of other stakeholders in the company: "The image of the ideal executive was transformed from one of a steady, reliable caretaker of the corporation and its many constituencies to that of the swashbuckling, iconoclastic champion of 'shareholder value'."[15]

To counter this, Khurana and Harvard Business School Dean, Nitin Nohria, argue that all MBA graduates should submit to an examination with the aim of establishing that all graduates understand the norms and standards of the management community, and in return for which they would be given a license as a Certified Business Professional. This license in turn which would have to be renewed periodically.[16]

However, I believe that this attempt misses the real essence of what management is. To illustrate my point, I will refer to the guilds, one of the most interesting social phenomena that appeared during Europe's Middle Ages, the origins of our modern trades and professions. The expansion of the city and the spread of a money-driven economy from one based on barter saw the guilds' stature grow over the course of the thirteenth century. Among the time-honored professions that developed into guilds during this epoch were jewelers, carpenters, blacksmiths, and glaziers. Many guilds were established on the basis of a letter of patent or a concession by the local ruler, in exchange for which the guilds agreed to pay the said ruler taxes and to bear arms on his behalf in times of conflict.

Germany's *zünfte*, the *métiers* in France, the craft guilds in England, or Spain's *gremios* were all variations of this model of association, out of which vocational studies would eventually emerge, and characterized by long apprenticeships under the supervision of master craftsmen. The guilds were also the forerunners of the trade unions, providing their members with a rudimentary health insurance in case of illness, and in some cases an old-age-pension. The guilds also became fiercely guarded repositories of know-how accessible only to members; equally, the guilds laid out the first career structures and established specialist niches in their particular professions.

Over time, the guilds disappeared or adapted to the needs of the market economy, giving way to chambers of commerce, professional associations – such as those of doctors, architects, or engineers – and to more sophisticated, increasingly open, trade bodies. Nevertheless, some modern-day professional organizations, such as the bar associations, retain something of the guild, although many of their privileges are now endangered by supranational legislation such as the European Union's 2006 *Services Directive*[17] that aims to create a single market for services, eliminating cross-border barriers in the process.

In a world where a growing number of professional services can now be bought and sold widely via the Internet, legal or corporate obstacles to services rendered beyond a country's border is nothing less than protectionism and a limit to competition.

Historically, management has never attained the status of a formal profession, in the sense of setting up a guild or association by managers. In large part, the reason there are no managers' organizations – apart from chambers of commerce or sector networks – is due to the flexibility and presence of management throughout such a wide range of activities, its all-pervasive nature, as explained before. Would it really make much sense for the head of a hospital's surgery department, the partner-director of a law firm, the founder of a high-tech start-up company, and the CEO of a consumer products manufacturer to create their own guild? They are all managers, and it may be that some of them have MBAs, but their shared professional interests would not extend much beyond ideas on how best to manage a budget or to motivate their workforce. In all likelihood, they are going to be more interested in learning all there is to know about their respective professions – medicine, architecture, law – and applying these techniques, tools, and ideas on management within the framework of these professions.

Management is to be found in just about every area of our society. Looked at in detail, all forms of work reveal the presence of some kind of management. As with design, we become aware of faults in the objects we use only when they don't work. In the same way, we realize that a professional activity is being badly run when we notice the absence of the basic principles of management, for example: human error during a medical procedure resulting in a wrong diagnosis or even death; or when an architect repeatedly goes over budget on a project, or fails to meet deadlines – sadly all too common among the field's *starchitects*.

The need for management in all activities has helped drive the growth of management studies, along with the appearance of so many new business schools and the decision by professionals from diverse fields to take an MBA. It has also prompted some sociologists to predict that business studies will form part of the syllabus of primary schools in the future, in the same way that literature and mathematics have up until now.

Nevertheless, returning to our point, the presence of management in so many areas makes it very difficult to meld the various executive fields into a single profession, one that stands out from the rest of the applied professions. In which case, what are the main arguments for turning management into a regulated profession like any other?

1. *The keeping out the under-qualified argument.* In many cases, professionalization has been introduced to prevent those without the necessary training and skills from practicing certain trades and careers. For example, in medicine, professionalization means that doctors have been trained sufficiently to carry out their job. But as experience shows, keeping out those who are not properly qualified doesn't mean that some patients won't seek the services of those providing alternative medicine anyway. It should also be said that the justification of maintaining professional standards has often been used to prevent professionals from other countries being accredited, typically on the basis that they have undertaken a different line of studies, or that they have not completed their training, or that the standards in the country in question do not match ours.

   For the purposes of our analysis, the main task here is to identify whom we would keep out of our professional association, and on what basis. I would say from the start that it is virtually impossible to determine who should be kept out of management. What about entrepreneurs, the most authentic representatives of management, men and women who, in the best sense of the word, are rule breakers? Do we foresee setting up formal accreditation procedures for entrepreneurs for joining the management profession? Would they be considered professionals only if their startups had proved to be a success over time, or would they be allowed in even if their businesses had failed? The answer to such questions is obvious: there is no point in professionalizing entrepreneurs.

Interestingly, almost all business schools these days say they want to develop entrepreneurs: trying to professionalize them would surely be the best way to frighten them off. Clearly, the argument of maintaining professional standards or keeping out the under-qualified would not justify professionalizing management.

2. *The necessary skills argument.* Closely linked to the above, this argument says that professionalizing management would guarantee that those in charge of organizations have the necessary skills to carry out their tasks. The tendency for multinationals to recruit MBAs indicates that business school graduates possess certain skills and that they have developed certain abilities that will increase their likelihood of being successful managers. But we find a number of respectable exceptions to this rule, notably in the form of successful business people who have had no formal education. That said, my main objection to the argument that managers must possess certain skills is that a qualification obtained in the past doesn't necessarily enable anybody to face the challenges of the future. Which is why business schools always insist that continuing the learning process throughout a management career is *sine qua non* for success, even for entrepreneurs.

   Management is a clinical profession practiced in a constantly changing environment. As with medicine, where doctors update their knowledge and their techniques constantly, managers should keep abreast of the latest business theories and concepts if they are to make their decisions on the basis of right criteria. The course contents of an MBA today are significantly different from those taught 20 years ago. MBA graduates should update their skills by taking short courses regularly, maybe every five years. It is only by guaranteeing that management professionals update their skills on a regular basis that we can really start to talk about management as a profession.

3. *The improving professional practices argument.* A popular one this, it lies at the heart of Khurana's proposals arguing that the professionalization of management would not only promote a more ethical approach to doing business, but would also result in better management practices. In effect this would be akin to managers taking an oath or making some kind of commitment to society, as is the case with other professions with an ethical code. Lawyers, for example, sign an ethics code when they join their respective bar associations. That said, in the case of bars, as with guilds, these ethical codes are based more on sticking to technical principles associated with a profession than on any wider-reaching values.

   For example, the New York State Bar Association's Rules of Professional Conduct[18] overwhelmingly focuses on the responsibilities of a lawyer to their client. In its preface covering the general responsibilities of lawyers, it is established that a lawyer "is a representative of clients and an officer of the legal system with a special responsibility for the quality of justice." That reference to "justice" needs to be understood more in the context of respecting the judicial system and procedural principles rather than as some kind of search for abstract or absolute justice. It is often said that lawyers are committed to their clients and the judicial system, but not to society. In any event, as mentioned, any authority that ethical codes might have, would depend in large measure on the extent to which their infraction could be punished.

Codes of conduct are to be found throughout the business world, even if management is not a regulated profession. The majority of chambers of commerce around the planet have ethics codes and mechanisms for expelling members who do not abide by them. A great many businesses, particularly multi-nationals, also have codes of conduct. In this sense, I believe that the eventual professionalization of management would not add much to the already existing process of self-regulation that has spread so rapidly and widely throughout the business world in recent years.

For their part, many business schools have codes of conduct that must be adhered to by those attending their MBA programs. As with the legal profession's definition of its commitment to justice, establishing the exact nature of a manager's responsibility beyond that of creating economic and social value, along with the use of reason to resolve moral dilemmas, would be a tantalizing and controversial exercise.

4. *The regulatory argument.* Finally, a less persuasive argument, but one implicit in the idea of professionalizing management, and certainly the protectionists' goal, would be to regulate the activity. The creation of associations or guilds for managers would involve granting licenses and authorization to practice their profession, and eventually the requirement of belonging to a specific association. Such a solution would be in nobody's interests, and furthermore, would be counterproductive in terms of creating value. That said, in the European context at least, professionalization is generally associated with setting up some kind of regulatory framework involving limits and restrictions.

We need to advance the process of making management one of the best and noblest of jobs. In my opinion, professionalization is not the way to do this and would be a step backward – something that many jobs and sectors have already consigned to history. Business schools are comparatively much younger than other educational institutions, but more innovative when it comes to facing challenges. It is through better research, better programs, and a faculty more focused on the needs of the real world, as stated in this book, that we would be better equipped to provide creative responses to the demands that society puts on managers.

Richard Barker, a professor at Judge Business School, is among the detractors of professionalizing management: "The difference between a business education and a professional education is stark and fundamental: The former may help individuals improve their performance, but it cannot certify their expertise. The role of the manager is inherently general, variable and indefinable."[19]

In sum, rather than look to the past for answers by reviving guilds, we need to come up with new ways to help advance creative and socially committed management in the future.

Beyond a profession

Peter Drucker owes his position as one of the fathers of modern management theory to his understanding of the importance of the individual, something that came to him when attending a class given by John Maynard Keynes at Cambridge University in 1934. "I suddenly realized that Keynes and all the brilliant economics students in the room were interested in the behavior of commodities, while I was interested in the behavior of people," said Drucker.[20]

In recent decades, business schools have further developed and refined theories on corporate governance, the role of the CEO, or the defining characteristics of business leadership, producing any number of biographies and profiles of the business world's great and good. Management is about people and this fundamentally flies in the face of hard and fast professional structures. The human element also has a profound effect on how and what is taught at business schools.

It is worth noting that the case study, pioneered at Harvard Business School as a way of teaching management, emphasizes the importance of personal factors in a manager's decision-making processes, recognizing that it is people who either create or destroy value, above and beyond immediate circumstances or factors. Most business schools teach early on that the understanding of the perspective of the individual, or groups of people, is as important as economic theory.

Yet if management is not a profession – and this is my view – then how should we understand it? And, more importantly, how can we codify and improve it as an educational experience? Of course, one answer is that we assume management to be synonymous with what is taught on MBA programs. This is patently not the case. Management goes beyond the boundaries of a formal degree and entails a constant effort to combine education and the practice of managerial virtues, along with experience. The reality is that it is very difficult to implement effective leadership without a proper business education. At the same time, reflective practice makes managers to climb down the curves of experience. Monroe Stahrs are now in short supply.

"Leadership and learning are indispensable to each," is a quote taken from the speech that John F. Kennedy prepared for delivery in Dallas the day he was assassinated in 1963.[21] There has been much debate as to whether leadership is an innate or an acquired ability, or a mixture of both. That is a debate I am not going to get into here. Future advances in biology will reveal whether there is a specific gene responsible for leadership.

In the meantime, education and training seem to be the best way to develop leadership and managerial skills. Now, it is almost inconceivable that a leader could reach the top without strenuous preparation or the dedication to maintain and improve his or her skills. Leaders seem increasingly eager to update their outlook on society and business, and to anticipate the future. It is part of their role. This in turn requires a constant striving for learning and adapting to permanent change, as most management educators will confirm. In my personal experience of dealing with CEOs, I am impressed by the importance they give to learning new management concepts, and how they procure relevant information for their decision making. Lifelong learning is their reality. I used to believe that managers, particularly those at the top, were people of action rather than reflection, but now I know that this is not the case. Indeed, if we look at the published diaries of top executives, we see long working days of up to 17 hours, filled almost solely with meetings. But what those diaries do not show is the time CEOs dedicate to preparing for those meetings and increasing their knowledge base.

I had the opportunity to talk with the famous financier and philanthropist George Soros. From our conversation, I became aware of just how much time he devotes to reading and dealing with academics. Soros may not be such a good example of the studiousness of managers since he was formerly an academic, but numerous studies show that successful managers spend a substantial part of their busy days reading and studying. Some studies suggest that one of the reasons senior executives read is to get relief from the solitude of being at the top. According to a quote attributed to C. S. Lewis: "We read to learn that we are not alone."[22]

Tycoons of tomorrow

Leadership is neither about chance or luck nor genes. Business school educators play an important role in helping potential leaders to rethink their basic assumptions and to broaden their vision of the future.

A multi-disciplinary education, and one not limited solely to management, is particularly important for business leaders if we bear in mind the large number of tasks they must address, and which are often more of a political nature than just purely technical. Leading multicultural teams, talking to a wide range of stakeholders, developing a strategic vision, and other management skills are carried out better if done on the basis of a humanistic education, by applying emotional intelligence and relationship skills, and are boosted by an understanding of how other cultures work.

Interestingly, Fitzgerald's description of Stahr confirms that while experience and a knowledge of the sector a CEO operates in are vital, generally speaking leaders carry out political rather than technical roles. "Tycoon," the word Fitzgerald uses to describe his character, comes from the Japanese word *taikun*, which literally means "great lord/prince" or "supreme commander."

The tycoons of tomorrow need educational and training support to meet their changing needs. But, before we get onto a blueprint for the future, let us look at some of the issues that have clouded this agenda as business schools have developed.

CHAPTER 2

Out of the crisis, confronting the critics

Thorstein Veblen, one of the shrewdest economists of the past century, invested a significant proportion of his wealth in the stock exchange shortly before the Great Depression, with disastrous consequences. The author of *The Theory of the Leisure Class* was saved from the experience of seeing the collapse of Wall Street on October 24, 1929, dying a few months before. Nevertheless, Veblen serves as a stark reminder that even the wisest heads can lose themselves to stock market fever.

In recent years, we have given ourselves up again to the fantasy of eternal prosperity. But, as history shows, untrammeled growth is always followed by a period of adjustment: the Book of Genesis tells the story of the Pharaoh of Egypt's dream of the seven lean cows and the seven fat cows, and how, in interpreting it, Joseph came up with one of the first theories of economic cycles. Among the most prevalent failings in recent years was the belief in the fantasy of unlimited growth, along with their inability to grasp the notion of financial risk, to be concerned at the lack of transparency in the financial system, or to see the failings of a bonus system that rewards short-term results over the long-term survival of the company.

Articles on the financial crisis tended to focus more on adjudicating responsibilities rather than on providing clear diagnoses of what happened or on prognoses of how to get out of the downturn. Many business stakeholders, including managers, bankers, regulators, rating agencies, academics, gurus, financial journalists, and even the customers of financial products were myopic or bewitched by a tantalizing vision of an ever-growing economy, and so were careless in assessing risk and immature in ascertaining the complex consequences of financial decisions in a global economy. Some formerly respected opinion makers have turned from heroes to villains.

Like flotsam washed up on the beach, after the storm we are left with examples of criminal activity and unprofessional practices. Trust, the cornerstone of finance, has been hit severely, and it will take time and considerable effort to restore it.

Along with other major stakeholders in the world of commerce and finance, business schools must accept a shared responsibility for the world's current financial mess. To deny this would be a denial of the relevance of business schools in the real world.

That said, I do not believe that business schools have encouraged a limited understanding of managerial duties. Moreover, the "greed is good" maxim of the 1980s that led to the junk bond crisis has not been taught in any business school that I know of. On the contrary, the past decade has witnessed a significant growth in corporate social responsibility (CSR), which is now embedded in many MBA courses and reflected through many initiatives at major corporations. But it seems that such efforts have not been sufficient. Either the assimilation or implementation of CSR was superficial, or the directors who mismanaged their companies did not apply the golden rules taught at business schools. Or maybe the system was already corrupted and impossible to right. On the other hand, teaching business ethics and deontology does not immunize students and graduates from engaging in unethical behavior. This is something we have to live with, as in other recognized professions such as medicine or law.

In early 2009, *the New York Times* published an article critical of business schools, pointing out: "With the economy in disarray and so many financial firms in free fall, analysts, and even educators themselves, are wondering if the way business students are taught may have contributed to the most serious economic crisis in decades."[23] A few months later, the *Harvard Business Review's* blog featured an article entitled: "How to Fix Business Schools."[24] It was intended to generate a debate on the changes needed in management teaching in the post-crisis era.

Jay O. Light, then Dean of Harvard Business School, concluded:

> Business schools must share some of the blame, but there is plenty to go around...there were imbalances both on campuses and in the economy during an extended period of growth, when people became less focused on systemic risks and more focused on the upside and on making money...But to suggest that business schools and the MBA are the root cause of the global financial crisis is simplistic nonsense that ignores the obvious reality of the many complex and interrelated factors.[25]

Later in the same year, *BusinessWeek* opened a debate on its website under the headline: "Business Schools Are Largely Responsible for the US Financial Crisis. Pro or Con?"[26] It is worth pointing out that for the prestigious news weekly, the problem seemed to be uniquely American, rather than global. In favor of blaming business schools were Harvard's Jay Lorsch and Rakesh Khurana:

> In the run-up to the crisis, many business executives were so self-interested they failed to consider themselves as custodians of their own institutions. All of us involved in business education need to ask what our role has been in fostering a culture that allows executives to walk off with millions of dollars while their firms lay in tatters and society is left with the bill.[27]

At the same time, Andrew W. Lo, director of the MIT Laboratory for Financial Engineering, countered on behalf of the con side:

> The current crisis highlights the growing complexity of the financial system and underscores the sea change in business education from the generic to the specific, from the old boys' network to the global financial network, and from boardroom tactics to risk analytics. By training tomorrow's leaders to manage the risks of the financial system effectively and ethically, we'll have a fighting chance of surviving even the largest crises. This is what business schools do, and we need to do more of it, not less.[28]

Managers, not MBAs

The flurry of criticism of business schools ignited by the financial crisis was not the first time that business schools have come under fire. Perhaps the most outspoken and persistent critic of business schools is Henry Mintzberg, a professor at McGill University in Canada and a world-acclaimed expert of business strategy. Mintzberg's fundamental challenge to MBA programs is that they do not produce managers; they produce MBAs – an altogether different species.[29]

For Mintzberg, management is neither a science – not even an applied science – nor a profession, but rather should be described as an art or craft, where experience, intuition, and practice are the bases for learning. In his opinion, business schools have got it wrong in three main areas.

First, they've got the wrong people. Aspiring MBA students are young professionals lacking the experience required to learn management. "It's like trying to teach psychology to a person that has never known anybody,"[30] he says in his 2004 book *Managers, Not MBAs*. Generally, business school candidates are chosen for their analytical abilities, measured in a GMAT test, rather than on the basis of their professional experience, which is reduced to a requisite two-year internship of questionable use. Furthermore, the reasons that candidates give for wanting to take an MBA are questionable: most are looking to earn as much money as possible and to boost their career prospects; they typically lack the professional zeal required to teach and lead people, or to generate value in society.

The second error, Mintzberg says, is that MBAs teach people in the wrong ways. The teaching and methodology used in most business schools, he argues, do not produce the results the schools promise. They aim to create managers, but what they really do is to develop specialists, experts in coming up with solutions to specific problems, but who lack an overview and broad understanding of business. Mintzberg is equally critical of business schools in this regard, accusing them of taking the "academic approach" of Stanford, Wharton, or Chicago, or the "pragmatic approach" of Harvard and others that use the case study. For Mintzberg, both approaches may seem different, but they lead to the same results.

Although the different teaching methods used in business schools – for example, the case study, business games, or projects carried out in real companies – may appear to be practical, they are nothing more than simplified representations of a much more complex reality. As a result, students acquire a series of skills, such as the confidence to take decisions quickly, to simplify complex situations, or solve technical problems. The students become skillful formulators of strategy, but lack the ability to implement solutions.

Third, and perhaps most damningly, Mintzberg argues that MBA programs produce the wrong consequences, producing MBA graduates who are overconfident, arrogant, skilled in analyzing partial problems related to business requirements such as accounting or marketing, and who lack any sense of the reality of business.

Mintzberg summarizes his typical MBA profile through the equation: "confidence minus competence equals arrogance."[31] However, Mintzberg's statistics on value generation in businesses where the CEO has an MBA, on start-ups created by business school graduates, or on the absence of MBAs among the list of entrepreneurs who are household names are controversial, since there are also studies that show the contrary.

It is hard not to sympathize with many of Mintzberg's ideas. His book predicts many of the ideas that would later be developed by other writers, and who have dominated the debate on management education over the past decade. He is a visionary and deserves recognition for his pioneering work. For example, the importance given to admitting managers with work experience to MBA programs, as opposed to Masters in Management, which is aimed at students with no professional experience, is now common practice in business schools, at least in Europe. That said, I would like to outline my objections to several of his arguments with which I disagree, on the basis of my own experience of business schools.

To begin with, I believe that it is possible to develop management skills in students and young people who have no experience of business. I am thinking here about programs such as a Bachelor in Business Administration or a Masters in Management attended by younger students, particularly those programs directed towards the entrepreneurs of tomorrow. This type of educational environment can create the conditions within which the entrepreneurial spirit can flourish.

As *The Economist's* Adrian Wooldridge has pointed out, one of the myths about young entrepreneurs is that they are "orphans and outcasts," to borrow the phrase used by US thinker and writer George Gilder. They are: "Lonely Atlases battling a hostile world or anti-social geeks inventing world-changing gizmos in their garrets. In fact, entrepreneurship, like all business, is a social activity. Entrepreneurs may be more independent than the usual suits who merely follow the rules, but they almost always need business partners and social networks to succeed".[32] Here he is obviously thinking about people like Steve Jobs or Bill Gates, who left college to create their own businesses, and who are frequently used to illustrate the irrelevance of university studies in becoming a successful entrepreneur.

Nevertheless, my main problem with Mintzberg's view is his belief that it is only on the basis of experience, and thus to a certain degree, age, that managerial talent can be fully developed, and leaders created. I think that some of the challenges for business schools involved in training young people is to identify young leaders, and to find a way to channel their nascent entrepreneurial abilities, and to put them in contact with the main stakeholders in the business world.

The second strand of my critique of Mintzberg addresses his questioning of the efficacy of the teaching methods used in business schools, particularly the case study method, business games, and simulations. The limitations, in addition to the virtue, of such approaches are that the decisions taken by students in these situations have no real repercussions. Perhaps the best analogy for such methods is the flight simulator used by trainee pilots.

The advantage of flight simulators is that when things go wrong, the airplane doesn't crash for real. For this reason, pilots understand the value of simulators as a way of preparing to fly a plane: it gives them the opportunity to deal with problems and situations that will undoubtedly come up when they do pilot one for real. Mintzberg's criticism of the use of such methods brings to mind the problem set to students of cognitive psychology, known as "the map and the territory." A map tries to be the best representation of a real territory, but it can never reproduce all the aspects of a real territory. The problem with the journey to knowledge is that we need maps to better understand how to recreate the geography of a specific territory; we also know that it is a mistake to confuse the two things. Mintzberg is right to point out that some educators insist on believing that a case study is the same as reality, thus falling into a cognitive trap.

At the same time, Harvard Business School case studies always include a footnote pointing out: "HBS case studies are developed solely as the basis for class discussion. Cases are not intended to serve as endorsements, sources of primary data, or illustrations of effective or ineffective management." The point of this clarification, among others, is to establish that the user is dealing with a map, not a territory, and that the case study should not be confused with reality.

On the other hand, Mintzberg is mistaken if he believes that the anecdotes told by a manager in the course of an interactive class within the context of a program designed for senior directors are also much more than an abstraction of reality, largely drawn from memory with all the corresponding advantages and disadvantages. In any event, in my experience, the testimonies of many MBA graduates, even after many years, show that the use of case studies is beneficial in dealing with management situations. I fear that the case study, along with other interactive methods used in business schools, with all their imperfections, is the most effective methodology when it comes to teaching management. After all, many of our ideas and decisions, in management and in life, are based on the experiences and emotions shared with us by others.

The reality is that many of Mintzberg's suggestions are being adopted by business schools. Business education is one of the most dynamic and responsive sectors in higher education, a sector where self-criticism is not only welcome but also essential. Proof of this is the growing body of revisionist literature, put out mostly by publishing houses linked to business schools. This ongoing review of the methodology and content of our teaching methods has led us to emphasize the teaching of both hard and soft skills, or to develop both their analytical abilities and emotional intelligence. In the case of directors, it relates to developing their professional ethics or commitment to social issues, or in a more technical approach aimed at transmitting functional knowledge, or in a more general and overarching approach to the world of business.

Making sense of the critics

That business schools receive such a vituperative press is somewhat bewildering. As I have stated, management is universally practiced and is an important force for good. There is widespread acceptance that leaders need development of one form or another. Furthermore, the modern corporation is one of the institutions of our times. And yet, the existence and modus operandi of business schools is routinely questioned.

In an attempt to better analyze the issue, I have organized the most relevant critiques of business schools into five groups. First, that they teach that business justifies greed. Second, that they are a breeding ground for arrogant managers. Third, that the high salaries commanded by business school graduates are counterproductive. Fourth, that they place too little emphasis on financial risk. And finally, that by failing to emphasize ethics, they encourage dishonesty and cheating.

Do B-Schools teach that business justifies greed?

At the core of this argument is that the theories and models taught in business schools encourage greed among the student body. British journalist Peter Walker encapsulated this critique in an article in *The Observer* in 2009. "Too many MBA programs, the simplified version goes, draw in young, greedy types with little business experience and indoctrinate them with half-baked management and finance theories, along with an unshakeable belief in their own talents, before sending them out to earn ill-deserved fortunes in investment banking and consulting."[33]

Walker admitted that the picture he was painting was essentially a caricature, but that many readers would believe that much of what he said was true. Another harsh critic of the pernicious effect of the theoretical models used in teaching management was London Business School's Sumantra Ghoshal, who, in a well-publicized article published after his death, warned: "Our theories and ideas have done much to strengthen the management practices that we are all now so loudly condemning."[34]

Ghoshal argued that research carried out at business schools, and the models used in teaching there, are based on false criteria. To begin with, management has aligned itself with the social sciences, adopting a methodology and scientific suppositions that have on occasion been called "physics envy." In the physical sciences, causal and functional paradigms predominate, while in the social sciences it is functionality that explains how individuals behave. According to Ghoshal, no scientific theory "explains the phenomenon of organized complexity"[35] that are companies.

This reductionism of management to little more than scientism has led to a "gloomy vision" of humans, along the lines of *homo economicus*, which reduces human behavior to the satisfaction of our most basic instincts, said Ghoshal. Parallel to this, the liberalism of Milton Friedman argues that the fundamental responsibility of directors is to maximize shareholders' return on their investment. These basic principles have been used to build a theory of corporate governance on the basis of the need for independent board members, the separation of the CEO's and the chairman's functions, along with the need to give directors stock options to align their interests with those of the shareholders, thus avoiding the risks derived from "agency theory."

In short, as Ghoshal explained, this leads to a supposedly amoral theory of business, justified by a questionable vision of people and their behavior in companies. He warns: "Unlike theories in the physical sciences, theories in the social sciences tend to be self-fulfilling."[36] This in turn creates a vicious circle in which theory and practice feed off each other.

The result has generated ideas that "have shaped the intellectual and normative order by which all day-to-day decisions were made."[37] Ghoshal said cases such as Enron and Tyco are hardly surprising within such a system.

Any solution, explained Ghoshal, must start by recognizing that behind all management concepts there is always an ideology or an intention: "Social scientists carry an even greater social and moral responsibility than those who work in the physical sciences because, if they hide ideology within the pretense of science, they can cause much more harm."[38] He argued for a more optimistic vision about people and company directors, along with better social excellence objectives that relate to the interests of a larger group of stakeholders, rather than simply to those of the shareholders. He cited the example of positive psychology pioneer Martin Seligman, who calls for: "As much focus on strength as on weakness, as much interest in building the best things in life as in repairing the worst, and as much attention to fulfilling the lives of healthy people as to healing the wounds of the distressed."[39]

In a similar vein, Ken Starkey, a professor at Britain's Nottingham University Business School, has argued the case for changing both the content and the teaching style of business schools:

> Leading business schools will need to develop a different language and a new narrative to legitimize their function and to overcome their fascination with a particular form of finance and economics. Business schools need to broaden their intellectual horizons, not least by spending more time looking at the lessons of history ... They will need to cultivate an appreciation of the role of the state and of collective action to counter the fixation on markets and individualism (i.e., greed and selfishness).[40]

Bob Sutton, professor of management at Stanford, echoes this approach:

> Most of the models and assumptions they pass on to their students reflect a fundamental belief about human beings: We are hard-wired to be selfish. They assume that it's a dog-eat-dog world, and that humans want and take as much for themselves as possible and to stomp on others along the way.[41]

Ghoshal, Sutton, and Starkey's views have been countered by fellow academics. Chicago Booth's Steve Kaplan, answering the claims of Sutton (and Podolny), says: They "pine for a world that does not exist."[42] Self-interest is innate to humans, and looks likely to remain so for the coming years, says Kaplan, adding that the results of business school teaching have been overwhelmingly beneficial and that the world has experienced an unparalleled period of growth as a result.

Kaplan also dismisses the idea of business schools' "gloomy vision":

> There has been a huge increase in entrepreneurship courses and activities at every business school with which I am familiar. At HBS, entrepreneurship is a required first-year course. More recently, social entrepreneurship courses have been introduced and met with substantial student demand. Many of our students do, in fact, want to change the world.[43]

Even if they do, as Frank Brown, the former dean of INSEAD, says, few business school graduates have challenged conventional thinking during the boom years: "Today's troubles have been driven not just by greed, but by a lack of confidence. I think the average employee, maybe a business school graduate, lacks the confidence to ask the tough questions."[44]

Brown attributes this lack of confidence to the failure of employees at say, Enron or Worldcom to challenge the decisions of their bosses. However, MBA courses encourage students to question things that are taken for granted, to think outside the box, and to challenge proposals that do not fit with their principles or personal values.

Criticism of a culture of greed in business schools is exaggerated. That said, I agree with Ghoshal's assertion that behind every management theory there are values and principles that need to be explained. Management is philosophy in action: every management theory has come from philosophy. Furthermore, every manager has a view of the world, consciously or inadvertently, explicit or emergent, that conforms to a specific philosophy. Even to affirm the contrary is in itself a philosophical proposition.

The same applies to leadership theories: they can all be traced to a philosophical movement or school of thought. Modern theories of leadership owe a great deal to Friedrich Nietzsche, the nineteenth century German philosopher famous for his assertion that "God is dead." Nietzsche distinguishes between two types of morality: the "master morality" and the "slave morality." The first is applicable to the leaders of society, who create their own values for themselves. The "slave morality" is applicable to the herd, and sees the behavior of masters as evil. But masters, sustains Nietzsche, stand "beyond good and evil": they are subject to their own principles, different from the norms that apply to the herd, favoring mediocrity, and preventing the development of higher-level individuals – the true leaders.

Some of Nietzsche's writing would not be out of place in management literature on leadership in the 1980s:

> To give style to one's character – a great and rare art! He practices it who surveys all that his nature presents in strength and weakness and then moulds it to an artistic plan until everything appears as art and reason, and even the weakness delights the eye ... It will be the strong, imperious natures which experience their subtlest joy in exercising such a control, in such a constraint and perfecting under their own law.[45]

Nietzsche's theory brings to mind a number of fictional characters from the 1980s. Among the more enduring of them are Gordon Gecko, the protagonist of *Wall Street* and its recent sequel, the preacher of the "greed is good" maxim – a part of the Reaganite credo of the time – and Sherman

McCoy, the grieved executive of Tom Wolfe's *The Bonfire of the Vanities*, and described as a "master of the universe." Both characters seem to use the Nietzschean expression, to be "beyond good and evil" and exempt from the standards that apply to mere mortals. A passage from one of Nietzsche's works is again appropriate to describe their attitudes to life:

> For believe me! – the secret of realizing the greatest fruitfulness and the greatest enjoyment of existence is to live dangerously! Build your cities on the slopes of the Vesuvius! Send your ships out into uncharted seas! Live in conflict with your equals and with yourselves! Be robbers and ravagers as long as you cannot be rulers or owners, you men of knowledge! The time will soon be past when you could be content to live concealed in the woods like timid deer![46]

Eventually both stories end similarly. Gecko and McCoy are caught and punished, losing Nietzsche's superman status. Their finales are moralistic – a trend increasingly reflected in real life.

The increasing transparency required of companies and their directors, along with the close scrutiny that their decisions are subject to, make it hard to conceal major fraud for a long time. Francisco González, the chairman of BBVA, one of the world's biggest commercial banks, told me that one of his guiding principles, and which he required his employees to follow, was to bear in mind that all his decisions could be published in the press the following day. This is similar to Warren Buffett's rule of thumb: "I want employees to ask themselves whether they are willing to have any contemplated act appear the next day on the front page of their local paper."[47]

Over the course of the past decade, business schools have witnessed the flourishing of postmodern theories of leadership that disregard Gecko and McCoy's attitudes and propose new, renovated archetypes of business leaders. This has happened during a renaissance of business ethics, contemporaneous with some widely publicized business scandals. If we search recent literature on leadership, we find interesting examples of this new approach. Let me mention just two.

Jim Collins, the business best-seller author, proposes a new concept: the "Level 5 Leader,"[48] an executive who blends classical leadership virtues – such as ferocious resolve – with attributes not traditionally associated with the charismatic leader, such as humility and the tendency to give credit to others and assign blame to themselves. These two latter attributes were, according to Nietzsche, virtues of the "slave morality" and not applicable to masters who carry out their will to power. In management theory, they were considered in the past as naturally closer to the attitude of subordinates than that of leaders.

Another inspiring contribution is *Resonant Leadership* by Richard Boyatzis and Annie McKee.[49] They argue a similarly "anti-Nietzschean" proposal, defending managers who aspire to become effective, and saying that enduring leaders need to be attentive, hopeful, and compassionate.

Do B-Schools breed arrogance?

The second frequent criticism fired at business schools is that they inculcate arrogance in their graduates. "Humility is not a word often pegged onto MBAs,"[50] writes Henry Mintzberg. One analyst of management education wrote in an article entitled "The Top-10 MBA Program's Weakness" that: "It is not the course material of an MBA curriculum that is in the program's weakness, but the attitude of superiority it tends to instill in people."[51] In similar vein, Philip Delves Broughton, a journalist who took an MBA at Harvard Business School, asks whether part of the blame for the financial crisis might not be attributable to having given too much power within companies to, "a single, narcissistic class of spreadsheet makers and PowerPoint makers."[52]

Arrogance and a sense of belonging to an elite can be parts of the same attitude. Business schools certainly try to inculcate this spirit, usually in three phases: First, during the admission and interview process, there is constant emphasis on how the school selects only the best. Second, during the program, feelings of belonging are reinforced to a select group, the crème de la crème. Third, before and after graduation, students are encouraged to look only for the well-paid jobs, those near the top of their professional tree, or those with the high status.

Such sentiments are handed down from generation to generation both by the school's management, and by graduates. As Jeffrey Pfeffer pointed out in an article called "The Narcissistic World of the MBA Students": "Even if students didn't arrive at the leading business schools already narcissistic, orientation activities would soon make them so. One of the first things they are told is how accomplished and wonderful they are."[53]

There is no denying that these accusations are rooted in reality. That said, it must also be accepted that many institutions, including many in higher education, are based on the idea of meritocracy, that is to say in the recognition and promotion of those individuals with the best education and highest level of skills. Admission, grants, assessment of work, and selection for jobs are all on the basis of the concept of meritocracy.

There are procedures to avoid excessive elitism, such as positive discrimination or the use of alternative methods to measure a person's qualities, or changing the rules of our institutions, but these are generally counterproductive and undesirable. Of course, business schools are far from being the only institutions guilty of practicing elitism; it is a cultural characteristic of all well-regarded educational institutions. Similarly, candidates, their families, and all stakeholders tend to want to belong to elite institutions.

Given that the concept of meritocracy is intrinsic to the functioning of many institutions, the objective of educators, and of business schools in particular, would be better focused on how to instill in pupils a real sense of confidence and self-recognition, underlined by a sense of commitment to society and the virtue of modesty. The first thing that is needed, as Pfeffer points out, is to

> change the typical admissions director speech at business school orientations from one of singing the students' praises to, while acknowledging the accomplishment of their selection, emphasizing the responsibilities that come with attending school and entering a profession.[54]

Business schools certainly try to instill a sense of confidence in students that will allow them to analyze, establish goals, and assume risks. This confidence is essential for action-oriented future managers. The challenge for educators and for students is how to balance the self-assurance needed to lead people and to take decisions with the modesty required to avoid over-confidence and losing touch with reality.

Openness and modesty are two recommendable attitudes to start any learning experience with. In fact, they are key for those entering an MBA program, since much of learning comes from fellow participants. "Wisdom is how little we know," a sentence attributed to Socrates, the father of some of the best learning methods still used today.

I tend to kick off the inaugural speech I give to MBA students at my school with the same words Socrates used when addressing new students: "The only true wisdom is knowing that you know nothing." I then add that they may feel a little bemused, since MBA students normally have a pretty high opinion of themselves, have followed a competitive selection process, and have respectable professional experience.

But I believe that this is the proper way to welcome a group of motivated students who are going to start a very challenging learning experience and who have invested an important amount of their time and their resources. To focus on cultivating their self-esteem as based on a sense of belonging to an elite would be misleading.

Another initiative that business schools can use to tackle their graduates' arrogance is to encourage diversity in class. Having graduates from a wide range of cultures, with different world views, or different ideas of what constitutes a "good life," aside from encouraging tolerance and an openness to new ideas, is an effective means of avoiding narcissism: pupils are immediately confronted with a reality of multiple references, thus making it harder to see themselves as belonging to a single, elite group.

Are the high salaries of MBA graduates counterproductive?

A third criticism leveled against business schools, particularly in the context of the global downturn, is that MBA graduates are overpaid. But this is beyond the domain of business schools as it reflects supply and demand. That said, studies show that having an MBA increases the likelihood of access to better-paid jobs.

For example, the Association for Financial Professionals' 2010 report concludes that "financial professionals with advanced degrees received higher compensation than those without. Those with an MBA showed strong salary potential: In 2009, financial professionals with an MBA earned an average salary 24 per cent higher than their counterparts with bachelor's degrees earned."[55] It also showed that having an MBA is a key factor when it comes to being promoted.

Another survey by *Chief Executive* magazine showed that 32 percent of the CEOs of the top 200 most important companies in the US had MBAs. But members of this minority ranked, on average, a full 40 places higher than their colleagues in the non-MBA majority.[56]

But the market isn't the only factor in determining the high salaries that MBA graduates enjoy. There are other reasons, such as a business school's ranking, which is partly determined by the salaries paid to MBA graduates. The *Financial Times* and *Forbes*, for example, include this criterion in their rankings.

Such rankings are often used as a benchmark by applicants when deciding about which business school to apply to. Including MBAs' future salaries as a factor in ranking a business school has been criticized by some in the teaching community. Nottingham's Ken Starkey highlights the link between over-ambition and high wages, pointing to the responsibility of league tables that "are heavily biased to the salary returns that accrue to MBAs who join these 'professions'. It is time to develop a more robust measure of what constitutes effective, sustainable management education and value added."[57]

What all this shows is that the market, companies, and recruiters value a business school education. However, from my experience, and from talking to managers in other business schools, it is clear that when MBA graduates look for a job they place importance on aspects other than just the salary. Money is a key factor, and for some, decisive, but young graduates also tend to look for opportunities for personal development, also taking into account a company's reputation, in addition to the atmosphere and culture of a company, along with opportunities to continue learning.

These factors are reflected in the popularity among the MBAs of *Fortune*'s "The Best Companies to Work For,"[58] which ranks companies on the basis of factors other than the salaries they pay. Then there is the growing number of MBA graduates who decide to set up their own companies, who will have to face stiff investment and other costs in the initial years of operation that will limit salaries. We are also seeing graduates who take time out after completing their MBA to do not-for-profit work.

At the same time, a significant number of graduates decide to work for the government, hoping to apply their new management techniques in the state sector. Blair Sheppard, Dean of Fuqua School of Business, said this of his school: "Over the last five years the number of people who want to do public-sector or social entrepreneurship at Fuqua has actually gone up about twentyfold."[59]

The ambitious MBA graduate, grasping, and motivated solely by money is a caricature, and doesn't correspond to the majority of graduates, who end up working in a wide range of sectors, in addition to finance, carrying out a variety of roles in a wide range of countries.

Do MBA programs focus too little on concepts such as financial risk?

Business schools' teaching has also been criticized for having failed to see the current and previous financial crashes, and for having failed to generate models to analyze financial risk. What we might call financial science is still nascent. Although the first business schools were set up more than 100 years ago, it wasn't until the 1960s, acting on the recommendations of two key reports by the Ford Foundation and the Carnegie Corporation, that they began to systematically develop research techniques in specialist areas, as in the other social sciences.

Compared with teaching in other social and life sciences, such as Medicine, Management is still in its infancy. Henri Fayol and Frederick Taylor, considered the founding fathers of management science, lived just

100 years ago. We are horrified when we read of medical practices such as bloodletting to relieve hypertension, recommended in many medical textbooks as recently as early twentieth century. Similarly, we are dumbstruck by arguments that sub-prime mortgages were a way of diversifying financial risk.

Management science's relative youth may explain the imprecision of many theories used in our discipline, but of greater concern is where it is headed within the framework of the social sciences. In recent years a significant number of major companies, particularly in the financial sector, have developed their in-house research divisions.

For example, investment banks or ratings agencies' analysis departments have produced important work on countries, sectors, or companies, which have been traditionally used by managers when assessing investment policy. This in-company research has been criticized since it may sometimes lack the neutrality of free academic research, given the connections between said companies and their evaluated clients. At the same time, the economics departments of many universities have focused their work on the same issues, albeit using different methods and based on different approaches. Perhaps more could have been done to avoid the crisis and understand the realities of the business world, had both spheres worked together. Corporate research departments lack the independence and methodological rigor of universities. That said, universities need to put more emphasis on researching areas that are of greater relevance for businesses working in the real world.

The fact is that, as an academic discipline, Management has a very complex object of study: how humans interact within organizations to produce value. Even if the development of Management over the past century has provided us with some reliable tools and theories, along with valid golden rules, it still has some way to achieve a reliable status as a science, and it is continually evolving in many different directions. For example, we have seen recently the upsurge of new areas and disciplines, such as Behavioral Finance, this one focused on the analysis of the cognitive and emotional elements that explain the market behavior of individuals and groups. The complexity and evolving nature of Management has also been illustrated by Aswath Damodaran, Professor at Stern School of Business, who, reflecting on the lessons from the crisis commented that "the market collapse and investor reaction has been a humbling experience and has revealed how much I do not know or fully understand about finance".[60]

In an analogous vein, Paul Danos told *The Economist* in 2009 that a main takeaway from the financial crisis "was not that it was an ethics problem, not that people were cheating overtly, it is that people were using the wrong mental attitude when they approached extremely complex problems that they hadn't seen before. Practice can hypnotize you into using old models and old ways of thinking. When you talk to people about the risk management systems in the big banks and at the Fed and at the regulators, it's amazing how they put together old models and old ways of thinking and tried to lay it on top of a new system".[61]

Do MBA graduates lack a sense of business ethics?

The final recurring criticism aimed at business schools is that they do not give sufficient importance to teaching business ethics. This may have been true in the past. But for several years now, most MBA programs have included at least one module on business ethics and social responsibility. Furthermore, the international accreditation agencies, such as EQUIS, AACSB, or AMBA, include business ethics among their criteria. So it is simply not true to suggest that MBAs are not exposed to ethical issues.

Whether this is sufficient, of course, is open to question – and goes to the heart of the debate about what sort of managers we want to produce in the future. An arguably effective and nuanced alternative is not to make ethics a specific subject, but to incorporate it into all subjects. This is the option recommended by the Aspen Institute's Center for Business Education. Its *Beyond Grey Pinstripes*[62] survey assesses business schools in terms of how they incorporate ethical and sustainability issues into their teaching.

Thomas Piper (co-author of *Can Ethics Be Taught?*) argues that the best way to teach business ethics is not just through a specific course looking at leadership and social responsibility, but by addressing these questions throughout the whole MBA program. First, he says, because, "ethical dilemmas arise in all functional areas and at all levels of the organization."[63] Second, because when teachers avoid the subject, "we send an unintended but powerful signal that they are not a priority."[64] Effective business ethics teaching depends in large part on its inclusion across the board as an integral part of acquiring a business education.

At the same time, it is essential that ethics teaching be done with the same rigor and with the same high standards that characterize the rest of a school's teaching. Aine Donovan, the Executive Director of the Dartmouth Ethics Institute, has asked: "Does teaching ethics in general help counter individual cheating and group collusion?" Her answer was no. "Unless taught properly by people who understand what they're doing, the result can be worse than no ethics training at all."[65]

MBA students have also been accused of unethical behavior in their studies. In 2006, a report on cheating surveying 5,300 graduate students in the US and Canada, conducted by Donald McCabe, Professor of Management and Global Business at New Jersey's Rutgers University and President of the Center for Academic Integrity (CAI) was picked up by a wide range of media. The report revealed that 56 percent of graduate business students admitted to cheating in the past year, as compared to 54 percent of graduate engineering students, 50 percent of physical science students, 49 percent of medical and healthcare students, 45 percent of law students, 43 percent of liberal arts students, and 39 percent of social science and humanities students. Previous reports published by the CAI were as alarming: the results of a 2005 survey of 50,000 undergraduates at more than 60 US universities showed that on most campuses, 70 percent of students admitted to some cheating. The reality may even be worse, since it's likely that more students cheat than admit to it.

Do more students cheat nowadays than, say, four decades ago? It is debatable, although some analysts explain that easy access to almost infinite sources on the web and the flourishing of virtual communities of cheaters have contributed to rampant cheating. Cheating is always unjustifiable. That said, we should avoid embarking on a crusade that may damage the very pillars that sustain education and prestigious institutions, hitting those students who play by the rules. Although eradicating cheating may be almost impossible – in the same way that we cannot prevent people from cheating on their partners – we can at least impose mechanisms and procedures to make it difficult or too risky.

To do so, first we need to clarify a conceptual issue. Normally, cheating is considered wrong because, as the Oxford Dictionary explains, cheating is "to act dishonestly or unfairly in order to gain an advantage." [66] But educators and academic managers must also point out that it is the cheater who loses out most: firstly, by potentially exposing one's personal reputation – perhaps for life; and secondly, and more importantly from a personal point of view, by relinquishing the benefits that the learning process brings. We all know the intellectual satisfaction that results from understanding and discussing theories, ideas, and concepts. Those who take the shortcut and skip the wonders of learning are giving up a decisive part of personal development that is directly linked – I believe, in line with many philosophers – with happiness.

During a discussion with colleagues on the results of the study conducted by Donald McCabe, some of my colleagues pointed out that MBA programs are very demanding, sometimes beyond realistic expectations. To cope with these unrealistic demands, some students simply cheat. Other colleagues referred to the prevalent culture at many business schools that emphasizes performance at any cost, thus exacerbating competition and prompting disloyalty among fellow students – in line with Sumantra Ghoshal's views.

So far, we have established the importance of management and briefly charted the rise of business schools. I have gone into some depth to look at common criticisms of business schools. I don't believe they will easily disappear. As we have seen some of these criticisms may have some basis, while others distort the reality. I guess that these criticisms have helped business schools to better educate managers.

CHAPTER 3

Developing better managers

I began this book with the assertion that what the world needs now is good entrepreneurs, good managers, and good business leaders. So what do we mean by good entrepreneurs, managers, and business leaders? And how can we develop them in business schools?

My belief is that what is needed now is a return to the classical notion of virtues.

Virtue ethics is an approach to ethical thinking based on the character of the individual involved rather than on a set of rules or consequences. This is very different from the approach of *consequentialism*, which argues that the outcome or consequences of a particular action determine whether it is morally acceptable or not. It is also different from deontology, which asserts that the rightness or wrongness of an act is determined by the character of the act itself. In practice, the difference in these three alternative views of morality tends to lie in how issues are approached rather than in the conclusions reached. For example, a consequentialist may argue that stealing is wrong because of the negative consequences produced by stealing – though a consequentialist may allow that certain consequences might make stealing acceptable. A deontologist might argue that stealing is *always* wrong, regardless of any potential "good" that might come from it. A virtue ethicist, however, would focus less on stealing in any particular instance and instead consider what a decision to steal says about a person's character and moral behavior.

With its origins in the writings of the ancient Greek philosophers Plato and Aristotle, virtue ethics was the prevailing model in the ancient and medieval worlds. It emphasizes the character of the individual rather than the rules. In this sense it places responsibility and accountability firmly with the conscience of the individual rather than with the interpretation of law or regulations. In essence, bankers would have to ask themselves not whether their actions are allowable under the rules as they are currently interpreted, but whether this is the right thing to do? This is an idea that has developed in my mind over many years, and was brought into sharp relief by the recent financial crisis. It is inspired by a deep respect for the lessons of the past as well as the opportunities of the future. There are a number of reasons why I believe that the notion of virtue ethics has much to recommend it to modern management.

Managers as architects of social structures

The first point to recognize is that the business and social environment is changing. In this new environment, the new business heroes will be entrepreneurs – the people who create wealth for society, either by creating new companies or by rejuvenating big corporations and even public institutions. By their nature entrepreneurs tend to operate outside of the existing norms or rules. They are the creators of their own rules; they change society and cause new ways of organizing and structuring human activity. Consider Facebook, for example, or Wikipedia, or Twitter, all of which were created by entrepreneurs and which are now shaping society. In the coming years, entrepreneurs will be the architects of the new social structures – and the engines of social progress. As *The Economist* argued in 2009: "The entrepreneurial idea has gone mainstream, supported by political leaders on the left as well as on the right, championed by powerful pressure groups, reinforced by a growing infrastructure of universities and venture capitalists and embodied by wildly popular business heroes."[67]

In which case, what advice should we be giving to entrepreneurs and directors? In the first place, we need to return to basics, to the golden rules of good directive practice, something that many will have learned at business school: basics driven by the need to come up with a long-term strategy for a business, to identify plausible formulas for generating value, to evaluate risk appropriately, to adopt contingency plans to deal with negative scenarios, to draw on a company's most valuable asset, without doubt, its personnel, and to look for new opportunities to innovate and renew the company they are leading. And one effective way to innovate is to also reduce costs and to increase productivity, both likely to be applied to companies at times of crisis.

But alongside the contingency plans, output increases, and savings, we need to provide business leaders the skills to address other key questions: how to rejuvenate their original business; how to renew products and services; how to identify new overseas markets; how to know when it is the moment to diversify; and how to be on the look out for strategic alliances that can reduce operating risks. Recent generations of business school graduates contain a high proportion of young men and women with just these skills. Below are a few examples.

In 2009, Marcela Torres, an IE Business School MBA graduate from Colombia, founded Prospéritas, a microcredit company based in her native country. Prior to joining IE she had worked in a wide range of areas: she started at Microsoft, later worked for the hospitality industry, then became a financial consultant, and finally worked for the government on reintegrating ex-combatants into society. During her MBA, she decided to set up a microcredit company, an area she had explored before coming to Madrid. She joined forces with other MBA students, who were equally passionate about her initiative, developed a detailed business plan, and won IE Business School's 2008 Best Entrepreneurial Project of the Year Award. Prospéritas, now incorporated as a microfinance institution under Colombian law, provides small-amount loans to low-income entrepreneurs, solely for productive uses. Although the company's customer list still only features in the dozens, it aims to attract millions. Torres' vision is not just to offer loans to small entrepreneurs, but to offer a wide array of advisory services and products to keep their ventures sustainable. She also says that Prospéritas' industry is not as high-risk as many believe: her clients repay better than regular borrowers. "The market is still way bigger than we would like it to be and there is plenty of room for a lot of us to jump in. The more competition we have, the more clients get better conditions," she said.

The emerging microcredit business is not the only new ocean where today's MBA graduates are exploring innovative ways of creating social wealth and breaking the mould. A significant number of IE's new generation of alumni are exploring business opportunities in fields like biotechnology, renewable energies, or the green industries. Phillip Pausder, a German graduate of IE Business School's 2008 MBA Class, moved to the Cayman Islands, where the company he set up, TripleP, has helped a local mobile operator to increase the energy efficiency in its network. TripleP was founded after graduation and focused on sustainable advice for corporations, merging with another Berlin-based company, resulting in a company named CleanVenture.

The new company will enable client's companies to run as sustainable and profitable businesses at the same time. It will unlock value and transform its client's business by providing advice on how to reduce their carbon footprint and energy expenses. Philipp puts sustainability at the core of management values, and rejects its confinement to CSR (corporate social responsibility) departments, but at the same time realizes that the best way to sell sustainability is to show cost-saving returns. He also believes in the high potential of this business. A first assignment for CleanVenture will be helping big mobile-phone operators to reach isolated rural areas and offer competitive costs to consumers with low incomes.

Philipp's new company is just another example of how true entrepreneurs come up with new ideas and concepts that will renovate entire industries. It also shows the way to new MBA career paths for future business school graduates. Traditionally, MBA graduates looked mainly for jobs in financial services and blue chip consultancies. But today we live in a different environment where business schools are able to produce not just good financial engineers or accomplished management technicians, but also a significant number of entrepreneurs who are at the same time good global citizens.

Another example of a start-up created by MBA graduates to provide solutions for the needs of the players in the new cognitive economy is Busuu.com, founded by IE graduates Bernard Niessner and Adrian Hilty in 2009. This is a Web 2.0 company for people interested in learning or improving their language skills. The site boasts of a large online community of native speakers taking a step beyond traditional methods of language learning through the use of Busuu's multimedia software material and language exchange. In 2009, Busuu.com was nominated for a number of prestigious Internet awards, such as the European Tech Crunch Awards, and the AlwaysOn Global 250 Winner in the category of emerging innovators for technology. In September 2009, the company won the European Language Label, a prestigious award for innovative projects in language learning, which is coordinated by the European Commission. I believe that the company may become, with time, one of the leading organizations in providing foreign language learning solutions on a global scale.

Managers of the future

Despite the economic crisis, applications for MBA programs increased – proof that the credit crunch will not curtail demand for MBAs in the future. Business will remain the hottest ticket in higher education with the widest career opportunities. As *Financial Times* columnist Lucy Kellaway remarked in *The Economist's* "The World in 2010": "In future those who stump up [for the cost of a business education] will do so because they want to learn the skills, not because they think they are buying entry into a cool end exclusive club."[68] The MBA should mainly be a transformational experience, a hub where participants become entrepreneurs and innovative managers.

Management can still be one of the noblest vocations in the world. It can create growth, wealth, and development in society, and it provides jobs, fosters innovation, and improves living conditions in the community. Good management is one of the best antidotes to most of the world's ills, since it promotes convergence and understanding among civilizations. In times of crisis, what are needed are more entrepreneurs and better management.

Cultivating managerial virtues and continuous education

There is no magic formula for turning somebody into a consummate manager. Good managers are made over time, on the basis of systematic exercise of good habits and routines, and as a result of accumulated experience of their sector and their relationships. To reach the heights of management excellence requires discipline and hard work. It is not achieved simply through the passage of time. The learning curve is steep. I would like to discuss two aspects that are closely connected: systematic practice of what might be called the virtues of management; and lifelong learning. I am also in favor of integrating the different management disciplines within the context of the social sciences and the humanities.

Education can and should be a personal transformation process. Some people argue that it is not possible to learn or develop basic traits of character beyond a certain age. I believe that this view is based on outmoded Freudian theories according to which the basic features of personality are acquired and fixed before reaching adolescence – more extreme versions of this say that they are formed in the womb. But a growing number of contemporary education theorists and psychologists accept that many skills and traits can be learnt and developed in maturity if the necessary attitudes are cultivated. An example of this is explored in *Can Ethics Be Taught?*,[69] which concludes that ethics can be taught and learnt at business school by young managers, as cited by several Harvard Business School scholars. Indeed, at business schools we work on the premise that junior and senior managers can not only update their knowledge of the latest business tools but also improve their skills and further shape their personality – hopefully for the better – through education.

Business schools can provide a valuable platform for cultivating a series of virtues such as hard work, endurance, self-organization, sociability, curiosity, modesty, and common sense, all basics for good management. For example, curiosity – in the sense of openness – is the door to wisdom, and a necessary virtue for the advancement of knowledge and even for achieving self-fulfillment and happiness.

Management virtues are operative good habits. They are not innate, but are achieved through constant exercise. It is never too late to start practicing or perfecting these good habits, and they can make management education a transforming experience. How can business schools help their students cultivate these virtues or competencies? To answer this question, the best analogy is from Michelangelo. The great artist believed that the job of the sculptor is to free the forms that were already inside the stone.

The job of teachers might be interpreted in a similar way: freeing students' potential.

Developing virtues, understood as habits or routines that form our character – and not necessarily in the religious sense – has been a core aspect of teaching in all societies throughout the ages. In Ancient Rome, the young were taught the virtues of *dignitas, pietas et virtus*.[70] *Dignitas* meant adopting greater decorum as one assumed more responsibility. *Pietas* involved respect for the family, law, and tradition. *Virtus* included a bundle of skills such as bravery, trust, and moral courage. Military training throughout the ages has also involved developing virtuous habits. Jeffrey Pfeffer suggests that business schools could learn from military academies, where humility is an important part of the code of conduct, as is discipline, along with punishment for failing to observe the rules.

Virtue is also a key element in many philosophies, starting with Aristotle's. The concept has been further developed by contemporary philosophers such as Elisabeth Anscombe[71] and Alisdair McIntyre,[72] who have developed a theory of morality that attempts to go beyond the rigid principles of most ethics, based as they are on Kant's categorical imperative or John Stuart Mill's principle of the greatest happiness. Anscombe and McIntyre argue that the key questions related to "how to live" and "how to behave" are best answered by identifying and then practicing virtues, rather than through a rational exercise on the basis of the principles outlined in other philosophical models. I would say that this approach is the way to teach and learn what constitutes good management.

Good managers are forged over the course of their career, based on the repeated practice of the basic skills required for management, such as self-awareness, determination, prudence, or a vision of the future. The learning curve is again a valid analogy, suggesting as it does that managerial virtues are acquired through experience, sensitivity, analytical skills, an ability to assess problems, and the application of reasoning. These are all the result of continued learning over an extended period of time. This approach seems to me to be the most realistic, although the toughest, compared to trying to inculcate into MBA students a compendium of principles or recipes that they should apply to whichever situation comes up in the future. Business ethics is too wide and complex a field to be summed up in a few case studies, and yet the practice of these virtues will prepare managers for how to deal with these moral dilemmas in the future.

The development of these core virtues has had an impact on the Positive Psychology movement, whose aim is to find and nurture genius and talent and to make normal life more fulfilling and not simply to treat mental illness, the traditional objective of psychology studies. Christopher Peterson

and Martin Seligman, two of this movement's most distinguished representatives, are the authors of *Character Strengths and Virtues*,[73] which
looks at the six most important virtues for the development of a happy life.
Figure 3.1 below lists these virtues, along with a series of initiatives that
in my opinion could usefully be implemented in an MBA program. I will
comment on such initiatives in later chapters.

A genuinely integral education should combine general teaching methods such as classes, with individual attention to students through one-
on-one teaching, tutorials, coaching, and mentorship. This personalized
approach identifies weaknesses and builds strengths in students though a
focus on the professional development of each person, bringing out their
virtues where necessary. For example, the EFMD-Carrington Crisp report
entitled Executive Education Futures notes: "A large number of employers
use coaching to enhance the value of learning and this may be a growing
field for executive education purchasers to maximize the value of individuals learning. Looking ahead, one of the main requirements of purchasers is
a greater focus on personalized learning plans."[74]

The other important theme that I identify is the need to provide a more
integrated and rounded education. Extreme specialization has come in

Character Strengths and Virtues and ways to develop them in MBA Programs (adapted from Peterson & Seligman, 2004)
Wisdom & knowledge: All MBA Courses, life-long learning, interactive learning methods, integration of pedagogy and technology
Courage: Work pressure, peer competition, entrepreneurship courses
Humanity: Social responsibility initiatives, emphasis on sustainability, team work, international exchanges
Justice: Courses on business ethics, Law and leadership
Temperance: Peer evaluation, 360° evaluation, emphasis on modesty, coaching and individual learning solutions
Transcendence: Courses on humanities, Design thinking, Internships

Figure 3.1 Character strengths and virtues and ways to develop them in MBA
programs

Source: Adapted from Peterson and Seligman, *Character Strengths and Virtues*.

for criticism because of its undesirable consequence: "silo syndrome," in which academics deal only with colleagues in their subject and students gain only a narrow perspective on knowledge. Universities can combat this by restoring the value of humanities in the tradition of American liberal arts colleges. Making humanities a core part of all degrees will cement the learning experience and develop open-minded and well-rounded graduates.

At IE Business School, for example, we have introduced a number of humanities' courses as a core part of the MBA curriculum. We believe that by learning the history of different civilizations or by the appreciation of modern art, for example, we produce well-rounded graduates, who will become enlightened managers who may also behave as global citizens.

Lifelong learning: The norm for managers' careers

Management evolves over time. Although some golden rules are still valid, the environment, the institutions, the nature of companies, and the ways of assessing risk, for example, have changed in recent years. Consequently, managers need to come back to school to learn new concepts, new tools, and to update their managerial skills. Managers cannot simply rely on what they learned many years ago in their MBA programs. This is a clinical occupation like medicine or architecture, where professionals need to update their knowledge and skills. One conclusion that may come out from the current financial crisis is the need for managers to return to school to update their knowledge and validate what they do in the real world.

Lifelong learning must become the norm for all executives. Several writers and analysts have already highlighted this, among them Frank Brown, the former dean of INSEAD, who points out that over the course of his career as an accountant, he has had to complete a series of courses to be able to revalidate his Certificate of Public Accountant. He asks:

> Why don't we, as business schools, develop a curriculum for continuing education post-MBA? It would make sense to me that we develop one week modules for general managers that are 'refreshers' to be given every five years after graduation from an MBA. These would be designed to deal with changes in environment, financial products, developing world issues, etc. We could also develop a series of 'electives' of say one week, which each MBA could select based upon their

current responsibility, industry, geography, etc. Maybe for a start, to continue to use the title MBA, a minimum of two weeks every five years should be required.[75]

Interestingly, at the time of writing Wharton and Harvard announced wide-ranging changes to its MBA curriculum – including the provision of free top-up training to MBA alumni after seven years. Other business schools will follow suit.

Businesses and business sectors change, just like circumstances. By the same token, we live blended lives, and the career of most managers is also a blend. Advances in medicine will increase our life expectancy, and retirement ages are already being put back. This means that managers will witness profound change over the course of their careers to a previously unseen extent. The need to adapt to new environments will repeatedly require extra training and the acquisition of new skills. Peter Drucker said that the segment of higher education that will experience the biggest growth in the coming years is lifelong learning, because of the significant increase in the adult population and the need to learn new skills. We will also see the growth of senior entrepreneurship, led by managers with accumulated experience, along with the resources needed to face new ventures in areas yet to be discovered.

Are business schools in a state of maturity?

Given the dynamism of business, management education is in a state of permanent transformation, something that academic insiders are sometimes reluctant to accept. In fact, management education is changing in terms of its business model and not just as a phase within a cycle. Income sources for many business schools are changing, as are the needs of students and customers, as are traditional channels of distribution – both regarding the promotion of management programs as well as the diffusion of knowledge – and the entrance of mega-players and "new species." Business schools are the icebreakers of higher education. Where they go other higher education providers will follow.

Some commentators argue that the management education market in North America is approaching maturity. For example, Paul Danos, Dean of Tuck Business School, says: "the U.S. market is mature in that there are many university-based programs in every region of the country, and there are many levels of quality and prestige. The real growth in MBA programs worldwide will come from outside the U.S. and there are many varieties of programs including two-year, one-year, part-time, executive, and distance."[76] (January 25, 2008, Deanstalk http://www.deanstalk.net/deanstalk/2008/01/paul-danos-in-w.html)

The US market is the largest in the world, meeting the largest demand globally. The idea that sectors mature is an anthropomorphic analogy whereby each industry evolves consecutively through the stages of introduction, growth, maturity, and decline. The main advantage of this model is its simplicity and intuitiveness, but it does have its shortcomings too. Professor John Stopford's maxim is helpful to understand how innovation takes place even in mature industries, often giving birth to new businesses: "There are no mature industries; there are only mature companies."[77]

Stopford's words are indeed pertinent when considering the supposed maturity of the MBA. Those who make the maturity argument point to the high number of schools offering MBAs, the stability of the numbers of GMAT applicants, and the threat of some other substitute educational offerings. Maybe the truth is not so much that MBA programs are maturing but that there are simply some mature business schools out there.

There are a number of reasons for supporting this view. Firstly, if we look at the broad family of MBA programs, which includes Executive MBAs, MBAs specialized in sectors or particular disciplines (such as Finance or Marketing), with traditional or online formats, the fact is that the aggregated market has grown in the past decade and the prospects are positive.

Secondly, there is still ample room to grow in mature markets if schools aim at attracting more women to MBA programs. This is still a pending issue in many MBA programs, where the percentage of women is still below the average of other equally demanding degrees such as Law or Medicine. The average percentage of women in MBAs is still very low, although it has grown in recent years (around 40 percent at top schools) compared with other degrees.

Thirdly, there are still big opportunities to internationalize the student body at many business schools. The Bologna Accord in Europe, for example, may represent a historic opportunity in the future, not to mention other regions with faster growing economies, fundamentally Asia.

Fourthly, some of the statistics we are using may be misleading. Although GMAC[78] reports discrete growths in the number of participants in the GMAT test in the past years, many schools are using alternative instruments to select applicants, including their own tests.

Management education: An agenda for change

"It was the best of times, it was the worst of times [...] it was the spring of hope, it was the winter of despair, we had everything before us, we had nothing before us..." These familiar lines are from the start of Charles Dickens' *A Tale of Two Cities*, one of the most celebrated literary openings ever written. They seem as opposite today as they were to the French Revolution – the context of the novel – and even to Dickens' times.

Supposedly, every century brings a revolution and we are, more or less perceptibly, living through ours: a major societal shift, where the economic crisis, along with other factors like developments in technologies, the changes in the profile and values of younger generations, along with the conflicting forces of globalization and local diversity, are shaping a new model of society. Caught in the middle of this maelstrom, many managers feel uneasy and anxious. At the same time, the current circumstances provide an arena where true leadership can be tested, and where managers can identify new opportunities or reinvent their existing businesses: it is time for the survival of the fittest, in Darwinian terms, or for the birth of new species that better adapt to this new environment. Times of crisis provide the breeding ground for entrepreneurs and innovators, and many major companies, such as Google, were created under adverse circumstances. To paraphrase Dickens, the worst of times often provides the best of times too.

We live in a brave new world where business schools face the challenge of preparing not just good financial engineers or accomplished management technicians, but also global citizens. My purpose here is therefore to identify a number of initiatives that business schools' deans, directors, and faculty can implement in order to confront future crises and to better serve their mission.

They must initiate constructive interaction with various management stakeholders, particularly governments, since they will become pivotal players in the economy as regulators, shareholders, and investors in the coming years. Given the increasingly active role played by governments in the economy today and the foreseeable structural and cultural changes of the management landscape, business schools must find a new paradigm for their relationship between business and government. Entities such as public-private partnerships may well offer opportunities for research, teaching, and consultancy, as well as potentially suitable careers for MBA graduates.

To conclude this chapter, and Part I of the book, I would emphasize the need to dismiss any sense of elitism or arrogance among our management students, real or not. Management, if performed with personal modesty and a sense of service to the community, can be a noble occupation. We need true leaders, good managers who continually strive to improve their knowledge; and good management is synonymous with ethical management, nothing more, nothing less.

PART II

Today's pressing challenges

CHAPTER 4

The changing landscape

Back in 1976, Steven Spurrier, the former vintner turned world French-wine champion, organized an international wine tasting competition in Paris. The categories he selected were Cabernet Sauvignon for the reds, and Chardonnay for the whites. The competing wineries were from the US and France. The judges were French, and the tasting would be done blind so that the tasters would not know which varieties they were sampling. Everything about the event pointed to the French wines taking the day. But to the surprise of all concerned, the US wines came top in both categories. What's more, among the top ten wines of both colors, six were from California, and just four from France. George Taber, in his book *Judgment of Paris*,[79] argues that this event marked the beginning of the globalization of the wine sector: for the first time, New World wines had beaten those of the Old World, and what's more, on the basis of the decision of French judges.

Unlike wine, which originated in Europe, business education was born in the US around the beginning of the twentieth century. A similar analogy to that of *Judgment of Paris* in the business education world took place in 2010 when the *Financial Times* awarded first place in its ranking of MBA programs – business education's red wine category – to the London Business School, unseating Wharton, which had alternated the honor with Harvard since time immemorial. Furthermore, four of the top ten programs were not from the US. At the same time, in the Executive MBA category – the equivalent to white wines – the *Financial Times* ranked the program offered by the Kellogg-Hong Kong UST Business School, a Sino-American *coupage*, first; while among the top ten, six were not from the US, or were joint programs organized between US and overseas business schools. Business education may have its origins in the US, but the *Financial Times'* latest rankings suggest that it has now gone global. The Americans' loss of hegemony has been highlighted by Della Bradshaw, the Business Education editor of the FT. "When the FT began ranking MBA programs in 1999, 20 of the top 25 schools were from the US, with the remaining five from Europe; however, in 2010 there are just 11 US schools in the top 25, a further 11 are in Europe and three business schools are in Asia."[80]

In reality, the globalization of business schools began three decades ago. Globalization, a process that has taken place through the economy and other social activities, has been the most important driver in the development of higher education in recent decades.

Along with business schools, the entire educational world is going through a massive transformation. Driving this change are three powerful trends: the said globalization, new technology, and the changing nature of knowledge and its multifarious sources of creation and delivery. In Part II, we examine each of these trends in turn, and how they are redrawing the educational landscape.

First I examine some of the prevalent trends of this changing educational landscape – and in particular the new educational models that are emerging as a result, along with the generic strategies that traditional business schools may implement to achieve competitive advantages in a global context.

Trends shaping the new learning curve

Business schools are probably the most dynamic segment of higher education in terms of market orientation, curriculum changes, models of governance, and development of new programs. There are five elements affecting the sector that I would like to draw attention to:

1. *Increased competition and commoditization.* This, in turn, is stimulating the need for differentiation. Competition is now international. Increased student access to international programs and the growing standardization of MBAs, Executive MBAs, Advanced Management Programs, and Diplomas in Management means that business schools' offers are increasingly homogeneous and comparable across the board. This will further increase competition, requiring business schools to find ways to set themselves apart.

   Standardization means that programs have to reflect a series of characteristics or specifications. For example, to be ranked by the *Financial Times* or to be approved by the international accreditation agencies, MBA programs require applicants to have professional experience.

   In parallel, business schools are searching for new ways of differentiation from a global perspective, for example, offering specialist MBAs, focused on particular sectors – health care, energy or telecom, or on management functions – finance, supply chain management – or exploring new modalities and formats, like blended programs that combine face-to-face modules with online modules.

2. *Multi-polar competition.* Until a few years ago, the US was the center and the major player of business education. However, today, business education is a multipolar sector. This multipolarity demands that business schools aiming at competing on a global basis cannot rely solely on the attraction of international students to their home-based campuses, but they also need to have a presence in different continents.

Robert Zoellick, the president of the World Bank, often talks of a multi-polar world in the context of the changes sweeping the global economy.[81] Accenture Consulting has also taken up the term multi-polar competition to describe the way that multinational firms have grown.[82] This multi-polar world is reflected in the growing number of multinational firms from the emerging economies. Among *Fortune* magazine's top 500 companies worldwide for 2010, 46 are from China, up from 16 in 2005.[83] At the same time, the number of business schools from emerging economies, mainly in Asia, has grown in recent years, with more and more making it to the *Financial Times'* league tables and being accredited internationally.[84]

3. *The consolidation of university-based schools.* This is fast becoming the age of the university-based business school. Many business schools have traditionally functioned as independent institutions, even if they belonged to a university. Harvard Business School, located in Soldier's Field across the Charles River, separated from the rest of Harvard University, is a good example of this institutional and locational separation from parent universities. Most US business schools were created for post-graduate students, and enjoyed considerable autonomy. But in Europe, they were even more independent. INSEAD and IMD, for example, were not set up by universities but by business people, while in France, almost all the most prestigious business schools are part of the *Grandes Écoles* system, functioning under the auspices of regional chambers of commerce.

But the rise of globalization has questioned this independence. Recent years have seen more and more business schools join forces with their parent universities to try to exploit as many synergies as possible. Colin Mayer, former Dean of Oxford's Saïd Business School, told me that this is the age of the university-based business school. Mark Taylor, Dean of Warwick Business School, told the *Independent* newspaper that his "vision for the school is to become Europe's leading university-based business school."[85]

This increased integration of business schools with universities is reflected in the growing number of double degrees or joint programs with other schools in the university, such as medicine, law, or engineering. In the future this could lead to more business schools amplifying their focus on the post-graduate market to develop programs aimed at undergraduates.

The growing importance of business schools within the universities they were set up by, could also make them benchmarks for other research and teaching institutions on the basis of the income they generate, the number of students they attract, or the popularity of their programs. Business schools' growing contribution to their universities will also limit the resentment that has sometimes been expressed towards them by other departments within the social sciences.

4. *Hybridization.* A fourth element of the changing landscape is what is awkwardly labeled "hybridization." We will be witnessing experimentation and the development of new programs and educational approaches in business schools. These may include:

   • cross-disciplinary courses (merging management with design, the humanities, psychology, biology, and other sciences);
   • mixing the public and the private, and the emergence of MPAs (Master in Public Administration programs);
   • symbiosis between pedagogy and technology, along with a variety of delivery formats (face-to-face, online, distance learning);
   • integration of academic and clinical faculty, particularly given the shortage of academics with PhD degrees in management;
   • promotion of cultural diversity in the composition of MBA classes to enhance the learning experience; and
   • double degree, joint degree, and multiple exchange programs, that may allow participants to live in different countries and learn from diverse cultures.

5. *Need of achieving critical size and scale.* As a result of international competition, business schools will look for new ways to increase their size and scale, and thus establish a greater presence in the global market. As with other multinational institutions, business schools will require the resources to do this, such as faculty, research, or facilities. The way to establish a greater international presence lies with the opening of their own campuses abroad, when resources or financial support from local governments are available, or doing so with local partners, as has happened in other sectors.

Another way for business schools to achieve a bigger presence in the global market is through acquiring, or merging with, other educational institutions. While mergers and acquisitions are common in the business world, they were previously taboo among educational institutions. Yet, over the past decade, Europe has seen a spate of such mergers, particularly among business schools, although mostly within the confines of the same country. These include:

- the "new" Manchester Business School, which was formed in 2004 as a result of the merger of UMIST's Manchester School of Management, the Institute of Innovation Research (IoIR), the Victoria University of Manchester's School of Accounting and Finance, and the "old" Manchester Business School;
- TiasNimbas, the largest business school in the Netherlands, the result of a merger between Tias (a private company with limited liability, 80 percent of its shares being owned by Tilburg University and 20 percent by Eindhoven University of Technology) and Universiteit Nimbas in Utrecht;
- Aalto University, established on January 1, 2010, when the Helsinki University of Technology, Helsinki School of Economics, and the University of Art and Design Helsinki were merged; and
- Henley Business School, the result of merging the previously independent Henley Management College, formerly the Administrative Staff College, with the existing business school of the University of Reading.

We can expect to see an increase in mergers and acquisitions in the future, both in the private and public sector, particularly if legal restrictions are lifted. In the case of public institutions, the search for synergies, the need to achieve greater economies of scale, and the reduction of the number of programs will all lead to consolidation in business schools, as well as in universities in general. For example, the United Kingdom, a country that historically has anticipated many of the forthcoming reforms in other countries, will likely see this process very shortly, due to the educational reforms being implemented by the coalition government of Prime Minister David Cameron, and outlined in the *Browne Report*.[86]

All these trends are fostering competition at a national and global level, and making business schools adopt new strategies to adapt to a new environment that will change more rapidly than ever before. The business education landscape has grown beyond its traditional academic borders and comprises a number of new species, new forms of education, which are altering some of these basic suppositions and changing the rules of the game. In the following sections, I analyze some of this new phenomena.

A new species: The "Big Education Retailers"

The past two decades have seen an increase in business and management schools of all kinds, some within Academia, others independent. The latter belong to a new species, many of them with different missions, but all focused on teaching and spreading knowledge rather than in generating academic research.

Generally, they are commonly denominated for-profit educational schools and colleges, given that their premises are usually privately owned, held by partners, or even built with money raised on the international money markets.

That said, distinguishing in terms of for-profit and not-for-profit is not an entirely helpful exercise, and largely fails to explain the phenomenon of these new schools, as pointed out by the 2010 annual report by Universities UK, which represents 133 universities and higher education centers. "Almost all UK not-for-profit universities now work on a businesslike basis and are expected by their funding bodies to accumulate surpluses in order to finance expansion and capital investment," reads its crisp assessment.[87]

The report notes that many prestigious universities move into the business sector, or are clients of investment funds – at least for the management of their endowments –, which means that their results and activities are analyzed by ratings agencies such as Standard & Poor's or Moody's. As things stand, and on the basis of their strategic mission, the legal status of the so-called for-profits, or the fact that they are privately owned, doesn't necessarily determine their worth or nature.

That is why I prefer to use the name "Big Education Retailers," rather than "for-profit universities," to refer to those institutions that are basically concentrated on teaching activities with large-scale programs supported by online methodologies, good value offerings, and in some cases with global presence. Table 4.1 includes some of the main operators in this segment.

The best way to assess the contribution of these institutions to society is by their activities, as well as what the people running them do with the profits generated. For this reason, it is hard to understand the criticism directed at them from some sectors – mainly academic – who tend to dismiss them for "commercializing" education.

This approach is based on the belief that education and teaching should not be subject to business criteria such as efficiency, or having a market outlook – characteristics of many institutions – as this exposes them to the risk of distorting such a basic and supposedly disinterested activity as education. The argument is that the independence of academic institutions guarantees their neutrality when it comes to generating knowledge, rather

Table 4.1 Big education retailers

	Revenue/Net Income ($million)	Students/ Countries	Mkt Cap./ Value	Brands	Employees/ Faculty
Apollo	4,926/568	315,350 (2005) 2010: Phoenix, 470,800	NASDAQ: APOL $6.28B	University of Phoenix, Apollo Global, Inc. $1 B joint venture (2007)	(2010); 22,220 (empl) 35,194 (fac)
Laureate	1,420	550,000; 21 countries, 55 institutions	Private Buying price in 2007 est. $1.3B	Don't know which of 50 to include, see list: Laureate online education	28,500 (empl)
Devry	1,915/280	80,000+	NYSE:DV $3.71B	Keller Graduate School of Management Becker Professional Education and DeVry Inc.::	10,009 (empl)
Kaplan Subsidiary of Washington Post	4,569/91	70,011 (online campus)	NYSE:WPO $3.76B	Kaplan Higher Education Kaplan Test Preparation Kaplan International and Kaplan Ventures	Full-time: 15,000 (empl); Part-time: 19,000 (empl)
Capella Education Company	(2010) 114.7/17.9	38,000 (purely online)	NASDAQ:CPLA $898.88M	Capella University	1,358 (empl)
Corinthian Colleges, Inc.	1,764/146	86,000	NASDAQ:COCO $429.61M	Everest, WyoTech, or Heald	11,500 (empl)
Strayer Education, Inc.	512/105	54,000	NASDAQ:STRA $1.81B	Strayer University, Inc	334 (empl)

Continued

Table 4.1 Continued

	Revenue/Net Income ($million)	Students/ Countries	Mkt Cap./ Value	Brands	Employees/ Faculty
Education Management Corp	2,508/168	158,300	Buying price 2006, est. $3.4B Back in 2009 to NASDAQ:EDMC; $ 2.54B	Argosy University Brown Mackie College The Art Institutes	13,400 (empl)
ITT Educational Services	1,590/374	80,000	NYSE:ESI, $2.04B	Daniel Webster College (DWC) ITT Technical Institutes	5,500 (empl)
BPP Holdings (Part of Apollo Int since 4Q2009)	251/loss (186.6)	BPP has more than 5,500 law students	2009, BPP was acquired by Apollo Global, Inc. and delisted from the London Stock Exchange.	BPP University College of Professional Studies BPP BPP Law BPP Business School	

than their being subordinate to the spurious interests of stakeholders outside the educational sphere.

There is no denying that there are a great many mediocre institutions among the for-profit business schools. Furthermore, the poor image of for-profit universities has been tarnished by a number of scandals in the US to do with fraudulent admissions procedures, as well as misuse of federal funding for grants. *The New York Times* published a story related to the "Pell Grant fraud controversy" in August 2010 regarding a number of for-profit colleges that had received more than US$4 billion in federal grants and an additional US$20 billion in loans from the US Department of Education in 2010.[88]

However, Jennifer Washburn, in her book *University Inc: The Corporate Corruption of Higher Education*,[89] argues that many universities are also subordinate to the commercial interests of the companies that finance their research, for example, through technology transfer offices. Washburn argues that universities' integrity is at stake when commercial interests dictate what research is carried out, and how. However, her argument misses a key point. In addition to the idea of "research for its own sake," universities, and particularly business schools, as producers of knowledge, should focus their research on solving social problems. In our market-based system, one of the most effective channels for identifying and responding to social needs is through businesses themselves.

At the same time, it is also true that many big education retailers or for-profit universities fulfill a valid role in training executives and in other areas of higher education. Many of these schools are perfectly open about their mission, which is to teach rather than to carry out research. This didactic role means that they are able to offer courses at more competitive prices than many other institutions, and thus reach a wider public, while at the same time carrying out their mission to offer lifelong learning to all the professions and to people from all walks of life.

As noted earlier, differentiating in terms of for-profit and not-for-profit is not necessarily the best basis for analyzing the education management market, at least in terms of the programs on offer. Companies such as Apollo, which owns the University of Phoenix, Kaplan, Capella Education, or DeVry University, have their own schools, an international presence, and aggressive expansion plans until 2020 in the Americas, Europe, and Asia. Some of them are traded on the stock exchange, and are listed on indexes such as the NASDAQ, a strategy that gives them access to external financing to fund their expansion plans. Laureate, another for-profit educational conglomerate, defines its mission as making "quality higher education accessible and affordable so that more students can pursue their dreams."[90] The company's objective is clearly to provide education in the "good value" segment and to reach a large market of students who would not normally have access to the top universities; this in itself is a respectable enough mission. Value, as far as the company is concerned, is "defined by our students and those who employ them."

The question here is whether these educational conglomerates can continue to notch up the double-digit growth of recent years, even at a time when education is undergoing permanent growth and demand remains steady. In large part, the growth-through-acquisition policy of these companies has been to then rationalize resources and procedures, to increase efficiency and profitability, and to look for synergies. But the economies of scale achieved through this process may turn out to be limited, and they expose themselves to the risk, as some analysts[91] have pointed out, of creating financial bubbles, particularly bearing in mind that growth through acquisitions has largely been financed through leveraged buyouts of property, the value of which will have fallen sharply in value due to the economic crisis. They are further limited by new restrictions on funds for grants in the wake of the Pell Grant fraud controversy mentioned earlier.

I believe that the needs of education and professional development can be met only through a combined approach by private and public institutions, of for-profit and not-for-profit schools. Or better, of big education retailers, on the one hand, and of research universities, on the other. The former are focused on teaching and/or distribution of knowledge, the latter, on the development of research and the delivery of high-quality differentiated programs, combined with a wide offer of complementary services to students.

Corporate universities

Many large corporations, from a range of sectors and across different continents, have their corporate universities (CUs), where they train their staff, identify potential senior managers, and inculcate the core aspects of their organizational culture and strategy. Normally, CUs rely economically on the budgets of their matrix companies. During the 1980s, when such institutions flourished, business schools saw them as dangerous competitors, particularly their executive education departments.

But experience has shown that the relationship between the academic world and the CUs has been largely collaborative, and many in-company programs developed by business schools are carried out jointly with the heads of CUs. Furthermore, several directors of CUs come from the business school world, for example, Joel Podolny, former Dean of Yale School of Management, who now runs the still embryonic Apple University.

Most CUs are, strictly speaking, neither universities, nor do they pretend to be: they neither have their own teaching staff, nor do they carry out research. As such they cannot compete with the business schools. Furthermore, they are often seen as training centers with a captive audience: the company's own employees.

As such, it seems unlikely that CUs will ever offer open programs for executives from other companies. Were they to do so, we might usefully ask whether they would admit employees from competitors, or whether they would be obliged to offer jobs to all the graduates from their programs.

Networks of CUs have been set up across continents with the aim of sharing expertise, identifying new tendencies, and developing joint knowledge. The best known is Corporate University Exchange, an association headquartered in the US and with members around the world, along with the corporate division of EFMD, the European Foundation for Management Development, which has developed its own system of accreditation for CUs, known as CLIP, the Corporate Learning Improvement Process, which has already recognized 16 institutions, all of them European.

Business schools and CUs have also worked together to create several interesting initiatives in management education. These emphasize the applicability and value for money aspects of training, reflected in talk of "learning solutions," among them coaching, one of the growing trends in executive education, or the development of initiatives to identify and strengthen executives' leadership skills. In general, collaboration between business schools and the CUs is growing, although the academic and corporate worlds remain wary of each other.

I would argue that CUs have the capacity to become laboratories for testing many of the theories and models developed in university departments. At a meeting in 2010, Leslie Teichgraber, VP of Pepsico University, told me that CUs increasingly look to business schools to come up with new concepts and to identify the trends that will allow them to improve their executives' training and education.

Consultancy-based education centers

Consulting firms are also natural candidates to enter the management-training sector, and many of them have developed educational courses for their executives. It is noteworthy that McKinsey talks about its graduates as alumni, and set up the McKinsey Global Institute in 1990 to carry out economic research. It also publishes the well-respected *McKinsey Quarterly*.

Many of the management tools taught in business schools were in fact created by consultancies: Boston Consulting Group's growth-share matrix, or McKinsey's value chain are just two examples. The perceived advantages of CUs as information providers are applicable, *mutatis mutandi*, to consultancies.

One particularly interesting case of a consultancy that moved into the educational field is the Arthur D. Little School of Business set up in 1964 by the company of the same name. Inspired by MIT, and located close by in Boston, over the years the school has developed its own programs, initially for its own consultants, later making them available to the wider market. By 2002, it was offering Masters in Management, and an MBA, both online and at the school. It had attracted a significant body of foreign students, although its overall student body barely numbered one hundred. The Arthur D. Little brand name gave the school international presence, but by the same token, when the company went bankrupt following a series of scandals involving its senior management, the school went down with it. The school was then bought by Bertil Hult, the well-known Swedish businessman and founder of EF Education First, one of the world's most important private-education companies, with more than 22,000 employees and a presence in 51 countries. The school changed its name to the Hult International Business School, occupying the ninety-fourth position in the *Financial Times* ranking of MBAs in 2010.

Education delivery through social networks

One recent development is the reappearance of management training based on home study supported by Internet-based social networks. Perhaps the best known of these is *The Personal MBA* (PMBA),[92] an initiative that came about when more than 100 applicants for Harvard Business School's MBA program and other top schools were turned down after hacking into the online application system ApplyYourself.com to find out whether they had been accepted before official notification by the schools in question.[93]

When the well-known blogger and arch-critic of MBA programs Seth Godin found out about the story, he wrote in one of his posts that the unlucky candidates had just saved themselves $150,000, and that they could match the MBA program they had just been turned down for by reading around 40 books and combining their home studies with work experience. This set in motion a movement to identify MBA programs' reading lists, which was led by Josh Kaufman, a young executive at Procter & Gamble, who soon set up a website that would play a key role in the development of the movement, attracting thousands of participants who read the book list, and then shared their feedback and professional experiences in online chat rooms.

PMBA participants do not graduate, or receive any certificate or formal qualification; they are not taught by academics, and of course there are no authorities to vouch for the quality of their studies. This is a uniquely peer-to-peer experience, as its proponents intended. The only cost is the purchase of the recommended books. (Kaufman discusses the first years of the initiative in his 2011 book *The Personal MBA*.)[94]

The appeal of the PMBA lies both in its entrepreneurial spirit and in it being a peer-to-peer experience. That said, there is no way that simply reading some books and sharing one's ideas about them with others can ever match the learning processes of a structured course led by academics and business people. Otherwise, all traditional learning could be substituted by reading an encyclopedia, an approach that so far has not been proven to be efficacious, and certainly lacks any appeal. What's more, with the breaking of the initial wave of enthusiasm, PMBAs seem to have settled into little more than a reading club for management studies enthusiasts to share their thoughts and experiences.

Advocates of PMBAs are also guilty of dismissing the reasons why people want to take an MBA at a top school in the first place, and which are to do with the experiences they will accumulate during study, their admittance to sophisticated networks, being able to associate one's professional career with a prestige brand, or being able to enter the professional market with the advantage of having an accredited academic qualification.

Social networks offer a powerful learning tool yet to be fully exploited by the education sector. Business schools could perhaps learn from the PMBA phenomenon by applying social networking to extend the learning experience beyond the classroom and by encouraging more peer-to-peer activities.

As seen, the upsurge of new business education providers with disruptive models and approaches to the learning process poses new threats to traditional business education players. How can business schools turn those threats into opportunities? The remainder of this chapter focuses on how business schools generate their income. I also propose two generic strategies that may orientate academic managers to build sustainable advantages from the new learning curve.

How business schools earn their income

There are a number of different economic models – or business models – for business schools. Traditionally, a business school's business model or income source determines its strategy, its mission, and the resources it relies on. There are, basically, three alternative models. In reality, they are not mutually exclusive, and most successful business schools are based on models that allow for a diverse ranges of income sources.

Type 1. *Subsidized business schools.* Typically to be found in the public sector within a large university, subsidized business schools' income tends to come from regional or federal (national) budgets. On the basis of an analysis of a sample of business schools belonging to this category, I found that around 70 percent of their funding comes from government subsidies. As a result, these business schools are able to offer low, or even free, tuition fees. Typically these are large institutions with a substantial teaching staff made up of high-profile academics with a track record of research. In countries such as China, where education is still largely funded by the state, business schools receive government money on the basis of the number of successful graduates they produce.

The survival of the subsidized model depends on the extent to which the state is prepared or is able to continue funding higher education. In the United Kingdom, for example, in recent years there has been a move away from government-funded university places. A mixed model has emerged in the US, where private business schools such as those in the Ivy League, many of them belonging to prestigious research universities such as Harvard or Stanford, exist alongside the major public universities such as Haas Business School in

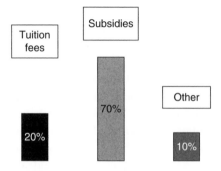

Figure 4.1 Subsidized b-schools

Berkeley, part of the University of California, and Michigan Business School.

In Europe, most of the major universities are publically funded, although many business schools were set up as independent institutions, or are funded by business organizations such as the local Chamber of Commerce. Examples of European subsidized business schools include Rotterdam Business School (Erasmus University), Vienna University Business School, or Louvain Business School.

Type 2. *Endowment-funded business schools.* Rooted in the tradition of "giving back," endowments are a characteristic feature of the US university system. The private universities of the Ivy League, for example, compete with each other in international rankings on the basis of their endowments, which are made up of the amount of money they have accumulated through donations from individuals and companies. Donors often subject their endowments to conditions regarding their use. Business schools with large endowments will generally have other sources of financing, as is the case with Harvard, Wharton, Chicago, or Stanford, where tuition fees and income from executive education also make a significant contribution. Figure 4.2 illustrates the average amount of income that the top business schools make from interest on endowments, which is around 25 percent.

The financial crisis has hit endowments hard, reducing their income-generating capacity. For example, Harvard Business School's endowment totaled $2.8 billion, more than triple Stanford's $825 million, but both endowments have shrunk as a result of the crisis. The business school expert John A. Byrne says: "Stanford saw a decline in endowment income in 2010 to $52 million from $58.8 million a year earlier. The school largely offset the decline by rising tuition and fees from students, which brought in $70.9 million last year, up from $64.5 million in 2009. The result: Student tuition and fees now account for 46% of Stanford's annual operating budget, up from 42% in 2009".[95]

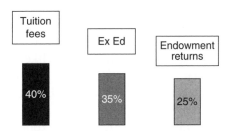

Figure 4.2 Endowed b-schools

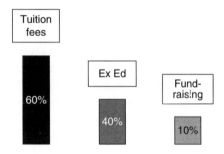

Figure 4.3 Tuition-led b-schools

Type 3. Tuition-based business schools. The defining model for most of Europe's top business schools is tuition based, with most funds coming from matriculation fees for their assorted programs, as well as from executive education and fund raising.

European business schools have long been envious of the generous endowments bestowed on the big US schools. The plus side of this is that, as a result of being financially needy, European schools have had to become more responsive to the requirements of the market.

On the basis of their present and future sources of income, business schools may develop different strategies and portfolio of programs. The discussion of different types of business schools according to the range of programs and international positioning, as well as the forseeable future moves of strategic groups follows next.

Two generic strategies for business schools: Vertical integration or specialization?

It is easy to talk of business schools in broad terms as if they are globally homogenous. This is what critics of business schools often do. In fact, business schools differ widely across the globe in terms of mission, program portfolio, legal status, and economic models. They may be part of professional networks (like the *Grandes Écoles* in France, belonging to the Chambers of Commerce), or be independent, like INSEAD. They may belong to wider universities with ample educational offerings, like most business schools in the US, or be part of small, specialized universities, like the polytechnics of Milan or Zurich in Europe. They may be public and large, like Arizona State University or Rotterdam University, or be small scale and selective like Dartmouth College in the US, Cheung

Kong Business School in China, or Sabanci University Business School in Turkey.

The "business models" of academic institutions and how they are funded also vary across the globe. The "Ivy League" institutions in the US are heavily endowed, and the returns coming from their endowments represent a major source of their incomes. In fact, the fund-raising culture developed in the US has created a distinctive economic model of universities that many have tried to replicate elsewhere with mixed results.

Alternatively, in Europe the nation state has traditionally been the main financial contributor of universities. At the same time, a new model of business schools has emerged in Europe in recent decades, their income based on the revenues mainly generated from a diversified mix of educational programs, degree and non-degree. This alternative economic model seems more inspiring and applicable to some emerging economies such as the BRIC countries.

Some business strategists argue that companies, based on their resources and capabilities, should focus only on those industries where they can excel. According to this perspective, diversification is not a preferred option for growth unless the industry newly entered into is closely related to the company's core business or unless there are clear synergies to be exploited.

This is also applicable to educational institutions and was very lucidly explained by Professor Peter Lorange, former President of IMD, the Swiss business school: "Strategy means choice, not only in business but also in educational institutes. In the short term, choices that break with tradition may be painful but I firmly believe that in the long term they pay off. Of course, choices must be made consistently and must be based on a clear strategy."[96]

Under Lorange's leadership IMD was fundamentally – and successfully – focused on executive education programs. However, the globalization of education, and management education in particular, is challenging traditional paradigms. The global evolution of management education will foster the polarization of business schools' models: on the one extreme of the spectrum, "focused schools," covering only one or two segments of higher education, and on the other end, full-service business schools, offering a wide array of educational activities at all levels on a global scale. Following an idea inspired by Harvard Professor Michael Porter's proposals,[97] schools that do not choose one of these models will become trapped in the middle and will lose their competitive edge.

The changes to the world of learning also mean that educational providers are adopting different strategies according to their strengths and

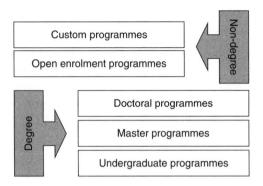

Figure 4.4 Segments of management education

opportunities. Here too, the patterns are most apparent with business schools. Business schools emerged in the US as centers of post-graduate studies. The model was then exported to Europe, where the majority of business schools that were set up in the 1950s and 1960s, such as INSEAD and IMD, taught masters programs for executives.

Figure 4.4 illustrates the main programs offered by business schools. Historically, the most popular segment has been masters degree programs, among them MBAs and Masters in Management, the latter being the fastest growing in Europe in recent years.

Considering the portfolio of programs that business schools may offer, they may be classified generically into two types: "Vertically integrated business schools" and "focused business schools."

Vertically integrated, or full-service business schools, offer every segment of management education, from undergraduate programs to executive education. The best example of this in the US is Wharton, which offers world-class teaching in all segments. In Europe, examples include Oxford's Saïd Business School, Rotterdam's RSM, IE Business School, or HEC-Paris. Schools that adopt these kinds of strategy may build up a teaching staff made up of a wide range of academics, typically leaders in their field, and whose responsibilities include undertaking research and teaching.

On the other hand, focused business schools concentrate on a particular activity in a bid to become the global leader in their sphere. For example, in the case of IMD, the focus is on executive education. The focus can also be on a particular discipline or specialist area of expertise, as in the case of the Center for Creative Leadership, one of the world's top schools for leadership programs and coaching. Schools can also seek to set themselves apart through their teaching methodology or learning system, as was the case with a number of the training providers that some years ago explored opportunities in the once successful *Second Life* online platform.

Future moves of business schools

"Strategic grouping" is a commonly used tool in sector analysis, which facilitates the creation of maps of the different companies operating in a given sector on the basis of the most relevant criteria for making competitive decisions. A strategic group is one that groups companies that follow a similar strategy. The criteria for classifying strategic groups vary, depending on their range of products or services, the geographic markets they cover, distribution channels, brand consolidation, the degree of vertical integration in their spheres of activity, the quality of their product or service, and price range.

From a global perspective, seeing business schools in terms of strategic groups allows us to compare their performance, as well as to benchmark them, measure the barriers that prevent mobility between different groups, and to orient stakeholders.

Different classification criteria can be applied to business schools, but when giving presentations or developing strategies for my own school, I have focused on two:

1. the global presence and reputation of the school, measured in terms of international accreditation, position in rankings, proportion of international teaching staff and students, international alliances, and programs they have set up in other countries; and
2. the range of programs a school has developed, as seen in the previous section, whether it is focused on specific types of programs, such as executive education, or whether it covers all educational segments, and is a full-service school.

Figure 4.5 shows these two criteria according to whether they are vertical (based on reputation and global presence) or horizontal (based on their range of programs).

In the upper part of the chart are the most prestigious global schools, ranging from the so-called boutiques, centered on a segment of specific programs (IMD, which earns most of its income from executive education programs, is perhaps the best example of this) to the other end of the spectrum where the integrated schools – or full-service – are found, such

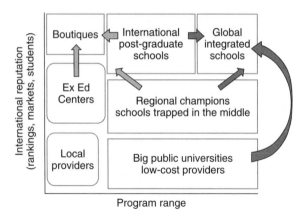

Figure 4.5 Strategic groups: Future moves

as Wharton, which runs programs from undergraduate level to executive education, all at the highest levels of excellence.

On the basis of this classification of strategic groups, the continuing process of globalization will oblige business schools – particularly the elite institutions – to choose between two strategies:

1. to find ways to set themselves apart from the competition through specialization in a particular aspect of management education (for instance, IMD in executive education, or the Center for Creative Leadership in the area of leadership); and
2. by becoming full-service business schools, thus attaining the critical mass that will allow them to cover all educational segments, and by having a broad-based teaching faculty, as well as a global presence.

The failure to opt for either of these strategies will result in being caught in the middle, that is to say, lacking sufficient differentiation as far as programs go, and by not being large enough to compete internationally.

I believe that this trend is already underway in Europe, as shown by London Business School's decision to enter the Masters in Management segment of the market. Talking to the deans of US business schools that until now have offered only MBA programs, some say that they are looking at entering the undergraduate segment, or designing new Masters in Management for graduates with no business experience.

Obviously, there are strategic groups that will be able to survive based on other models than the two mentioned above, either because their reputation or global prestige are not key factors for them, or because they have a competitive edge through lower costs. This will be the case with distance-learning providers, or with providers of local education such as public universities offering management programs targeted at domestic constituencies and that are financed through government subsidies – factors that block them from competing in the global market.

In sum, business schools cannot rely on the "business as usual" maxim to compete in a global higher education world. I have proposed two generic strategies that provide a solid basis for future growth, but intense competition will however remain a constant reference in the future. It is now time to concentrate on the next shaping force of education, the impact that new technologies have on the learning process.

CHAPTER 5

E-Learning

Let us take a step back and look at the bigger picture: what are the big trends that are re-shaping higher education? The first and perhaps most easily observed trend is the arrival and adoption of new learning technologies. Witness the impact of IT on the creation and distribution of knowledge, teaching methodologies, and communication in general. These technologies and online teaching will transform the role of the teacher, who will cease their traditional role, instead morphing into a kind of orchestra conductor of the learning process. Teaching materials will increasingly be in digital format, and the speed and procedures developed on the Internet to create, spread, and validate ideas and theories will profoundly change the nature of research, along with the very concepts of authorization or academic verification.

The impact of IT on the learning process is unquestionable and unstoppable. One obvious effect is the huge increase in distance learning at educational institutions across the globe. This is one of the areas where business schools have led the way. Of the business schools that used to offer only face-to-face learning, probably over 80 percent are now running online courses.

Traditionally, distance learning was confined to the larger education providers. They had a high volume of students that made investing in distance-based technologies and learning materials more cost effective. Today, however, as technology costs continue to tumble through technologies such as Cloud Computing, the opportunities for remote learning are becoming available to all. Indeed, one of the most exciting and alluring prospects that I see in the new learning curve is the potential to provide access to education for people who were previously denied it, in particular, the poorest segments of society.

For example, there is no reason – other than a failure of our collective imagination and will – why the very best educational materials should not be made available to the poorest people in the world. Imagine, for example, a young person in a remote village in Africa who is able to download learning materials designed and created at one of the top universities in the world. Or think of a young woman in India who can access learning modules from Harvard or Oxford or my own institution, IE, via their mobile phone. Imagine how that could transform her life. Imagine how it could transform the world. Fortunately, this is increasingly becoming a reality.

As noted, business schools have played a leading role in adopting remote-learning technologies. They have also been pioneers in adopting learning materials. My school IE, for example, in common with several others has invested in producing interactive online case studies. The development of new technologies and their use by schools that have a leading role in conventional classroom-based learning are not only altering the boundaries of this educational segment but also the very nature of the learning process. Many people believe that online programs cannot entirely match the human experience and vividness of face-to-face education. That may be true in some regards, but I would argue that remote learning technologies have other advantages. For example, they can be asynchronous – they don't rely on all the participants being in the same place at the same time. A student on one continent and time zone can download and use an online learning module while the professor who created it and their fellow classmates sleep on another continent or in another time zone.

This means that a plethora of new learning methodologies is coming of age. Today, for example, it is possible to replicate the classroom experience for people on different continents using the latest telepresence technologies. And this is just the start.

The first wave of e-learning providers

For me the technology issue really began to take centre stage one bright, chilly November morning in 1999. I was at the Boston offices of Batterymarch Financial Management, looking out across the city from the landmark John Hancock Tower. The IE Business School board of directors met with its advisory board to outline our strategy for the coming decade.

The presentation had been preceded by several months of intense preparation led by three key figures: IE's President, Diego del Alcázar, a man characterized by his vision, intuition, and commitment to change; Julio Urgel, the then Dean; and José Mario Álvarez de Novales, a peerless strategist, who, sadly, passed away in 2006.

Tania Zouikin, the President of Batterymarch, and the meeting's host, had dubbed my contribution *The Red Book*: I had chosen the color for the background of the final part of my PowerPoint presentation to press home the importance of the event. That meeting marked the beginning of

IE Business School's active development of online programs and a series of alliances with business schools across the globe, exemplified by the creation of Sumaq, a consortium bringing together Latin America's top business schools with IE.

One of the main conclusions of my presentation was recognition of the need to find new ways of delivering our programs. I outlined the following ways forward: adapt faculty to new needs and forms of delivery; amplify the range, internationalization, and variety of new programs; explore distance and online education forms of provision to reach international clients; and make outside IT providers a key link in the value chain.

Even by the 1990s, few business schools had thought about offering online courses, and most still saw online learning as part of distance learning, associating it with autodidacticism, and as something of an inferior educational product. But, alerted by the threat from players such as the Apollo Group's University of Phoenix – although not a direct competitor, it was shaking up the lower echelons of business education, and had acquired an aura of innovation – we had come to understand the enormous potential of online input for our executive education courses.

Some of the more prestigious business schools in the US had already begun to take tentative steps in this direction, setting up consortia and forming alliances with IT companies to develop platforms and new teaching models. The thinking behind these alliances was that the business schools had the content and teaching staff, and that IT companies had the ability to develop the software and the platforms for the courses that would be taught online. It seemed the perfect synergy, and would broaden the business schools' horizon without weakening their brand, given that the consortia would function independently and were not going to offer university qualifications.

Among the most important consortia that had been already set up by the last year of the millennium were Unext, bringing together Columbia Business School, the London School of Economics, Stanford University, the University of Chicago, and Carnegie Mellon among its partners; Pensare, whose main partners were Fuqua School of Business (Duke University) and Harvard Business School; University Access, backed by North Carolina at Chapel Hill; and Caliber, whose associates were Wharton School of Business and the University of Southern California.

These initiatives generated considerable expectation in the market, attracting major investors and the attention of analysts such as the *Financial Times'* Della Bradshaw, who in October of 1999 wrote: "All the talk these days is of technology partners."[98] A growing number of business schools in Europe and the US, encouraged by the example of these pioneers, began approaching IT companies to find ways to get into these consortia, a process that was quickly dubbed "musical chairs" by the pundits, as the schools sought desperately not to be left out of the innovation game.

There was speculation as to which of these consortia would end up dominating the market, which platform would win out, and which would become the global benchmark in attracting the hundreds of thousands of students worldwide that the market potentially offered. At that time, the two main platforms were IBM's Lotus, and Blackboard. UNext and Pensare had also developed their own platforms.

Also under discussion was whether this new approach to education would turn out to be more costly than traditional methods of teaching. Developing platforms and new courses was a costly affair, particularly if prestigious business schools produced the contents. Furthermore, although some economies of scale could be found through distribution – the more the participants in a program, the lower the cost of producing the modules – student expectations of permanent feedback, along with the need to customize courses for businesses, did not offer much hope for huge economies of scale.

The dream of Icarus: The case of UNext

Five years later, by 2004, many consortia had either folded or been bought out. The only commercially successful online initiative over the long haul was Fuqua School of Business, whose blended-format Executive MBA gave it the lead. The story of UNext offers a salutary lesson regarding the huge expectations created by the new consortia set up by some business schools and IT companies at the height of the dot-com years.

UNext and its affiliate Cardean University were set up in 1997 with an initial investment estimated at US$180 million. UNext was owned by Knowledge Universe, set up the year before by junk bond supremo Michael Milken, the man who had been jailed and was fined more than US$1 billion for securities law violations in the 1980s.

Conceived as a B2B company with the aim of developing exclusive online educational programs, UNext had no physical teaching staff or campus, unlike other for-profit institutions such as the University of Phoenix or DeVry University. One of its major strengths lay in the academic partners it had managed to line up, among them Columbia Business School, which had the right of veto over future partners, along with the London School of Economics, Stanford University, the University of Chicago, and

Carnegie Mellon. UNext had also managed to attract a stellar line up of academic heavyweights, including Daniel R. Fischel, the then Dean of Chicago Law School, and the three renowned University of Chicago economists Gary Becker, Jack Gould, and Merton H. Miller, who sat on the board.

UNext was meant to be fully operative from day one. In the words of Richard P. Strubel, its President and CEO: "This is a very expensive undertaking. And the whole business model depends on making a huge up-front investment rather than a business-to-consumer model of selling individual courses. I don't know that anyone will ever do it again, and they certainly won't do it the way that we did it."[99] This meant hiring a large staff comprised of software engineers, specialists in cognitive knowledge, psychologists, and teachers, among others. After looking into using IBM's Lotus, it was decided to develop an in-house platform, the cost of which was estimated to have run into the dozens of millions of dollars. Among UNext's first corporate clients were Barclays, AOL Time Warner, Bertelsmann, IBM, and General Motors.

It wasn't long before the first major problems surfaced. On May 4, 2001, the *Chronicle of Higher Education* ran an article headlined: "Rich in Cash and Prestige, UNext Struggles in Its Search for Sales".[100] The article was about UNext's high burn rate and growing skepticism about its viability. In the months that followed, other articles reported on decisions to cut back on staff, as well as problems with the academic staff's contracts, and the lack of demand to generate the kind of income needed to keep the project afloat, with speculation that communications giant Thomson (now Thomson Reuters) was interested in taking it over.

So where did UNext go wrong? Like so many of its equally unsuccessful contemporaries, the project was overly ambitious and costly, and its vertical integration failed to cover both the development and commercialization of its programs. Another factor was the cost of developing the technology, which, in the end, differed little from the already existing platforms in the market.

It was also erroneously thought by its founders that UNext could get away with so-called differentiated programs – costlier than those offered by competitors Apollo and DeVry – via an exclusively online delivery rather than via including face-to-face teaching in its programs as well: the so-called blended approach. Once again, unrealistic growth and earnings estimates were at the root of the project's problems, and to top it all, UNext pointedly failed to understand the importance of in-house teaching staff for an educational institution's identity, and instead opted to subcontract out knowledge generation. The adventure of UNext reminds of

Icarus to reach the Sun with unsuited equipment: too far, too fast, and too ambitious.

It's not about the platform

What we have learned is that technology alone is not the answer, but that it is a significant part of the answer. Blended delivery, combining online and face-to-face teaching offered, continues to offer tremendous potential for management teaching. Among its advantages are:

- Easier and friendly access: where and when the participant wants, allowing for participation from remote places.
- Flexible and tailored to student needs, with asynchronous sessions.
- Participation in "Learning Communities", since technologies allow for a wide access to social networks.
- Continuous feedback and personal assessment through sophisticated applications.
- Keeps the momentum of learning, as opposed to the static and transilient experience of the traditional classroom session.
- Creates new markets and clients, with the potential of reaching the entire world.

Over the past ten years at IE Business School we have fine-tuned the blended approach to teaching management, with excellent results according to the opinion of participants: *The Economist* ranked our Executive MBA in 2010 as the Best in the World.[101] We have taken a trial and error approach, but always being aware of the need for prudence when making new investments, and with a weather eye on developments in the sector, both within and beyond our cluster. Perhaps where we got it most right was by understanding from the start that developing our particular brand of blended educational delivery wasn't so much about inventing a new model that was radically different from traditional teaching, but about replicating as accurately as possible time-honored methods through the combination of teaching with accessible technology.

Furthermore, we understood that involving our teaching staff in this process was essential. We knew that tutors or teachers lacking the qualifications and experience of our professors in the classroom could not deliver blended teaching. The solution was to give our professorate intensive training and support in how to teach online. At the same time, we understood that new teaching materials, such as multi-media case studies, needed to be developed by the same people who produced traditional format teaching materials, and not subcontracted out. To do this we set up a special team to help our professors.

Finally, and no less important, we have seen that the success of these blended programs is not based on some magical technological platform able to solve every problem associated with the learning process. Instead, as with traditional teaching methods, it takes place through interaction between students and staff, program directors, and the technicians who keep the platform running, along with the practice we have developed along the way to make the learning experience as satisfying as traditional methods. In a sentence: it's not about the platform; it's about the quality of the learning process.

Along the way, we have seen that most of the challenges we have come up against in developing blended delivery could be overcome or got around. But one aspect that has proved problematic is the amount of time that teaching staff need to dedicate to each online student – if students are to be taught by the same professors who teach in our classrooms, as opposed to being taught by tutors, as is the case with most online education.

An online session can extend over several days. Our experience shows that teachers often end up putting about four times as much work in answering students' questions and advising them as they would in a normal classroom situation, which obviously means that teachers need to be paid more.

Another aspect of our blended programs is that we require students to finish their studies within the same time frame they would if they were attending face-to-face. In other words they belong to a class, or cohort. We feel that this approach builds a stronger sense of belonging because students establish rapport with their fellow participants. This might seem less flexible than the approach taken by schools such as Warwick or Henley – which allow participants to complete their studies over a series of years – but we believe that the sense of continuity this approach confers outweighs any disadvantages, and makes for a more complete educational experience.

Blended format education will continue to grow and improve in the coming years. The three main challenges that I can see are: dealing with market segmentation, insomuch as more and more schools will seek to set themselves apart from the mainstream online competition; the need for ongoing training by teachers to improve their ability to combine technology with educational delivery; and developing new content, formats, and networks by making use of the growing number of new resources and relationships available through the Internet.

We live blended lives

Managers live blended lives: their careers change; they move to different companies; they even jump into diverse industries. Management knowledge also evolves, as do the skills needed by managers. Education should also be blended, accommodating these changes.

In January 2006, *The Economist* and *Fortune* dedicated respective articles about the challenges posed by the digital world to the media industry. In the words of *The Economist*, we are going towards a business world where "what you supply matters far more than how you supply it", a world with "an abundance of virtually costless ways to supply consumers with what they want to watch, whenever they want it."[102]

Fortune interviewed Bob Iger, the Disney CEO, who announced the search for a new business model on similar lines. The digital revolution, in the words of Iger, "is creating an even more voracious appetite for content."[103] The net winners of these transformations were content producers, and the potential losers, as *Fortune*'s Marc Gunther anticipated, were broadcasters and traditional channels of distribution.

Those articles made me think again about the implications of the digital revolution in education and management education in particular. One of the key questions that b-school deans should ask themselves is "How am I driving my school in this digital world?" Of course, this question has consequences not only in the field of learning methodologies, but also in the rest of the processes and activities run by b-schools.

Certainly, many of the classical myths on management education are questioned nowadays. Look at the following equation, which many people believe intuitive and right:

E-Learning = Low quality and cheap

How many of you would agree with this equation? I do not, for one. First, most top b-schools, even the most recalcitrant, are already combining face-to-face methodologies with those of e-learning, via online campuses, interactive communication, multimedia case studies, video-conferences etc. Therefore, e-learning is already part of the stuff of MBA programs: it is not anymore a matter of black and white, online versus off-line methodologies; it is just a matter of intensity and integration within the other elements of the program. Furthermore, some players are even demonstrating that e-learning offerings can be of the highest quality and produce the same or even better results in terms of learning productivity, developing analytical skills, and interaction and networking with other participants. In addition, e-learning has the advantage of being better adaptable to a given student's circumstances of time and geographical location. All this has a clear consequence: today, some of the best blended educational offerings are more expensive than the traditional face-to-face ones because they provide better quality and are better adaptable to customer's needs.

These new and competitive forms of e-learning result from an improved conception of how we view management and understand our lives. As a colleague once told me: "We live blended lives," and the education we receive should also be blended.

A richer blend

The survey published in 2006 by the Financial Times on online management education showed that distance learning was thriving across the board and that many business schools – over 65 percent – that used to offer only face-to-face programs were already running online courses.[104] As I said before, I guess this figure is at least 80 percent today. Traditionally, distance learning was the domain of big education providers that played on scale, had a high volume of students, and based most of their offerings on self-learning modules. However, the development of new technologies and the entrance of schools that have a leading role in conventional classroom-based learning are not only altering the boundaries of this educational segment but also the very nature of the learning process.

Many people believe that online programs cannot entirely match the human experience and vividness of face-to-face education. Are those two intuitions right? Is online education a second or third class education? As I said before, I do not believe so.

From childhood, we are trained to use our senses as an important vehicle for learning. Sight, hearing, smell, touch, and even taste are employed from the early stages of education to develop conventional behaviors and to associate names with qualities, and actions with effects. As the learner progresses, though, using the senses becomes less pivotal for learning, which is rather based on the exercise of other intellectual faculties such as reflection, introspection, or analysis. The need of "animal feedback," if you can pardon the expression, that attaches decisiveness to exercising the senses for learning, becomes much less relevant and gives room to more abstract forms of acquiring knowledge and developing intellectual skills. Antoine de Saint Exupéry summarized this idea brilliantly in his masterpiece *Le Petit Prince* (The Little Prince); the fox tells the protagonist that "what is essential is invisible to the eyes."[105] This sentence of profound and multiple meanings may be fully applicable to learning and particularly to online education.

Indeed, senses are not so decisive for learning, and being physically in the same room with your classmates throughout a whole year may not necessarily be the most productive learning experience. When I meet participants in our blended programs – those that combine intense online periods with some face-to-face sessions – I notice that they know their fellow students very intensely, and they also show a superlative degree of enthusiasm about the experience. Let me clarify that I do not refer to conventional distance learning offerings where the student may feel anonymous. I am talking about delivering a comparable or even a better learning experience than the traditional classroom session. This includes rigor in the process of selecting students – normally absent in big distance learning universities –, employing the school's full-time faculty and offering equivalent support and services to participants.

My impression is that students of sophisticated online programs are methodologically forced to interact with their classmates, more than in face-to-face programs. One of our participants in the Global MBA who lives in Shanghai told me that when you learn online you need to get known by the others because "otherwise you don't exist." This requires an effort that people who come to a conventional class and sit passively may not need to take. In addition, in high quality online programs everybody has a chance to an equal slot of participation, which is not the case in classroom sessions where time is limited.

Indeed, experiences in good online programs are the closest thing to how many multinationals manage communication and decision-making nowadays, and they may provide experiences at least as intense as in face-to-face offerings.

I am fascinated by the effects that high quality online education can have on its participants. I attended some sessions of the "integration days" of our Global MBA, a program with a substantial proportion of online sessions. "Integration days," the only face-to-face part of the program, aims at gathering participants with other members of the IE community – alumni, corporate clients, recruiters, and the like – at different cities across the globe. I was amazed at the intensity of the relationships between program participants, many of whom had only been in contact online in the previous three months. Amazingly, it seemed as if they knew each other for a long time. Indeed, the experience at my school is that our online offerings generate a much deeper interaction between participants, fostering true and long-lasting relationships, and even –although it may sound counterintuitive – a strong sense of identity with the school. Actually, student questionnaires indicate consistently that blended programs enjoy the highest degree of satisfaction among participants.

I was particularly interested in the feedback from program participants about what distinctive skills they feel they were developing, as compared to the skills fostered by traditional classroom methodologies. One of the participants referred to the diplomatic skills that are enhanced by online exchange. When people address each other verbally, they use body language, gestures, as well as tone and other sensitive mechanisms to modulate the message. However, in written communication, language is only what you sense. The added reflection of written communication helps avoid any undesired faux-pas that may cause an unwanted negative reaction. Effective written communication, among persons belonging to diverse cultures and expressing themselves in non-native "working English," can be more efficient while being neutral, amiable, and respectful.

The second interesting finding is that online education fosters solidarity among participants, since they all have to contribute and work in different timeframes. Students who take a face-to-face class can just sit and listen without doing anything else, which of course is not recommendable. However, if a student taking an online course does not take an active role it shows and affects the quality of the class discussion, since groups are composed of less people, and the methodology requires a dynamic dialogue.

The difference in timeframes – we have students from Hawaii to Shanghai, covering all continents – makes some participants work with their team peers in the early hours of the morning, an effort that their classmates recognize and appreciate and that helps cohesion and commitment.

There is a lot to study about the pros and cons of online education, and I am talking here about top-quality offerings, about the best possible replica of conventional classroom methodologies, and not about massive distributed learning. It seems that online education may help its participants become not only good managers but also better people.

As we have seen, technology is revolutionizing education. In the next chapter, we examine the second big trend driving the new learning curve – globalization and the internationalization of stakeholders.

CHAPTER 6

International stakeholders

A main reason for the globalization of business education is the internationalization of stakeholders. Marshall McLuhan's global village has its global school house.[106] As people move more freely and frequently between countries, they require education that is both portable and flexible. Imagine, for example, that you are half way through a three-year part-time Masters program and your company decides to transfer you to a different country. You would not be very happy if you had to start your degree all over again. You would expect your educational provider to find a way to allow you to complete your studies. Similarly, if you were on a full-time MBA program but had to go back to work, you would hope that you could switch tracks to a part-time program. These are just two of the issues that business schools have had to address in recent years. The overall effect is a much more flexible approach to degree programs and learning methods.

The upshot is an internationalization of "stakeholders," that is to say an internationalization of the different special interest groups active within higher education, from the teaching staff and students, to the management and sponsors of universities. For example, a growing number of companies now recruit graduates or finance chairs at universities, while the existence of exchange programs for students and teaching staff, such as Erasmus, have made universities more diverse places.

International reach is a particular challenge for education providers. Very few institutions have the resources to run their activities on an international scale without establishing alliances with foreign institutions. Here too, business schools have been in the forefront of new practices. International partnerships have evolved from simple student exchange agreements to joint degree programs and sophisticated collaboration. Some business schools have gone beyond this and opened greenhouse campuses abroad, following the model of related industries like consultancies and other professional services companies. For example, INSEAD has established campuses in Singapore and Abu Dhabi in addition to its traditional home in Fontainebleau near Paris. Similarly, Chicago Booth has campuses in Chicago, London and Singapore.

A number of other business schools have also forged relationships with peer institutions in other countries. The evolution of international partnerships among business schools is already underway. A number of different strategies are available to cope with the challenge of globalization – ranging from traditional joint ventures with new strategic alliances, multipurpose, more open and indefinite in time, where competitors join forces in collaborative initiatives. There are also new species emerging in higher education, such as for-profit universities, multi-branch campuses, and online institutions.

Transcontinental competition and protectionist reactions

Given the global shift in education, countries that adopt protectionist measures in education, preventing the entry of foreign universities or other higher education institutions, or refusing to sign up to supranational initiatives, will end up on the periphery of the educational world, and lose their best and brightest talents. Opting out of the international mainstream will mean stagnation and decline.

By the same token, globalization will mean that university programs are increasingly concentrated, as the big institutions join forces or major centers of learning are set up to focus on particular disciplines, setting a global benchmark in the process. For example, the University of London is now a consortium of autonomous centers where two business schools that are in direct competition with each other co-exist: the London Business School and Imperial College. Alternatively, IMD in Switzerland stands apart from the competition as a center of executive learning.

As we have seen, these two models represent the two extremes of a spectrum of possible competitive strategies. Universities can opt to develop a scale and number of resources – in terms of teaching staff, research, and programs – that will allow them to compete internationally. Alternatively, they can focus on a particular discipline, area of activity, or even methodology. The risk of not going for either of these two strategic options – scale or specialization – is to end up in the worst of both worlds: neither having the resources to compete globally, nor to be a global leader in some area, thus losing competitiveness and a key presence in the education market.

Another characteristic of the higher education environment and of business schools in particular, is transcontinental competition, that is to say, a multi-polar development of supply and demand. The US may still have more business schools than anywhere else making it the world's biggest market for business education, but in recent decades there has been widespread growth around the world of business schools. What's more, as is being seen in other global sectors, demand is increasingly originating in Asia, where the biggest growth in the market, in pupils, and in new institutions is taking place. It is estimated that the Asian nations, led by China and India, will represent 70 percent of global demand for university studies by 2025.[107] At the same time, more and more US and European students are applying to programs in Asia, prompted in large part by a perceived need to improve their international profile. It is worth looking in detail at the drivers behind the irreversible phenomenon of the internationalization of business schools, as well as the internationalization of their stakeholders.

Who are business schools' stakeholders?

Historically, educational activity has been limited to the relationship between teachers and students and to a lesser extent on the parents of the latter. Nevertheless, the concept of stakeholders in education has been taken from management studies to include others who are involved in, or whose interests are significantly affected by, education. An analysis and evaluation of stakeholders in the educational sector is fundamental for academic managers when it comes to designing strategies for their institutions, for designing teaching programs, or for planning how best to use their resources and funding. Business school deans know this, and in recent years have seen the time they are able to spend on their faculty and students reduced, as they must dedicate a larger slice of their agenda to dealing with external stakeholders. Figure 6.1 shows the most relevant stakeholders in business education.

The past two decades have seen a level of cross-border movement of teachers and students, unseen for seven centuries, when the first universities were set up. According to UNESCO figures, the number of students studying abroad grew 50 percent between 2000 and 2007, to reach 2.7 million individuals. Since 1980, the number of Americans studying abroad has quadrupled.[108]

As regards business schools, the figures point to an even greater increase in student mobility. Between 2005 and 2009 alone, the number of people taking the GMAT, the standard test required by business schools with an international outlook, grew by 32 percent. More significantly, over the same period there was a 40 percent increase in GMAT tests being sent to other schools, which clearly illustrates the sharp increase in students attending business schools abroad.[109]

In fact, Business Studies is the biggest growth area of higher education in recent years. It is hard to measure the worldwide demand for Business Studies, particularly bearing in mind that the most frequently used tools to measure it – such as the GMAT test – tend to be found in a specific

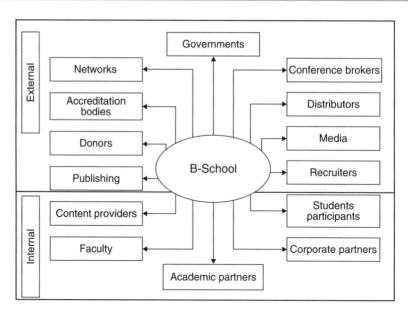

Figure 6.1 B-school stakeholders

market segment: applicants to US MBA programs or schools with international admission systems. Undergraduate programs in business would not be included, despite having increased significantly around the world. Furthermore, Executive MBA Programs increasingly tend to rely more on alternative criteria for admissions – including personal interviews – in addition to the GMAT.[110]

At the same time, there has been a proliferation of masters programs in management, along with programs aimed at graduates with no professional experience. What's more, executive MBA programs, along with non-regulated executive education offerings, are among the main growth areas, reflecting executives' need for learning over the course of their career. Greater international mobility on the part of business students is also explained by the fact that the cost of study is more easily recovered through access to better-paid jobs than other degree or masters programs are able to provide, along with a general willingness to study abroad. At an AACSB[111] presentation in 2010, Dan Le Clair estimated that there are approximately 12,000 institutions worldwide that grant business degrees at the undergraduate level or above.

The US receives more overseas students than any other country, followed by the United Kingdom and Canada. In recent years, several European countries, among them France and Spain, have earned a place among the ten most important destinations for foreign students. Furthermore, China's and India's economic development is favoring the entry of a growing number of students from other countries, while Hong Kong and Singapore remain important educational hubs. Australia, with its intelligent policy of inviting highly skilled students and workers, is also among the most popular destinations for international applicants. According to a study by EFMD in 2005, of the decisive factors that make one country a more popular destination for international students, 37.5 percent said language, preferably English, 21.7 percent said cultural attraction, 21.7 percent cited the country's reputation, while other aspects like a benign climate or closeness to friends and family were much less important, with just 6 percent citing such factors.[112]

At the same time, the study indicated that the key criteria for applicants choosing a specific business school were, in order of importance: the institution's reputation, post-graduate work opportunities, readily available information on the school, its location, and financing. With this in mind, as well as taking into account the most popular destinations for students, we can deduce that the language of the school's program is a key factor in deciding where to study, along with the ease of gaining a work permit after graduation, as well as the educational experience itself. These factors underscore the prevalence of English as the lingua franca of global education, and require business schools that want to compete in the international arena to offer programs in English. Equally, they also show that mobility and the possibility of working in the country of study are also important factors in attracting foreign students.

Capturing foreign students

There are many countries that have tried to attract foreign students in recent years, but the case of Australia stands out. Aside from its inherent advantage as an English-speaking country, and its proximity to the emerging markets of South-East Asia, forceful marketing by the government and by the country's educational institutions have set the benchmark for other nations looking to become centers of international education. Australia has 39 universities, of which two are private, and a further 70 business schools. It is estimated that its share of the global university student population is 11 percent. International students enrolled at Australian universities comprise 20 percent of the total, giving it in all likelihood the highest ratio of international students anywhere. In 2005, Australia overtook the United States and the United Kingdom as the destination of choice for fee-paying students. As an export, university education in Australia is worth around $15.5 billion.[113]

The international development of Australia's universities has been significantly facilitated by IDP Education, a consortium created in 1969 and jointly owned by the country's universities and SEEK, a private company. This consortium has actively promoted Australian universities by providing international applicants with information, organizing trade fairs, offering grants and subsidies, by researching on trends in international education, and by running IELTS, the test to assess a student's level of English. IDP has been much more active and successful than other agencies set up by governments to attract international students, and has some 29 offices around the world, backed up by an impressive online information service and response to applications. The success of IDP shows that public private partnerships (PPP) often work better than state-run, noncommercial initiatives when it comes to promoting a country's education system. Furthermore, it highlights the importance of using effective information to create a global higher education market.

At the same time, the Australian government has been proactive in helping students stay on in the country to work after they graduate, an enormously important factor for international students. Current Australian law allows international graduates at Australian universities to stay in the country for 18 months, extendible in some cases, a policy that contrasts sharply with the rigid policy of concessions and extensions of visas in Europe and the US. Furthermore, international students enrolled at Australian universities can obtain visas to carry out on-the-job training during their studies, which constitutes credits towards their grades. In 2007, the main Australian universities set up a "qualification passport," similar to a European diploma supplement, outlining a student's courses, which makes it much easier to continue studying abroad. All these factors, along with a largely benign climate and cultural life, and a tolerant atmosphere, have helped to make Australia one of the most popular destinations for overseas students.

Student mobility: The Bologna Process in Europe

The Bologna Accord is a process begun in 1998 in the Italian city to integrate higher education among 47 countries. It is backed by member states' education ministries, as well as by the European Union and the Council of Europe, among other institutions.

The first major objective of the Bologna Accord was completed in 2010 when university studies among almost all member states were standardized. This involved the adoption of a system that was essentially based on two main cycles, undergraduate and graduate, as already existed in the United Kingdom. Access to the second cycle requires successful completion of first cycle studies, lasting a minimum of three years. The degree awarded after the first cycle will also be relevant in the European labor market as an appropriate level of qualification. The second cycle should lead to the master and/or doctorate degree.

Undergraduate programs from now on will run for a maximum of three or four years, masters for one or two years, and doctorates for a minimum of three years. The objectives of the Bologna Accord are fundamentally to improve and integrate university education within Europe, with the aim of improving mobility by students, teachers, and better sharing of information and research. At the same time, it aims to boost competitiveness by raising educational standards, allowing European universities to better compete with US institutions. In the final analysis, the initiative aims to create a single knowledge space within Europe, improving education, and therefore the economy and social wellbeing.

The Bologna Accord has already brought about a transformation in higher education. As was to be expected, the reforms have been both praised and criticized, with strong opposition from some sectors within the university system. In the first ten years of its implementation, not only have undergraduate, masters, and doctorate programs been standardized, but also teaching content and their titles have been changed. As some analysts have pointed out, the results of these reforms have been far from even: some universities have taken the opportunity to undertake deeper reforms, and to adapt to the needs of the market; others have merely undertaken cosmetic change. For example, a report by the European Universities' Association in 2010 pointed out that the Bologna Accord "has not led to meaningful curriculum renewal but compressed Bachelor programs."[114]

That said, the Bologna Process is the best opportunity to overhaul Europe's universities, and to adapt research and teaching to the changing needs of society. Described by some as the educational equivalent of the Eurozone, the idea is to create a new knowledge-based single area, making Europe the destination of choice for international students. In recent decades, Europe's leading business schools have increased their share of international students at the US' expense.

Europe is becoming an increasingly popular destination for international students, although some countries within the EU were obviously more popular destinations than others. In 2005, the Academic Cooperation Association (ACA), the body that compares the US and European markets in terms of their ability to attract overseas students, found that Asian students, for example, focused their knowledge of EU universities on those in the United Kingdom, France, and Germany. While the US is associated with innovation, competitiveness, and dynamism, Europe tends to be seen in terms of its cultural heritage, its traditions, and the arts. But Europe and Australia are considered more accessible in terms of visas, and above all, the cultural and linguistic diversity of Europe is highly valued – even if the lingua franca of education in the EU is English.[115]

What is needed for real regional integration?

Oscar Wilde once wrote: "When the gods wish to punish us they answer our prayers."[116] There is no denying that the Bologna Process has raised the hopes of many of Europe's educators, but it runs the risk of achieving the wrong results. The thinking behind the initiative is to create a single European Higher Education Area (*EHEA*), concomitant with the creation of other single areas in policy, human rights, law, economy, and trade. The creation of this single space of academic free movement is supposed to allow people and ideas to circulate to all comers of the EU, improving European competitiveness in line with other "single spaces," and particularly with that of the US. But aside from the anti-Bologna movements that have emerged in some EU member states, most of them in southern Europe, the biggest danger the process faces is that it is used for protectionism. Some national or regional governments, or their academic and professional associations, might take advantage of it to protect certain programs or degree programs, thus blocking the movement of professionals and the recognition of their qualifications. This potential reality would be the nightmare. We have already seen trade unions and academic associations in different European countries questioning the idea of mutual recognition of qualifications. Some degree programs, particularly in the higher levels of engineering, have refused to recognize the new rules. But even taking into account the current global economic crisis, the Bologna Process seems irreversible, and any obstacles can be overcome with time and by reaching compromise, as have other EU initiatives.

What would constitute a successful implementation of the Bologna Process (my so-called noble dream)? To begin with, it has been seen as relating solely to adapting programs and study cycles in European universities, which was supposed to be completed by 2010.

But aside from this much-needed harmonization of the EU's myriad education systems, three other measures are required.

First, there is a need for accreditation systems and transnational recognition. At present, the recognition of the new degree programs, masters, and doctorates issued by universities is done by national or regional quality and accreditation agencies. But if we use other markets or segments that are genuinely international as the benchmark, it will be necessary to use transnational agencies. In the case of business schools, for example, there are three accreditation systems recognized internationally by the sector's stakeholders: in the US, the AACSB (Association to Advance Collegiate Schools of Business), and in Europe, AMBA (Association of MBAs), and EQUIS (European Quality Improvement System). The world's top business schools are accredited through these systems, which, in addition to verifying the quality of their programs also encourage best practices and the development of regional institutions. Were the European Association for Quality Assurance in Education (ENQA) to create a European register of quality assessment agencies, it would serve as the model for transnational agencies, which, if endorsed by other stakeholders and professional associations, would take on greater international visibility.

Second, it is important to make information comparing different graduate, masters, or doctorates much more widely available. A single higher education space in Europe means that the stakeholders of the system – students, teachers, and employers – must have access to detailed information about what programs are on offer, backed up by reports comparing the quality of different institutions, the main characteristics of programs, and assessments of the extent to which they meet the needs of companies and institutions that hire graduates. In the US, for example, the existence of several accreditation systems, like those mentioned above, along with guides, magazines, and other media specializing in education, are a key factor in providing transparent information that allows students to compare and contrast programs and colleges. As we know, these mechanisms have their weaknesses, but overall, they make a major contribution to improving information, which is essential for any single market.

Third, developing the financial instruments to provide the funding to support the new system is perhaps the most important factor in creating a single space for higher education in Europe. On one side, this would involve additional financing for universities, using public and private funds, allowing them to match US institutions in terms of investment into research, investment per student, along with resources for teaching. At the same time, grants and loans would be needed to encourage students to enroll at overseas universities. Once again, if we compare

Europe and the US in terms of grants and loans, it is clear that outside of funding provided by universities, Europe lags far behind the US. Any new funding programs for students would have to involve cooperation between the public and private sectors. Greater and more diverse availability of funding would help those countries whose universities face serious structural problems regarding financing, to catch up with the rest of the EU.

Regional integration of higher education may provide favorable winds for those business schools that have or aim at having an international positioning. It is now time to analyze some of the alternatives to develop this international presence.

Achieving global presence

There are many avenues that a business school can go down in trying to find a place in the global arena. Figure 6.2 lists these alternatives, based on the resources they require, along with their concomitant financial and operating risk.

Being recognized as an international business school does not necessarily mean having a physical presence in other countries, as is the case in other sectors. Nor does it mean opening subsidiary campuses on other sites. A school can be genuinely international by maintaining a single campus if it can attract foreign students, has teaching staff from abroad, and if its programs are genuinely global in orientation. In this sense education is different from other related business sectors such as consulting or services providers, which have to open offices abroad if they want to have an international presence.

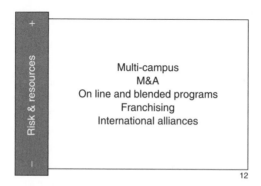

Figure 6.2 Avenues to achieve global presence

When business schools formulate international strategies, they have frequently drawn on the experience of companies such as McKinsey, Accenture, or PWC, which operate on the basis of the same strategic mission, a cohesive and organized culture, but still with a physical presence abroad. These companies also tend to be typical examples of "transnational organizations," as Christopher Bartlett and Sumantra Ghoshal dubbed them.[117]

Recent years have seen a growing number of business schools develop strategies to open campuses in other countries. INSEAD was the pioneer in this approach, opening its second campus in Singapore in 2000. Under the slogan, "One School, Two Campuses," the school offers the same academic program in both countries, including its MBA program, with the same level of supporting services. The same school has subsequently opened a third center in Abu Dhabi, albeit with a more limited range of programs. INSEAD's lead has been followed by other US and European schools. Duke University's Fuqua Business School, for instance, opened a campus in Frankfurt with the idea of setting up a European operations' base from Germany, the EU's leading economy, but where paradoxically, there remains a dearth of top business schools. Fuqua's experience in Germany was not a success, however, and the school closed after a few years. Chicago GSB initially opened a campus in Barcelona, to provide its Executive MBA to Europeans. It subsequently decided to move the campus to London, given the latter's importance as a financial and business center and its international connectivity. The UK's Nottingham Business School has opened a campus in China and plans to expand their operations there.

Pursuing a growth strategy based on opening schools in other countries is possibly the most risky in terms of the resources required. Generally speaking, schools that open international campuses tend to do so when invited by a country or city, usually backed by subsidies, tax breaks, and land donations.

At the same time, it is very difficult to replicate the way a business school runs its operations at its main campus. Academic institutions have an identity that is tied to their location. Ivy League schools, for example, attract people because of their history and reputation. I call it "Ivy syndrome." Basically, when applicants choose one of these schools they really care about its location, they want to live the experience, to be part of it, and to touch the ivy that grows on its walls. Ivy and classical architecture provide a reassuring appearance of permanence and longevity. Schools know this and play up to it. Indeed, replicating the original campus abroad is a real challenge. There is a perfect replica of the Parthenon of Athens in Nashville, Tennessee, for example. What's more, it is a near-perfect replica of the building designed by Phidias 25 centuries ago. However, the excitement and emotions experienced during a visit to the Acropolis, I am sure you will agree with me, have no comparison.

Perhaps the most difficult problem faced when running two or more campuses overseas is to maintain the same identity and academic standards. Inevitably, one campus – usually the original – will have priority over the others. Furthermore, assigning teaching staff to one campus or the other can be complicated, even if incentives are offered. Soon after taking up his post, and following a trip to Asia, Nitin Nohria, the first Indian-born Dean of Harvard Business School, dismissed the idea that either his appointment or his trip signaled that HBS is about to open a fully fledged campus overseas any time soon. "I don't think that is necessary and nor do we have the ambition to do that," he said. "We're in the business of chasing knowledge and not chasing demand."

Professor Nohria's comments make sense if one bears in mind that a significant percentage of HBS's income comes from its editorial division, particularly from the sale of case studies. The dean says Harvard's preferred strategy would be to maintain "a small physical footprint" in Asia through research centers and executive-education programs, which would provide the school with a "very large intellectual footprint."[118] "We will always be in some ways deeply rooted in America," Nohria says. "That is our heritage, that's where we are located." Nohria also says that roughly 40 percent of all Harvard Business School students are now from outside the US, and that there is no intention to deliberately increase this proportion. "Should that mix be 50 percent or 60 percent? We should always remain fundamentally a meritocracy," he says, concluding: "That's been a great strength of American educational institutions. I'm proof of that. If the student body becomes more international that's because that's what the best students in the world look like. It's not like we have targets."

These comments deserve some attention. For one thing, every business school in the world aims to attract the best and brightest students. The question, as we will see in Chapter 9, is how each school defines what it understands to be the best students. Are they those with an entrepreneurial spirit? Those who have better developed their emotional intelligence, as opposed to their analytical abilities? Those who have more professional experience and proven ability to meet targets?

Secondly, because above and beyond the objective of attracting the best students, defining an ideal class profile is part of what a school is offering. For example, if objectives are established on the basis of gender diversity, or minorities or nationalities, all with the aim of generating a pluralistic environment that is an integral part of the learning process.

The American way

So why is it that the country that invented the business school has such a questionable international profile?[119] The real reason that so many US business schools prefer the majority of their students to be domestic is their business model. Given that a significant proportion of their income, particularly in the case of the top schools, comes through endowments bestowed by former students, they cannot afford to jeopardize such funding by recruiting a significant number of foreign students, who do not share the "giving back" culture of the US, and who will in all likelihood return to their countries of origin to make their careers, a long way from their alma mater. Additionally, international graduates who return home will not be able to benefit from the tax breaks for such endowments in the US. So why should the schools risk changing a financing model that works, simply to increase supposed diversity? What's more, other means are available to the top US schools that want to raise their international profile through other means than by having a diverse student body, for example through exchange programs, overseas programs, and other extra-curricular approaches. These alternatives allow them to keep their business model, one of the pillars of which is fundraising among former students.

Strategic alliances and musical chairs

Strategic alliances are the preferred way of entering new markets when companies lack the resources to make heavy initial investments, or in heavily regulated sectors, both scenarios applicable to management education. Strategic alliances also offer incomers the benefits of the experience and knowledge of a local partner, a particularly important aspect in a sector that is highly susceptible to cultural differences.

These and other, related, reasons explain the recent proliferation of strategic alliances as an alternative to internationalization for many business schools. Such alliances go beyond the traditional student exchange programs, and have manifested themselves mainly in the form of joint or double degree programs, or through the setting up of consortiums for multiple, multilateral services, or strategic alliances covering a wider range of content.

So far, the most fertile ground for joint and double degree programs has been the Executive MBA (EMBA), with a global focus and a modular format. It is worth pointing out that 13 of the 100 EMBA programs in the *Financial Times'* 2010 ranking were joint or double degrees between two or more schools, including the three programs that topped the league table: Kellogg-HKUST; Columbia Business School; and London Business School; and the so-called Trium of HEC Paris, London School of Economics, and NYU Stern.[120] To judge from the number of alliances between schools to set up international EMBAs, it would seem that this is the way for schools to reach into markets that they would not be able to penetrate on their own: they pool resources and spread the risk, while retaining brand recognition. For example, Kellogg School of Management occupies four places in the *Financial Times'* 2010 ranking: in double degree EMBAs with HKUST (first place); with WHU Otto Beisheim in Germany (fourteenth); and with York University-Schulich in Canada (twenty-third), aside from its own EMBA, which came in at nineteenth. Kellogg also has a double degree program with Recanati School of Management in Israel, its first such initiative. Needless to say, this approach offers economies of scale – management and development costs, gathering all students in common modules – and significant insight into the global market, as well as the obvious synergies: Kellogg is an academic leader providing the highest-level curricula, while the commercial and marketing aspects of the operation are carried out by the local partner.

Another important area for strategic alliances between business schools has been the creation of consortia to tackle management education niches at the global level. An example of this is CEMS (conceived as a Consortium of European Master's of Science), which has brought together 25 schools from around the world to develop a shared degree in the masters in management area, as well as taking advantage of other synergies derived from sharing teaching, educational, and infrastructural resources. Such consortia also work together on laying out market rules or setting the standards for certain programs. Another example is Sumaq an alliance created by IE Business School, and which brings together seven other leading business schools in Latin America, with a mission to develop executive education programs and applied research in the region.

As in other sectors, alliances between business schools are not always successful, nor do they generate the revenue or activity that was hoped. Common experience shows that around 50 percent of strategic alliances fail. This failure rate might also be applicable to the academic sector, although it is difficult to make a full assessment, given that even when alliances are slow to take root, or die on the vine, they survive in formal terms. Similarly, although it may be difficult to determine their potential for generating revenue, schools will continue to try to form strategic alliances, as this is the only way to combat the uncertainty and change that characterizes the sector, along with globalization, the impact of new technologies, and the activities of competitors in a range of sectors and countries.

Compared to deep-rooted partnerships such as mergers and acquisitions – which are already underway in the educational sector – the disadvantages of strategic alliances are clear: they are vulnerable to how the relationship between the two parties develops; it is also difficult to establish the criteria for dividing profits between partners. But leaving these difficulties aside, I believe that no business school, regardless of its resources, can survive in the future without entering into strategic alliances. I believe that we will see a renaissance of them in the coming years, and that they will go beyond setting up joint or double-degree programs.

Strategic alliances also offer external advantages to schools, insomuch as they tie the image of school to that of another prestigious international institution, something that is perceived as adding value by external stakeholders, particularly by applicants and corporate partners. Furthermore, they boost a school's accreditation evaluation – such as those carried out by EQUIS and AACSB – or in the league tables and rankings such as those published by the *Financial Times.*

At the same time, strategic alliances offer internal advantages by allowing for synergies and other types of saving or pooling of resources such as sharing faculty – always at a premium – as well as providing the impetus to set up joint research projects, develop online educational platforms, or recruit new students. Figure 6.3 shows some of the activities along a business school's value chain that can be developed without losing either its identity or competitive advantage.

Yves Doz and Gary Hamel[121] have come up with a conceptual framework that is particularly appropriate for strategic alliances in the education sector. They argue that it is important to distinguish between conventional joint ventures, which are typically focused on an objective that is governed by time and a particular activity, such as the double-degree programs mentioned above, from the "new strategic alliances." The latter are characterized precisely by the lack of any clearly defined mission, and where there are no predetermined ways to create value, and where the relationship between partners can develop in any number of ways. In these sorts of relationship the management of the alliance over time is more important than the initial design, all of which makes it essential that both parties are able to adapt to changing circumstances.

I believe these new strategic alliances, with multiple missions and that are less sharply defined, have an important role to play in the future of the business education sector, principally with the aim of creating economies of scale as a way of facing up to growing international competition.

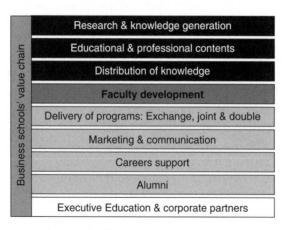

Figure 6.3 Business schools' value chain

These types of alliance, which will lead to consolidation in the sector, have already been seen in other similar industries, such as airlines, the media, publishing, as well as consultancies and professional services.

Ted Snyder, Dean of Yale School of Management, when addressing the EFMD Deans Meeting of 2011, discussed the growing trend towards convergence and increased competition among US schools. He asked the question as to how many schools with "multiple brass ring strategies" – those that boast top faculty and students, that undertake research, that have a global presence, and that have excellent facilities – can coexist in the US. His answer, which unsettled many in the audience, was no more than ten. Obviously, that forecast is based on the market remaining at its present size. It is also true that many of the "multiple brass ring" schools in the US have opened programs and centers in other countries, thus widening their market.[122]

At the same time, it should be borne in mind that competition is increasing around the world. I asked Tuck's Paul Danos whether he thought that any of the Ivy League schools might one day merge in a bid to create economies of scale, to boost their resources, and to face international competition. He said no, but he didn't rule out strategic alliances, given that they are quicker and simpler to put together.

If this is the likely outlook for the top business schools of the US, which generate twice as much income as their European competitors, along with much larger faculty and alumni, as well as having access to extracurricular income, such as income from endowments, then the imperative to merge is all the greater in the rest of the world, whether in Europe, Latin America, or even Asia. We may well see a kind of musical chairs in the coming years, with the creation of macro-groups of schools with high teaching standards, and with the ability to offer their services on any continent.

In the face of this likely scenario, and on the basis of my experience, I would like to put forward a series of recommendations that might help these new strategic alliances prosper. First, deans should take a leading role in defining the mission of any alliance, as well as in the negotiations. This will speed up the process of reaching agreements. Second, the personal relationship among the principal players in setting up the alliance will be key. Beyond simply having a positive personal relationship, it is important that they share the same vision about the future of the sector as well as on the appropriate strategies. Emphasizing factors such as operational performance over strategic objectives tends to lead to the failure of many alliances. Third, it is essential that partners commit themselves to a win-win outcome. As in personal relationships, there can never be a guarantee that an alliance will benefit both parties in the same way and at all times: the important thing is that in the long term, both parties believe that they have come out of the deal with more than what they put in.

Strategic alliances should be permanently at the top of every dean's strategy list, and something that their performance in the post is judged-on by the boards that appoint them. From the constant reports in the media, it seems that in the coming years we will see an increasing number of alliances, many of them highly creative. Deans should hope that they will all be able to find a chair before the music stops.

Educational hubs

Another interesting aspect of the globalization of higher education is the evolution of educational hubs. These clusters of educational providers attract other quality providers and students. They are spreading to emerging economies and can be a catalyst to raise educational levels in those countries and to develop knowledge-based economies. Several education-focused hubs have been established in the Middle East, for example, and are attracting the attention of some of the world's leading business schools. Dubai's Knowledge Village is a learning community with state-of-the-art facilities. It includes the Dubai Knowledge Universities campus, allowing international universities to have a presence in Dubai. There is a similar move in Qatar, where the Qatar Foundation for Education, Science and Community Development has created Education City, a 2,500-acre campus near Doha.

The government of Abu Dhabi has also wooed leading educational providers, including INSEAD, which has established a permanent campus in the Emirate, and is launching in Abu Dhabi a section of its Global Executive MBA (GEMBA) program. The Abu Dhabi government also has an international agreement with the Paris-Sorbonne.

India is also following the learning hub model with its Education City, located on a 60-acre site near Delhi International Airport. Lancaster University Management School will be working in partnership with GD Goenka Educational Trust, which owns Education City, to deliver a range of programs, including a two-year Global MBA starting in 2010.

In Europe some education hubs, like Oxford and Cambridge universities, have followed the principle for centuries. Indeed, being part of an already established education cluster gives their much younger b-schools an important advantage at home – and with the emergent educational hubs. The Saïd Business School at Oxford, for example, has benefited from its strong brand recognition in the region, winning executive education projects with both Abu Dhabi and Saudi Arabia. The Abu Dhabi Oxford Leadership Development Program was launched in January 2008 to deliver a development program for more than 200 of the Emirate's leading civil servants.

London Business School's Dubai-London Executive MBA (EMBA) opened its doors in September 2008. The 16-month dual-campus EMBA is taught by London Business School faculty at the Dubai International Financial Centre and LBS. Manchester Business School has opened a Middle East centre in the Dubai Knowledge Village, which it uses to provide support and coordination for its distance learning MBA students in the region. Warwick, another leading UK b-school, also offers distance-learning MBAs in the Gulf in association with local partner Knowledge Horizon.

The post-Bologna European landscape, too, will be characterized by the existence of distinctive education hubs, cities or larger areas that become references for academic excellence or that concentrate an important grouping of educational suppliers. In other global industries, hubs provide an important role and operate as magnets to attract companies of a given industry and related businesses, as some respected academics like Michael Porter have demonstrated. Think, for example, of Silicon Valley as a hub for e-business start-ups, or Milan as a hub for the fashion industry. If management education evolves in a similar way to other global industries, it could be expected that education hubs would appear and would stand out on the map of European higher education. Interestingly, the US management education market has some clear educational hubs, the Boston area and Chicago being two of the frequently mentioned ones.

Evidence of the "hubization" of management education is the fact that some analysts cite some particular cities as centers that host a critical number of leading business schools. The *Financial Times*, for example, listed New York, Chicago, London, and Madrid as hubs of executive education institutions in an article some years ago, and the *Wall Street Journal* has pointed out how some cities in Europe – notably London, Madrid, or Paris – host an important number of highly ranked business schools.[123]

What will be the key factors for the creation of management education hubs? The list would certainly include elements such as business concentration, number and quality of education institutions, cultural aspects – for example, the host city's cultural life, the relevance of the native language spoken, leisure, sport facilities – cost of living and even the weather. However, the viability of these hubs will also depend on the initiative of many different stakeholders, notably local or regional governments, as well as other external factors, such as infrastructure, communications, security, quality of life, and the like. City rankings will probably play a relevant function here.

In some ways the first two mega-trends affecting higher education are widely understood. Technology and globalization are the key drivers for change in many other sectors. The third driver is, however, something that is the sole preserve of this sector: our changing understanding of what constitutes, or should constitute, knowledge, where it is originated, and how it is distributed.

CHAPTER 7

Melting pots of knowledge

Allied to globalization, the third trend driving the learning curve of the future is the changing nature of knowledge. In particular, we can see a *glocalization* of knowledge – to use a neologism: that is to say the coming together of ideas and theories at the transnational level, so that they are accepted and applicable anywhere, while also being adapted and developed to fit local needs, the product of specific cultures. Once again, this is most evident in business schools because they have been at the forefront of the globalization of education. For example, the same management tools are taught in business schools around the world, but they are often applied through case studies of companies based in the same country as the business school. On any MBA program you will learn about Porter's Five Forces but the case studies used to which the strategic analysis is applied will be local to the school – Mexican companies at Tec de Monterrey, but Chinese companies at CEIBS.

If we accept the parallel between higher education and other areas of social and economic activity characterized by their global nature, then aside from the convergence of teaching programs and models, the consequences of this growing internationalization and global integration will be increased competition among universities. Educational providers will now be able to reach out to a wider market. As well as trying to capture the best talent in terms of teachers and students, they will also vie for the best resources, such as donations from individuals and institutions – widely practiced in the US as fund raising. Globalization also means lowering entrance barriers to educational institutions that want to set up shop in other countries.

The United Kingdom, for example, and particularly London, has become the world's most important hub for executive training, overtaking Boston, which for many years was home to a large number of the best business schools on the planet. London's success is the result of several factors: the high concentration of multinational companies, along with the capital's importance as a financial center. Also, UK legislation facilitates setting up of international universities, and even offers subsidies and tax breaks to attract the top names in higher education. It has good local services and transport and communication infrastructure, and of course English is the language of international trade. Examples such as London and Singapore will likely encourage other cities to follow suit and create educational hubs.

Inevitably, there are times when the irreversible process of the globalization of higher education is seen as a problem. In some cases, measures have been adopted to prevent overseas educational institutions setting up centers in particular countries. It is worth pointing out again that as with other areas of activity, protectionism when applied to education generally results in a loss of quality and competitiveness.

Knowledge is contextual

What is knowledge? It sounds like an easy question, but it is surprisingly hard to answer. The fact is that knowledge has a lot of different meanings and connotations. A glance in a dictionary reveals that it can mean "awareness or familiarity gained by experience; a person's range of information; or specific information, facts or intelligence about something."[124] All of these can apply to education, although the latter is probably the one we tend to think of first. The point here, though, is to realize that facts and information constantly change. The GDP of the USA is not a static piece of information any more than is the population of Japan. But it is when you add in the notion that knowledge is contextual – in other words its usefulness and application depends on the situation that the definition of knowledge becomes exponential in its range.

What constitutes knowledge for today's MBA student, for example, goes way beyond management models and theories. It includes the learning that comes from spending time in a truly multicultural environment and experiencing the latest technological learning tools. In short, our notion of knowledge is changing all the time.

The focus of research and teaching in business schools is management. And while management may be a universal phenomenon, it also reflects the values and traditions of the culture within which it takes place. For example, the Capital Asset Pricing Model (CAPM) –which allows investors to price securities, such as stocks, on the basis of risk-free rate, market returns, and the security's volatility – is taught via the same mathematical formulae in finance courses around the world.

At the same time, the factors that make up a CAPM formula are inevitably contextual, and the environment that a company operates within must be taken into account when assessing its worth. What's more, managers with experience of valuing assets also know that at the end of the day, the decision to buy a company, while inevitably based on a conceptual or theoretical analysis, also comes down to intangibles such as the expectations, and even the intuition and empathy of the prospective purchasers and sellers.

The globalization of management in no way means that knowledge has been standardized to the point that all business schools now teach exactly the same things in the same way. In addition to context, or the international or domestic outlook of a given program, other factors, such as the culture and the values of the school, its teaching staff's profile, the makeup of its students, and the choice of teaching content, differ significantly. Even when schools look at the same case studies, the learning experience is different, as sector analysts have often noted.

What's more, beyond any formal similarities among business schools belonging to the same strategic group, there are always profound disparities. In my capacity as an auditor for EQUIS and AMBA, whenever I take part in accreditation processes for business schools, the one thing that always strikes me is how similar their mission statements are. The common denominator for so many business schools is: "developing leaders for the global society." But my experience shows that there are huge differences in how business schools interpret leadership, development, and the global society.

One of the myths that John Micklewait and Adrian Wooldridge dismantle in their book, *The Witch Doctors,* is: "that globalization would usher in an era of standardized 'global' products; that big, global companies would triumph; and that geography would not matter."[125]

The reality, as they point out, is that globalization has produced two different, counterpointed effects, and which are actually two sides of the same coin: increased homogeneity of ideas, values, products, and practices, and at the same time a strengthening of local and national identities, of customs, and of other differential aspects.

Our concern here is to identify the prevalence of business school models, and whether these models reflect diverse management cultures; and if they do, then we must identify which of these models will be the most successful in the future, and which will likely be adopted by emerging economies such as China or India.

Mars and Venus: Management knowledge in the US and Europe

There exists a tradition of highlighting the different models that US and European business schools are based on, but in reality, they have more in common than divides them. Leading European schools such as INSEAD were in fact modeled on institutions such as Harvard Business School, and often set up by graduates of the major US institutions. But over time, the European schools have adapted to, and been influenced by, their immediate environments, which are very different to those in the US.

Venus and Mars is how some view European society and thinking as opposed to that of America (it's debatable whether that includes Canada). This metaphor has been used to illustrate the different general abiding attitudes on opposing sides of the Atlantic vis-à-vis social issues, philosophy, and religion. Does this same paradigm apply to management education?

Some differing cultural and structural features are at the root of this confrontation between the two different archetypes of American and European business schools. Historically, American and European business schools have put a different emphasis on stakeholders in strategy formulation and decision making. Two decades ago, references to stakeholders in the US were discredited as borderline communist; the only relevant constituency for managers was shareholders'. Conversely, European business schools have developed out of a very different management culture, open to a wider array of stakeholder groups beyond shareholders.

The European business environment is characteristically regulated and governments have a decisive presence, often as major shareholders in big companies but also through other instances such as awarding licenses, fixing tariffs, pre-emptively approving mergers or acquisitions, or keeping various other prerogatives over companies' decisions. For example, in Germany the law determines that unions should have a representative in public companies' boards. In France the word "dirigisme" is often heard among French managers, referring to their government's strong interventions in the market.[126] Don Antunes and Howard Thomas reflected this fact when they explained that each of the European schools "was influenced by the set of cultural, legal and regulatory characteristics in their home country."[127]

Furthermore, US universities rely heavily on the income generated by their endowments and their MBA market is the biggest, most homogeneous, and sophisticated worldwide. In Europe, management education is still very fragmented, and there is a coexistence of various business school models. If I were to choose a word to define higher education in Europe it would be "diverse." The size of the American education market and the resources available to business schools result in more research-oriented faculties and in the more decisive role of a school's brand name. As regards sources of revenue, business schools in Europe rely almost entirely on the revenues generated by their activities and, in the case of public universities, on state subsidies.

Table 7.1 lists the structural factors that are usually seen as differentiating the US schools from those in Europe.

Let's give credit to where credit is due: Management education was invented in America. In fact, the first MBA in history was launched by Dartmouth College in New Hampshire. However in Europe, the flourishing of business schools occurred only in the late 1950s.

It is worth noting that many business examples demonstrate that being the pioneer does not necessarily ensure continuing as the benchmark in the long run. The Wright Brothers' first flight heralded a subsequent US lead of the aviation industry for the rest of the century. However, Airbus, the European aircraft-manufacturing consortium, has overtaken Boeing in commercial aviation in recent years.

Table 7.1   US schools vs. European schools

US business schools: Structural factors
- Shareholder culture
- Degree-oriented education system sees MBAs as essential part of preparation for management
- Faculty is selected and promoted on the basis of tenure track
- Research community: Academic orientation
- Widespread fund raising: Big endowments
- Media culture, importance of brand name

Europe: Structural factors
- Stakeholder culture
- Heavily regulated educational environment, uncertainty about future regulation, MBA is a post-graduate experience
- Teachers are consultancy oriented: Promotion is performance based
- Research community: Oriented to the business world
- Welfare culture, discreet endowments
- Culturally and linguistically diverse

US: Features of MBA Programs
- Students are mainly young and local
- Average length: two years
- Academic content based on learning hard skills
- US-centered
- Main recruiters are companies from *Fortune* 500 and leading companies

Europe: Features of MBA programs
- Student profile is diverse and older
- Variable length, although tendency towards one year
- Content is practical: Soft skills, different methodology
- Decentralized study perspective
- Variety of recruiters: Entrepreneurship and SMEs
- Teaching done in different languages

During the past decade, European business schools would seemed to have caught-up with their American counterparts and have lost their historical inferiority complex. However, the primacy of American schools will last, at least over the next decade, if there are no clear innovative models being born in Asia. The higher education industry changes more slowly than other industries, particularly due to more regulation, and it is not foreseeable that there will be big disruptive movements.

Despite the two differing models of management education, the trend is, irreversibly, towards convergence: it is a consequence of globalization. Will the descendents of Venus and Mars take more after their mother or father? My belief is that the leading schools in China and India will continue to look to their counterparts in the US for inspiration when mapping their growth strategies, a decision largely based on the perceived brand power and historical presence of the US schools. That said, I also believe that the European schools are closer geographically and culturally, more accessible and easily copied. Perhaps the most likely outcome is that the Asian schools will create their own business school model, introducing new characteristics, albeit built on long-standing theoretical foundations.

India calling

American and European business schools look at India with increasing interest and fascination. Indeed, India's economic growth in the past decade has heightened the need to develop talented business professionals with an international outlook. This has led to a surge in demand for MBA graduates in the country and a corresponding explosion in the number of Indian MBA programs, becoming the fastest growing business education market worldwide with more than 1,100 business schools and executive-education centers and producing over 75,000 MBA graduates a year. However, demand for top managerial talent still exceeds supply in the country, with some of the top Indian business schools receiving in excess of 125,000 applicants for just 250 places on an MBA program, one of the highest admission selectivity ratios in the world.

At the same time, the number of potential students from India applying to foreign business schools is increasing at a steady pace. GMAC, the Graduate Management Admission Council, reports that, in the past year, at nearly two-thirds of US full-time MBA programs, the largest number of foreign applications were submitted by Indian citizens. In Europe, the phenomenon is similar. At IE Business School, for example, India is the third largest constituency in the MBA Program. Our experience also shows that applicants from India have better analytical skills and academic preparation than their average international fellows do, a fact that shows the high quality of India's educational system and sophisticated culture. My impression is that Indian students also have a distinctive cross-cultural openness that allows them to maximize the learning in very diverse contexts, such as the MBA class at our school. In trying to identify the reasons for this excellent cross-cultural disposition of Indian students, I encountered a good justification in the writings of Amartya Sen, the Indian Nobel Prize Winner in Economics. In his widely commented book *The Argumentative Indian*, he explains: "There was a great strength in the old Indian tradition, where you took plurality as the natural state of affairs. Ashoka in the 12th century BC mentions the fact that we have different beliefs, we should listen to each other, we must argue with each other. That was an acceptance of heterodoxy."[128] In his brief essay "A Lecture in India: Large and Small," he confirms this view: "The intellectual largeness of India links closely with the reach of our argumentative tradition".[129]

This argumentative tradition and openness to pluralism will provide a very fertile soil for the development of knowledge and, consequently, the nurturing of research and innovation at Indian business schools in the future. As compared with some other emerging markets, where governments are investing heavily in education, but where some basic liberties and democratic conditions are missing, India has been a democracy since the time of its independence in 1947, with a solid tradition of tolerance, the natural environment for the growth of new ideas. Interestingly, India has also provided management science with some of its best gurus, a term generated in Hindi culture and referred to those masters who are able to destroy the darkness and give meaning and illumination to complex problems, a function very much needed in the world of business today. C. K. Prahalad and Sumantra Ghoshal are just two out of a long list of leading Indian figures in management knowledge in past decades. It is not a coincidence that Harvard Business School and Chicago GSM, two leading American business schools, have chosen renowned academics of Indian origin to become their deans as INSEAD has chosen Dipak Jain, former Dean at Kellogg Business School.

All the signs indicate that India can become a superpower of business education very soon, helped by its economic growth and by the advantage of English being the vehicular language. However, I believe that some main changes and transformations are needed to reach that status. First, although the Indian Institutes of Management at Ahmedabad, Bangalore, and Calcutta have truly come of age and are now directly competing with their counterparts in the US in terms of work profile and salaries offered, there are still few Indian business schools listed in the worldwide recognized rankings. The *Financial Times* 2010 ranking of MBA Programs, for example, includes only one Indian business school – ISB – among the top 100, whereas there are three schools from China and two from Singapore. Strangely, Indian business schools are missing in some other key segments of business education: the latest FT ranking of Executive MBA programs does not include any Indian business school, while there are five Chinese and three Singaporean programs listed.

Second, there are still few business schools in India that have been granted accreditation by one of the major international agencies – EQUIS, AMBA and AACSB. The importance of international accreditation is that it validates the programs and activities of recognized schools according to international standards and, consequently, opens up the school's educational offerings to international students. Here again, Indian business schools underperform as compared with other Asian competitors. For example, there are currently only two Indian business schools accredited by EQUIS, whereas there are seven from China.

Third, there is a need for more information and transparency regarding the Indian business education market, as well as more research on the Indian business context. In recent years, we have seen a formidable flourishing of management literature on India, something that is expected to increase in the future. *The India Way: How India's Top Business Leaders Are Revolutionizing Management* portrays a number of successful case studies of Indian companies, including some of the popular emerging multinationals like Tata, Videocon Industries, Ranbaxy Laboratories, and HCL Technologies. One of the features I have identified is that Indian leaders place special emphasis on personal values, a vision of growth, and strategic thinking. I hope we can learn from this and use it in developing business education, both in the East as well as in the West.

China, the learning giant

In October 2010, I was invited to attend the celebration of the sixtieth anniversary of the foundation of the Renmin University Business School in China. The ceremony was held in the university auditorium, bolstered by an impressive multimedia display and a presentational style comparable with that of the Oscars. As the spectacle unfolded, two particular aspects of the event struck me.

The first was the way that it reflected the profound Chinese respect for tradition, illustrated on this occasion by a tribute to the university's older teaching staff, now retired, who had made a key contribution to teaching the new generation of educators. During its early years, the school was heavily influenced by the economics and engineering institutions of what was then the Soviet Union, a political and cultural ally in those days, something that the organizers of the event had no qualms in recognizing.

I think that this illustrates something that is essential to understanding China's development towards a market economy, and in the future towards democracy as we understand it: China's social and institutional development has come about gradually over the years and is built on traditions and reference points dating back thousands of years.

Furthermore, the country's social and cultural transition is based on continuity; it incorporates the past, regardless whether they are seen as good or bad periods. This sense of respect for tradition makes a vital contribution to institutional continuity and in the reverence shown towards the elderly, in this case, the university's veteran teachers.

The second thing that struck me, and this may seem to contradict what I have just said, was the university's openness towards new currents of management theory, its looking out to the global market, the sharp pragmatism of its ideas, reflected in the announcement of new initiatives by its business school, the launching of new programs, and its rapidly growing internationalization.

In the end, the seeming dichotomy I am referring to – respect for tradition while looking to the future – is really a manifestation of that most Chinese of philosophies, yin and yang, the two elemental forces, seemingly opposed, but complementary, in balance and harmony, and which are to be found in everything, even in the world of business. The application of this duality has provided China with a powerful stabilizing influence, while at the same time allowing for rapid change throughout society, including business schools.

At the time of going to press, there were 234 government recognized educational institutions offering MBAs in China, attended by an estimated 70,000 students. Almost all MBA programs are taught by schools belonging to public universities, and are therefore subject to regulation regarding their numbers and objectives. That said, there are two business schools that stand out, and which are not part of the public education system: CEIBS (China Europe International Business School), a joint venture set up in 1994 between the European Commission and the Chinese Ministry of Foreign Trade and Economic Cooperation, backed by the EFMD, the European

Foundation for Management Development. CEIBS has since become the benchmark for executive education in Asia. The other is the Cheung Kong Graduate School of Business, founded in 2002 in the Chinese capital, and supported by business magnate Li Ka Shing. The school is highly respected by China's business community.

There are three main management education hubs in China: Beijing and Shanghai, in continental China, and Hong Kong, which has a different educational statute, and because of its history as a former colony is still influenced by British traditions to some extent. According to the rankings and league tables, Beijing's most international business schools, all part of the state system, are Guanghua School of Management, Beijing University's Beijing International MBA, or BiMBA, Tsinghua University, Renmin University Business School, and Tongi University. In Shanghai, the most important within the state system are Fudan University Business School, and the Antai Business School at Jiao Tong University. Hong Kong, which has the greatest number of schools with an international outlook, has HKUST (Hong Kong University of Science and Technology), the Chinese University of Hong Kong, the University of Hong Kong, City University of Hong Kong, and Hong Kong Polytechnic University.

Attending many conferences with deans of business schools in China, I have always been struck by their growing awareness of international competition, the need to develop a presence outside their country, and the rapid adaptation of these schools to the new global business environment. At the same time, I have often highlighted the need to introduce changes that will allow China's business schools, particularly those in Beijing and Shanghai, to project themselves more effectively at an international level. I would point to four main areas.

1. Schools need greater autonomy to develop the strategies appropriate to their needs. At present, schools that are part of universities have very limited room to maneuver, with little say over their curriculum, number of pupils, and degree programs, which are highly regulated.
2. Schools need to increase the amount of research they carry out: they lag considerably behind their Western competitors in this regard. That said, research needs to reflect local and domestic issues, related to Chinese management styles: to date, most theory on the subject has come from the West. Chinese universities seem aware of this challenge, and in recent years have made an effort to attract talent, recruiting teachers born in China but who left to work in the US and Europe. In fact, demand is such that Chinese teachers are increasingly hard to find.

3. Standards of business education vary sharply. On the one hand, there are the elite institutions mentioned above, which enjoy domestic and international recognition, while "the great majority of the nation's B-schools are of poor quality"[130] and where teaching staff fall below the standards of the majority of schools in the West.

4. China's business schools need to meet the growing demand for online courses, both in terms of degree programs and lifelong learning. Distance and online learning do not seem to enjoy the same status as in the West, and have not been developed to anything approaching their full potential. A recent report states that although it is expected that online education will take off in the future, with a 40 percent increase in 2011, it warns of "unimpressive continuation of doubts amongst members of the public as to the worth of diplomas from online institutions."[131]

Management education in China would also benefit significantly from opening up the market to foreign players. As is well known, foreign schools wanting to operate in China must do so in partnership with local institutions. These partnerships have not always met Western schools' expectations, which are keen to establish a bigger presence in what is now the world's biggest and fastest-growing market. As Alison Damast noted in *BusinessWeek*: "Foreign businesses in China often start out with an unbridled enthusiasm that is gradually tempered by bureaucracy, difficult local partners, and fewer customers than the size of its population – 1.3 billion at last count, and growing wealthier – would suggest."[132]

From my conversations with deans from Western schools that have looked at or entered into joint ventures with their Chinese counterparts, most say that their initial enthusiasm at entering what seems like a limitless market, and one where stakeholders are keen to work with them is soon tempered by the complex bureaucratic procedures they come up against, the strong sense of educational sovereignty shared by most Chinese officials, and the cultural difficulties involved in adapting to local markets. In contrast, many Western schools are seen by the Chinese as looking for quick returns, and unprepared to make the kind of long-term commitment required in China to succeed.

Faced with what they see as insurmountable difficulties, some Western business schools have decided to pull out of the country. Among them are Cass Business School, which had a joint MBA program with Shanghai University of Finance and Economics, the University of Maryland's Robert H. Smith School of Business, and the SUNY Buffalo with Renmin University Business School.

It is not to say that there have not been any success stories, among them that of Nottingham Business School, which has opened a Greenhouse Campus in Ningbo in Zhejiang province, a hotbed of high-tech start-up companies. A significant number of Western business schools looking to get into the Chinese market have instead opted to enter through Hong Kong, which has both a significant number of important business schools of its own, as well as a more flexible approach to dealing with international players.

Something else that has caught my attention in recent years is Chinese business schools' growing interest in sustainability and corporate social responsibility, along with values rooted in their own culture such as Confucianism, to the extent that some have even included a commitment to them within their mission statements. Colleagues and friends such as Xiang Bing, Dean of Cheung Kong Business School, or Xiongwen Lu, Dean of Fudan University Business School, reiterate the need to incorporate aspects of the Humanities and Western thought into China's millenarian culture.

Indeed, the underlying argument of this book, the need to continue learning throughout life, is one of the cornerstones of Confucian thinking.

English is the new Latin

Globalization has fostered multiple interactions among members of different cultures to a stage never known before. Furthermore, it is foreseeable that modern technologies, such as the Internet, will intensify this communication to unimaginable extremes. It is very likely that in the near future you may have as many, or even more, friends on other continents than at home. The fact that your friends may live in your antipodes will not pose any problem since you probably have access to cheap, friendly, and very advanced technologies that recreate in a very vivid – even more intellectually intense – way current face-to-face conversations and relations.

This cosmopolitan online world will be greatly enhanced by the development of very sophisticated instant translation. Looking to the near future, Eric Schmidt (former CEO of Google) predicted simultaneous translation and truth prediction (the probability that a statement is true, sometimes difficult to judge in a foreign language).[133] However, even if this occurs, different cultures will still need to use a vehicular language, sometimes referred to as "lingua franca," that is, a language that is used by a relevant number of people worldwide and that serves as an instrument for effective communication. An illustrative historical example of vehicular languages is Latin, widely extended and imposed during the Roman

Empire and, interestingly, the language used by academics in the Middle Ages. Vehicular languages are different to vernacular languages, sometimes called "native tongue," and are used mainly or exclusively in a given country or region.

Today, English is the most widely used vehicular language and, in fact, the global working language par excellence. Its native speakers – if India is included – represent the greatest force worldwide, followed by Chinese and Spanish. The Internet is probably the main acid test to anticipate which will be the prevalent vehicular languages of the future. Here again, English keeps its supremacy, and it seems it will become even more widely used, the "Esperanto" of our times.

English has also become the language of global education, as described in *The New York Times'* article "English as Language of Global Education,"[134] There I referred to "working English," i.e., a vehicular language far from pure Oxonian English and used, effectively, by hundreds of millions of humans: a mixture of vernacular expressions and accents with standard English. This has driven many people to talk about mixed languages such as "Spanglish" or "Englisch." Some believe that this jeopardizes the integrity of the English language, others that it is English at its most sublime. What do you think?

The students of today, and the managers of tomorrow, should be able to communicate effectively in at least two vehicular languages, in addition to their native one. Vehicular languages are the key to open to other cultures. Indeed, a way to bring civilizations together, or to create new ones.

A clear evidence of this is the language of delivery of MBA programs: although English is increasingly the "lingua franca" of management education, prospective participants may apply to MBA programs delivered in Welsh or Basque languages, for example, a singular opportunity that did not exist years ago. Maybe language diversity represents a potential source of differentiation for b-schools.

In previous sections, I have concentrated mainly on different elements that foster diversity, as a reverse side of globalization. It is worth examining the role of two important agents that may balance this diversity and at the same time foster transparency and comparability across continents. I refer to rankings and accreditation systems.

Melting agents: Accreditations and rankings

Accreditation provides a form of quality control in a rapidly expanding market. There are currently several different accreditation systems operating in the management education field. The best known and most established is the AACSB – the Association to Advance Collegiate Schools of Business –, which started life in the US. Most domestic markets have their own national accreditation body. More recently, the pan-European accreditation system EQUIS was established and is now highly respected not just in Europe but around the world.

As a representative of AEEDE, the Spanish Association of Business Schools, I have had the good fortune to participate in the setting up of EQUIS. Its origins lie in EQUAL, the European Quality Link, an association set up by EFMD, the European Foundation for Management Development, which brings together Europe's business schools and national accreditation agencies. EQUIS was set up with the aim of building a European system that would recognize the need for a diverse range of educational programs, and which would be overseen using universally recognized quality standards to validate each country's business schools.

The meetings to set up EQUAL went on over a period of almost two years, and were largely the initiative of Bernadette Conraths and Eric Cornuel of EFMD, under the leadership of Gordon Shenton, and with the decisive involvement of experts such as Jonathan Slack, Chris Greenstead, and Gene Crozier.

Looking back, I remember those meetings fondly, as they provided us with the opportunity to discuss questions that would be key to the future of management education, and because we were also all aware that we were involved in the creation and development of an important European institution. We set ourselves the initial task of establishing an accreditation system on the basis of mutual recognition, and we thus decided to design one from scratch. This would result in EQUIS, which would be independent of EQUAL.

That approach turned out to be the correct one: after 11 years of existence, EQUIS is now one of the most-respected accreditation systems internationally, with approved schools all over the world.

Accreditation agencies and the ranking systems set up by newspapers such as the *Financial Times*, *Businessweek*, or *The Economist* have played a crucial role in the globalization of management education, improving information, increasing transparency, and facilitating comparison among the different programs offered by business schools around the world.

While accreditation agencies undoubtedly have helped to validate and assess the quality of business schools, it has also been pointed out that because their evaluation is based on certain fixed standards – in themselves ample and open to interpretation – they run the risk of preventing innovation, the search for new approaches, or sidelining models that challenge the status quo. As Gaye Tuchman, Professor of Sociology at the University of Connecticut, points out: "The coercive accountability associated with both an audit society and its culture helps to constitute an accountability regime – a politics of surveillance, control and market management disguising itself as the value-neutral and scientific administration of individuals and organizations."[135]

Accreditation systems, particularly those based on peer-reviewed audits such as the AACSB or EQUIS, can tend to evaluate candidate institutions on the basis of traditional or tried and tested criteria, or on conservative views of what should constitute an academic establishment. In my experience as an auditor on accreditation visits to business schools, I remember two occasions that illustrate this problem. The first involved our panel members, all of whom were deans, and who had developed a critique of business schools that they saw as "opportunistic" because their portfolio of masters programs was, in the opinion of the panel, overly broad, and had been developed in a bid to meet all the demands of the market.

I was surprised by this assessment, particularly bearing in mind that one of the things we drum into our students at business schools is the need to be entrepreneurial and to identify new opportunities – in other words, to be opportunistic. I suspect that this is not the only occasion that an academic institution has been criticized in these terms: over the years I have seen similar comments in several accreditation reports.

The second episode took place during a visit to a different school, during which the auditors asked its management how often they revised their mission statement. The dean of the school's reply was "every year," pointing out that this allowed the school to calibrate its objectives with new initiatives, given the rapid of pace of change of the market.

This was clearly not the correct "canonical" answer. The auditors believed that the mission statement of a school should not be revised so often, to avoid what they called "institutional instability." But as we know from our experience in the business world, innovative companies sometimes revise their mission and goals on a daily basis. I remember a conversation with the director of human resources of Spanish clothes manufacturer Inditex (the owner of high street fashion retailers Zara), considered one of the most innovative retailers in the world, in which she told me that the company had decided to not even bother formulating a mission statement, preferring instead to talk in terms of values, so as to give it greater flexibility in adapting to changes in the market.

Toward a global standard

One of the recurrent questions posed to representatives of accreditation systems by business school deans is whether they plan to merge efforts and launch a single common accreditation scheme. The reason behind this demand is that accreditation is a highly time-consuming activity and requires the allocation of many resources at business schools. For example, those business schools that undergo national and international accreditation processes usually assign specific teams to manage this operation. Consequently, some deans would like to simplify these requirements by reducing the number of accreditation processes they participate in.

However, I do not agree with this point of view for three main reasons. First, accreditation – particularly international schemes such as EQUIS, AACSB, and AMBA – contribute decisively to the reputation of the school: in an increasingly global management education sector, accreditation awards contribute significantly to the transparency and comparability of educational offerings.

Second, each accreditation process represents an opportunity to review strategies and improve activities at the examined school. Third, the existence of different accreditation agencies brings competition and variety, something that, I believe, is always desirable.

In 2010, the creation of a new accreditation system launched by AAPBS (Association of Asia-Pacific Business Schools) was announced. The new scheme was aimed fundamentally at the recognition of programs and schools of the region taking into consideration the singularities of management education there. Ultimately, the purpose is to improve the quality of management education offerings in Asia and to contribute to the transparency of the market. Many questions about this new initiative still remain unknown, but I believe that AAPBS can learn from the experience of other international accreditation agencies. However, the recent news regarding AAPBS is that the initiative has been postponed indefinitely.

Rank and file

Business schools' rankings, if conducted according to the basic principles of impartiality, transparency, and consistency, add real value to the market. In recent years, many new ranking schemes have entered the scene, evidence that the market demands them. Different stakeholders – prospective students, recruiters, and corporate clients – see rankings as additional criteria to gather further information and make the educational offerings more easily comparable. It is thus legitimate that an initiative that provides value to the market has its returns and becomes profitable for those who undertake such effort. I have no objections here. I appreciate the positive attitude of those ranking producers who contribute to the transparency of the activity by engaging in a constructive debate with representatives of the institutions examined.

The rankings phenomenon is not unique to education. Law firms, consulting companies, and even auditors live under the rule of the rankers.

Certainly, rankings are here to stay and will probably proliferate in the future. Once European higher education systems in Europe adopt the same structure and cross border movement of students increases, applicants to a diverse set of disciplines will need to compare many different elements and will use rankings as an instrument to decide where to study. The recent flourish of worldwide university rankings anticipates and evidences this.

One of the frequent criticisms of rankings is that they compare institutions that are intrinsically different. As one dean used to say "it's like comparing apples with oranges." How can you compare, for example, a Chinese executive education centre run by practitioners with an American research university-based business school mainly comprised of academics? These two hypothetical institutions may offer MBA programs, but their location, mission, faculty profile, and research output vary essentially and are thus not comparable. The basis of this criticism is the incommensurability argument: different values or things of a different genre cannot be weighted according to the same scale; you cannot compare apples with oranges.

The incommensurability argument is appealing from a theoretical perspective and has generated long debates in different disciplines such as jurisprudence or aesthetics. However, it is irrelevant in practice. Every day we have to evaluate different things and take decisions. Should I go to the theater tonight or dine with my friends at home? If I invite my friends for dinner, should I prepare sushi or paella? The irrelevance of the incommensurability argument for the practice has been evidenced by some proponents of aesthetics theory like Oscar Tusquets, who stated that "everything is comparable."[136] The epitome of this comparability thesis is probably the maxim stated by Marinetti in his *Futurist Manifesto* of 1909: "A screaming automobile that seems to run on grapeshot is more beautiful than the Winged Victory of Samothrace."[137]

Indeed, different offerings and diverse institutions are comparable from the perspective of the applicant who wants to decide where to study an MBA. One of the virtues of rankings is that they provide information that will help to reduce the scope of the analysis for applicants. For example, they may help identify which institutions are the best regarded in Europe, America, or Asia, or which business schools excel in a certain management discipline or which MBA programs are better considered by some selected recruiters.

But the crux of comparability is the data considered as the basis for comparison, the question about different sets of standards' data usable for rankings. Certainly, concepts such as "full professor," "foreign students," "starting salary," or "aims achieved at the end of the program," just to name a few, may have different meanings and be measured differently across the board. Who can legitimately give a standard meaning to these and other open concepts? My suggestion is that accreditation agencies such as EQUIS, AMBA, and AACSB International may play a major role here. EQUIS, for example, has a tradition of coping with diversity, and its managers have discussed for some time the idea of developing a glossary aimed at defining the basic concepts used in the accreditation of business schools. Can we expect to have a universal set of standards soon? Don't hold your breath.

The next learning curve

CHAPTER 8

The purpose of business schools

Most institutions and businesses will, at some time or another, set down in writing what they see as their mission. The objective of this exercise is to capture the essence of the organization's activity, lay out its fundamental goals, and highlight what sets it apart from other, similar organizations. The mission statement will include elements that reflect the past and present of the institution – what we might call its DNA – along with its aspirations, which represent the challenges of the future.

One of the advantages of creating a mission statement is that it helps stakeholders coordinate their activities, ideas, and decisions. Setting down a mission statement should be no mere formality or conceptual exercise, and the end result should certainly not be some superficial statement. This is a profound exercise, carried out to provide lasting meaning to the existence of a company or organization.

Most business schools regularly re-examine their mission statement, as well as including it on their website and many official documents issued by the dean or other senior members of the management and faculty. Analysis of the mission statements of the main business schools in Europe and the US reveals startling similarities in their values and ideas. The most common recurring themes are the international outlook of the institution, the development of business leaders, their commitment to innovation and excellence, along with the carrying out of research, or the generation of new ideas and knowledge. In recent years, we have also seen a growing emphasis on corporate social responsibility and citizenship in business schools' mission statements.

It is possible that the similarities between so many business schools' mission statements has to do with the increasing convergence within the sector, along with the homogenization imposed by the accreditation agencies and the league tables set up by newspapers and magazines. In my experience as an accreditation auditor for EQUIS, one of the most recurring issues I have had to address is disentangling the differential aspects of the school being visited, given that mission statements are so generic and so similar. There is little value in evaluating a school on the basis of a single model. It was precisely to identify diversity among different schools and strategic missions that EQUIS was set up.

So, on the one hand, we find a notable similarity between business schools' mission statements, and on the other, a genuine diversity among their respective models and their actual programs. Above and beyond questions of difference and similarity, business schools' mission statements seem to share two fundamental objectives: research or the production and/or distribution of management-related knowledge; and the education, training, and development of managers.

In short, research and teaching are the two basic activities of business schools, as is the case with other educational institutions. In addition to this minimal common denominator, what distinguishes one school from another are its delivery methods, the type of teaching or programs that it offers, the type of students it seeks to attract, its research methods or the knowledge that it contributes to society and promotes, and the place in the value chain of knowledge where it has chosen to position itself, among other factors.

Sometimes, a business school's mission is revealed by the very name it uses. Although most institutions call themselves "School of Business," some, such as Yale and Stanford, opt for the alternative "School of Management," suggesting a wider reach beyond the world of business, and that includes forming leaders and teams for government and administration, along with other types of organizations.

I believe that the activities of business schools, and by association their strategic mission, can be evaluated on the basis of a three-fold mission composed of the following principles.

1. Business schools are bridges between the Academia and the Agora, the names used by the ancient Greeks to refer, respectively, to the place where knowledge is generated and the place where business and trade happens.
2. Business schools are education hubs, whose function is to develop and train leaders, managers, directors, and entrepreneurs.
3. Business schools are catalysts in the process of transforming the local and the global society.

Bridging the Academia and the Agora

In the introduction, I spoke of the need for business schools to act as a bridge between the Academia and the Agora. In Plato's *Dialogues* we see that the participants in the philosophical debates with Socrates are the politicians and businessmen of the day. The Agora and the Academia were linked, not just because of their physical proximity, but because the same men were active in both spheres.

I was inspired to reconsider the idea of uniting Agora and Academia after reading *Point to Point Navigation*,[138] the second installment of Gore Vidal's memoirs – as prescient and witty as its preceding volume. In line with his innate irreverence, one of the favorite targets of Vidal's essays and articles is, again and again, the deeply entrenched prejudices held by some academics, as illustrated in this passage from the opening chapter: "Contrary to what many believe, literary fame has nothing to do with excellence or true glory or even with a writer's position in the syllabus of a university's English Department, itself as remote to the Agora as Academe's shadowy walk. For any artist, fame is the extent to which the Agora finds interesting his latest work. If what he has written is known only to a few of other practitioners, or to enthusiasts ... then the artist is not only not famous, he is irrelevant to his time, the only time he has."[139]

It is time to bring the Agora and the Academia closer, and business schools can play a leading role in making this happen.

Some business school managers – most, I hope – consider that an important part of their institution's mission is to bridge the business world and academia. Some others – few, I believe – emphasize that business schools are academic institutions, and they should seek their own identity, separate from the business world.

These attached and detached views are at the extremes. The detached view was brought home to me when I interviewed a candidate for my school's faculty. I asked this person about the content and purpose of his research, and at some stage he explained that he was looking forward to teaching on executive programs because it would provide an opportunity to check whether the findings of his research fitted in the real business world. I tried not to overreact, – my friends say I am too diplomatic – but I was very surprised. Could you imagine a scientist, whose research was on elephant-family habits, saying that he would eventually like to watch some real elephants in order to test the accuracy of his theories?

The academic world has always experienced a tension between theory and practice, in management as well as in other disciplines. This tension has sometimes resulted in the creation of an abyss between the two spheres, characterized by the "ivory tower syndrome," a phenomenon that, paradoxically, some academics take great delight in. A curious antecedent of this syndrome was when the abbots of Middle Age monasteries prescribed the principle "ora et labora" (pray and work) because their monks were spending too much time in church and abandoning their responsibilities in the orchard or the library.

Immanuel Kant, the great philosopher, dealt with this question in his opuscule "Theory and Practice," essential reading for academics, where one of his aims is to overcome the gap between speculative thinking and practical decisions. One of the conclusions of his work is that when theories cannot be applied to practice, they are just bad theories.[140]

Wharton's Paul J. H. Shoemaker recently said: "the history of business education reveals an elusive balance between business and society."[141] And it is true that recent decades have seen the pendulum swing increasingly towards academic excellence that was based on better qualified teaching staff and high-level research. In 1959, what was seen as an excessive focus on the technical and practical led the Carnegie and Ford foundations to recommend more rigorous and scientific research. These recommendations prompted the business schools of universities such as Carnegie Mellon, Harvard, MIT, and Chicago to highlight academic excellence and research. Since then, there has been an impressive growth in academic gatherings, specialist journals, and conferences and congresses addressing specific aspects of business education. The result is an academic marketplace that feeds and sustains itself. As Shoemaker points out: "the field has beefed up its academic standing by promoting faculty with deep scientific roles."[142] That said, he also notes, somewhat critically, that: "over time, however, these scholars often took business research in directions no longer comprehensible or relevant to business students and managers."[143]

I remember a conference organized by Roger Martin, Dean of Rotman School of Management, in Toronto in 2005. He had invited deans from more than 20 schools from all over the world, along with other leading academics, to discuss the future of management education and the MBA. Among the delegates was a well-known and highly respected scholar from one of the leading business schools in the US who said that in all likelihood, the papers that he now produced would not be published in journals that he himself had created.

Criticism of less-than-relevant research produced by business schools is a constant theme in articles written by many top academics. In the oft-cited article "How Business Schools Lost Their Way," Warren Bennis and James O'Toole outline the rise of what they call *methodolatry*, the system in which teachers at business schools fear being seen as focused on spreading ideas, and thus tend to focus their research on satisfying the interests of their colleagues, looking only into issues related to methodology, and avoiding matters of real use in the professional world: "The system creates pressure on scholars to publish articles on narrow subjects chiefly of interest to other academics, not practitioners,"[144] in the sense that "businesspeople are starting to sense that individuals in the Academy are not engaged in the same profession they practice."[145]

Similarly, Jeffrey Pfeffer and Christina T. Fong[146] questioned the direction that academic research has taken in recent years, and its impact on the professional world. They pointed to three barometers to assess the impact of research carried out by business schools on the real world. The first is an analysis of the origin of *BusinessWeek's* Top Ten business books over two decades. They say there were four books written by business school academics in the top ten in 1984, with just one in 1991 and in 2001.

The second is based on the list prepared by Darrell Rigby[147] of management tools – the concepts and analytical frameworks use to illustrate management practices and to enable decision making. Rigby selected the 25 most popular management tools, on the basis of a book list published by the Dow Jones Group, along with interviews with academics and company directors. His conclusion was that only eight of these analysis tools originated in business schools, while seventeen came from consultants or corporations. Pfeffer and Fong's final source to demonstrate the gulf between academic research and the real world is based on a study by Barley, Meyer, and Gash[148] on the language and tone used by academics and managers respectively when discussing organizational practice. They conclude that while academics are increasingly influenced by the literary constructs of managers, the inverse is not true of managers. These three barometers led Pfeffer and Fong to the conclusion that research in business and the real problems that business managers face in their daily lives are headed down increasingly divergent roads.

Business schools are not the only educational institutions under fire for the alleged lack of relevance of their research to the needs of professionals working in the real world. I have personal experience of the debates currently underway in the worlds of Jurisprudence[149] and Architectural Theory,[150] both areas where research must have a connection with the real world if it is to be of any relevance. I suspect that lack of relevance is a potential problem for all areas of research, particularly in clinical disciplines. More than 200 years ago, Kant pointed out that there is no such thing as pure or applied research, simply good and bad research: his words are as pertinent today. In Chapter 10 of this book, which explores the profile of teachers and the nature of research carried out in business schools, I will put forward some proposals to address this challenge.

Business schools as learning hubs

A few years ago, a dean with many years of experience in education told me that the only things a business school needs to be successful are good students and good teachers. The rest – campus, facilities, and equipment – are mere accessories. Over the years, my experience has borne out his assessment: the most important ingredients in the learning process are the quality of the students and the quality of the faculty.

As we will see, not all schools mean the same thing when they refer to having or attracting the best students and teaching staff. And this divergence may be truly legitimate, since missions differ across business schools.

Leaving aside the question of students and teachers for the moment, a business school's value proposal includes other differential elements. In my opinion, from this perspective, business schools can be seen as learning hubs – places offering educational programs and services based on a particular philosophy and position. To better understand this idea, let's look at the basic elements that make up the learning process, and which can be seen in Figure 8.1: Content and Curriculum; Modalities and Formats; The Experience; and Access to Networks.

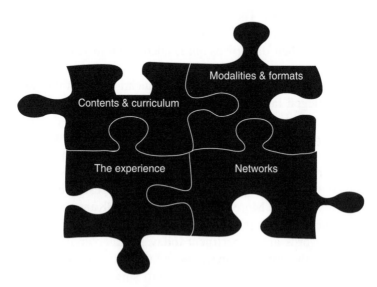

Figure 8.1 B-schools as learning hubs

Content and curriculum of programs

Considered by many to be the most distinctive aspect of a business school, the content of most schools' programs is a great deal more similar than might appear, at least at first look. This is partly explained by the market's standardization of programs, and, as said, particularly by the demands of the accreditation agencies. An MBA program will typically be made up of a series of modules. For example, AMBA (the Association of MBAs) may not include an exhaustive list of subjects that MBA programs must contain, but it does require that they include Accounting, Business Policy and Strategy, Organizational Theory, Information Systems Management, Leadership, and Marketing, as well as Finance and Operations Management, among others.[151]

That said, it is the balance or special blend of such components that makes a school stand out from the competition. Regarding this ideal blend of subjects, there has been a recurrent debate over the mix between "hard skills," such as quantitative methods for decision making, and "soft skills," those more qualitative areas related to the development of personal skills so important in leading teams or communicating effectively.

Recent research on the abilities that employers look for in business school graduates emphasizes the importance of soft skills, but it is also true that solid conceptual foundations, along with the ability to exercise quantitative analysis, continue to be among the main requisites demanded by recruiting companies. There has also been debate on the ideal balance between the transmission of theoretical and applied knowledge. And while there is no denying that the programs taught by business schools should be fundamentally focused on application, so that their graduates can use what they have learned in the world of work, it is equally true that learning theoretical models helps to strengthen graduates' capacity for abstract and conceptual thinking, beyond merely case-based reasoning. In line with Kant, I have always believed that in the real world there is no difference between applicable and non-applicable theories: there are simply good theories and bad theories.

In their *Rethinking the MBA: Business Education at a Crossroads*,[152] Srikant Datar, David Garvin, and Patrick Cullen make a comparative analysis of the curricular content of 11 of the top MBA programs, 10 in the US, and one in Europe, INSEAD. They conclude: "At the level of content – particularly the core curriculum and the subjects covered – we found programs to be much alike ... At times they even use the same textbooks and assign the same articles and cases."[153] Nevertheless, they add: "At the level of architecture – particularly regarding issues of structure, sequence and requirements – we found a large number of highly differentiated approaches."[154]

In which case, if there are few substantial differences among the content of the many MBA programs on offer, then how do schools differentiate themselves? They do so mainly by the emphasis or length of their core courses, by offering some courses that differ from the traditional, and above all by offering a range of elective courses to build on the basic concepts developed in the required curriculum. These differences are reflected in the way that stakeholders see a particular school's strengths. For example, Northwestern (Kellogg) is usually considered to be pre-eminent in marketing, while NYU Stern stands out for its teaching in finance.

In recent years, many schools have made a major effort to revamp their MBA programs, with the aim of integrating traditional courses and overcoming their fragmented or compartmentalized view of a company. Three schools offer interesting examples of this process of integration: Rotman School of Management in Canada, Yale School of Management (SoM), and Stanford GSB in the US, where all of them two-year MBA programs. It would seem to be the case that integration problems are more common in two-year programs than in their single-year counterparts, due to their being less compact and having a greater number and variety of contents, with the concomitant difficulties this brings in coordinating teaching staff.

In the case of Rotman School, the involvement of its Dean, Roger Martin, and Mihnea Moldeveanu, the Director of the Desautels Centre for Integrative Thinking, has been decisive. The pair are the authors of "The Future of the MBA: Designing the Thinker of the Future,"[155] in which they share their vision of the high-value decision maker of the future whom they call an "integrator," someone who solves problems through effective action, which the narrow specialist can often not solve even in theory. To overcome the fragmented nature of traditional subjects in MBA programs, Rotman School has included integrative thinking modules in its first year, which focus on understanding and analyzing how people use mental models in their everyday lives.

The school also teaches design thinking, a methodology for practical, creative resolution of problems or issues that looks for improved future results. It is the essential ability to combine empathy, creativity, and rationality to meet user needs and drive business success. Unlike analytical thinking, design thinking is a creative process based around the "building up" of ideas, argue Roger and Moldeveanu. As the pair explain, one of the main problems with business schools is the construction of bridges across different areas of knowledge: "even though business schools are already multidisciplinary (they are aggregates of representatives of many disciplines) and sometimes pluri-disciplinary (they are aware of being multi-disciplinary) collectives, they are not yet interdisciplinary (they do not cross disciplinary boundaries in ways that do justice to all of the bridged disciplines and successfully integrate across boundaries) or trans-disciplinary ones."[156]

With the similar goals in mind, Stanford GSM introduced important changes to its MBA curriculum in 2007, the result of lengthy consultations with a committee of 11 academics led by Gerth Saloner, the school's current dean. In Saloner's words, the committee took as its starting point the radical question: "If we were to develop an MBA curriculum from scratch, what it would look like?"[157] The result was an MBA program in which the first year is divided into two parts, the first called Management Perspectives –which combines subjects such as Accounting and Organizational Behavior with modules on critical analytical thinking and managing groups and teams – and a second titled Management Foundations, which explores the traditional core areas of an MBA, offering students three different levels for each subject, allowing them to choose those that best reflect their experience or knowledge. The second year of the MBA is made up of elective courses with varying methodologies, some of them very similar to a PhD, and involving the presentation of papers, along with academic discussions.

In the meantime, under the guidance of its then recently appointed Dean, Joel Podolny, in 2006, Yale SoM implemented a major reform of its MBA program. Yale's curricular amendments were also aimed at bringing about a more integrated approach to management. Under the heading Organizational Perspectives, the MBA's traditional subjects are seen from the perspective of various stakeholders: Competitor (the traditional strategy); Customer (Marketing and Sales); Investor (Finance); Employee (HR Management). The overhaul was completed with a module called Integrated Leadership Perspective, which involved case studies of companies at different phases of their life cycle, and which were taken from an international perspective to encourage participants to see things globally. Time will tell whether these radical changes to Yale SoM's curriculum will turn out to be anything more than a rejigging of traditional formulas, and whether they contribute to a more integrative approach to management. In any event, both students and the school's other stakeholders received them with considerable expectation.[158]

In general, the business schools that I have experience of, tend to update the content of their programs on a regular basis. There is an unwritten rule that says it is advisable to modify at least 20 percent of a school's curriculum each year to reflect the changes taking place in the real world of business. In my opinion, in addition to the updating of the content of core MBA subjects, or the creation of new modules focused on developing leadership skills, or the creation of transversal integrative subjects, as Yale and Stanford have done, the most important reforms in the MBA world are coming about through the introduction of subjects related to the liberal arts and humanities, which will have major implications for the world of management.

With this in mind, at IE Business School we have introduced subjects and sessions dedicated to the humanities in our MBAs and Masters in Management. Ours is a two-fold goal. On one hand, we hope to include management studies within the broad spectrum of the social and human sciences, with the aim of highlighting the inter-connectedness of the models, concepts, and theories of a range of disciplines, thus better understanding the social role of business. At the same time, we aim to create well-rounded managers, enlightened directors who are cultured, and who have a knowledge of the arts and history of their own and other cultures, thus better enabling them to lead multicultural teams. We believe that studying history provides key references that enable directors to take better business decisions, on the basis of an understanding of the experiences of the past.

Similarly, an understanding of the history of art can strengthen our observation and perception, two skills related to the ability to take more reflexive or considered decisions, in turn offering a counterbalance to the action-oriented approach of most directors. In this regard, the words of Drew Faust, the President of Harvard University, come to mind: "History teaches contingency; it demonstrates that the world has been different and could and will be different again. Anthropology can show that societies are and have been different elsewhere – across space as well as time. Literature can teach us many things, but not the least of these is empathy – how to picture ourselves inside another person's head, life, experience – how to see the world through a different lens, which is what the study of the arts offers us as well. Economic growth and scientific and technological advances are necessary but not sufficient purposes for a university."[159]

Different formats and modalities of programs

Over the years, business schools have experimented with a range of teaching methods that have featured traditional lectures, the case study, role-playing, action learning, game-based learning, simulation exercises, consultancy projects, and other approaches aimed at recreating the realities they will face in the world of management. As regards delivery, the top schools have tended to keep class numbers low, while online teaching largely remains the preserve of distance-learning universities. Early on in the decade, some pioneering business schools, such as Duke, began to introduce online modules, alternating them with face-to-face sessions, and which allowed participants to complete their teaching program within a similar time frame to traditionally taught courses. This approach gave students greater flexibility, particularly to executives who were required by their employers to travel a lot of the time, or who lived abroad.

There is nothing new about the modular method, and has been perfected over the years by online education providers, particularly by what I call "Big Education Retailers." In essence, it requires that students sign up for modules that they will finish over a period of time that suits them best, following guidelines established by the school or by the tutors assigned to them. These guidelines may refer to the order in which students complete their modules, or lay down a time frame within which the progam must be completed if they are to obtain their MBA. For example, MBA students on the United Kingdom's Open University distance learning degree programs finish their studies within an average of four years, while MBA students at Manchester Business School's Engineering Business Managers program take 4.2 years to finish their studies.

The modular approach has also frequently been a part of open courses in the sphere of executive education. By completing a series of modules, with their corresponding credits, students can obtain a certificate or diploma. For example, after completing the required four modules each year, students attending Oxford University's Saïd Business School can attain a diplomas in Global Business, Organizational Leadership, and Financial Strategy.

As Clayton Christensen, Michael Horn, and Curtis Johnson explain,[160] all services and products have their own internal architecture or design, typically made up of modules or components, and one of the defining characteristics of customization is that these components are interconnected. In an ideal world, these would be customized to a degree where the modules would reflect the interests and availability of each student. But programs are built and designed so that their component parts are closely linked, the result being that the better programs must be taught in the right order, and with time limits.

One of the reasons behind the success of the IE Business School's International Executive MBA is that it doesn't chop up its modules, and requires students to stick to specific modules. What's more, IE places great importance on an *esprit de corps*, the idea that students belong to a particular group. We believe that this fosters strong ties among students and facilitates learning. Furthermore, it imposes a sense of discipline and order that encourages the skills associated with an MBA: multitasking, and the ability to synthesize, time management, and working under pressure.

That said, the Internet offers business schools the chance to change the way they teach. Traditionally, classes are taught over a 60- or 90-minute period. Once the class is finished, the learning process can continue via note taking, reading, tutorials, or even by going over the whole class by watching a video recording of it. For example, the Kokkalis Foundation in Athens used to record classes, and then allow students access to these recordings. But in the traditional classroom-teaching situation, once the lesson is over, the class ends.

Schools like IE have developed new online teaching techniques involving the use of an interactive campus over a period of several days, thus overcoming the problem of having to teach a class, as it were, "in one go." This online campus, where professors coordinate forums and video-conference with students, is open 24 hours a day. These interactions are supported by digital learning tools that allow students to participate in videoconferences, send instant messages, access online documents, use blackboards, and communicate via VoIP (Voice over Internet Protocol). This allows students to participate at their convenience, regardless of the time zone they are living and working in. My experience of these kind of online sessions – my heavy travel schedule gives me no other teaching option – is that students participate more intensively, and they share their experiences, the result of which is a more effective application of the case study method.[161]

Needless to say, this online approach requires greater involvement on the part of teaching staff – at IE we estimate that academic staff put in up to four times that of the time they would if giving a traditional class – but the overall experience is much richer both for students and teachers. Students learn more, given that they are able to participate for much longer than they would in a traditional classroom situation, and they come away from each lesson feeling they have learned more. At the same time, class numbers are also lower: it is clearly not possible to manage an online chat session of more than 35 students. The teaching experience is more authentic, and students follow the lesson more closely than they would in a traditional classroom setting. It is my belief that although traditional teaching methods will continue to play a key role in MBA programs, the growing use of interactive online sessions offers a perfect compliment to classroom learning, as well as boosting the students' skill set. With this in mind, IE has decided to go for a blended teaching format consisting of traditional classroom assistance with online learning: we see this as the future of executive education.

The type of teaching materials used at a business school can also be a source of differentiation. One of the most frequent criticisms leveled at traditional case studies used in MBAs, particularly in programs for senior executives or in-company, is about their structure and content. There is too much information laid out in an orderly fashion and that allows students to identify the problem too quickly and to offer solutions. These critics say that such heavily processed case studies have little to do with the way that the way the world really works, where information is often scarce or fragmented. This has prompted some business schools to rethink their teaching materials and to take their case studies apart, providing students something that looks more like the kind of case they would face in the day-to-day running of a company.

For example, Yale School of Management has developed "raw" case studies[162] that are "open-ended, web based, multi-perspective presentations that often feature thousands of pages of relevant material that students must analyze, such as 10 Ks, 20-Fs, analysts' reports, news articles, stock charts, and interviews with key players."[163] In recent years, at IE we have developed multimedia case studies of a similar nature. They are deliberately left vague, reflecting the way that companies continue to evolve over time, with videos of the CEO and the directors of the company in question, along with information about their markets and links to external sources. These case studies allow for a more open and less predetermined discussion, an approach that we have found can sometimes make executives used to the ordered, predictable old case studies uncomfortable. From the school's perspective, such case studies mean that teachers must be more in touch with what is going on in the real world, as well as knowing more about the sector and company involved, but above all, they must be able to manage an unpredictable and open-ended discussion. But then, isn't that what a case study in the wild would be like?

What is the difference between one-year or two-year MBA programs? There is a Spanish proverb, attributed to Baltasar Gracián, which says "what is good, if brief, is two times as good." It is a proverb applicable to many different situations like presentations; and I can only think of only very few exceptions to the rule that I will omit here. Concision is a good virtue to cultivate and has been attributed to good writers, orators, musicians, and the like.

Duration is just one of the ingredients of an MBA program, but an important one. In the case of full-time MBAs, the trend in recent years has been to shorten the duration, and if you look at the European schools included in the *Financial Times* MBA ranking only a few remain that still have two-year length offerings.

There are good reasons why one-year MBAs are gaining ground. First, an MBA is no longer seen as the last chance to experience education. This is as it should be: education should not be contemplated as a one-shot, once in a lifetime option, but rather should be extended over an entire professional career. Indeed, updating business knowledge and perfecting managerial skills is a continuing need. This is in fact one of the main tenets of this book.

Second, the opportunity cost for students of being out of the market for a long time is becoming increasingly high. Third, many analysts believe that one-year MBAs satisfy the basic needs provided by the two-year ones. For example, George Bickerstaffe, former editor of the "Which MBA Guide," told me that in one-year programs participants seem to be covering the same things as those of two-year programs but at twice the speed. True, the intensity and workload of one-year programs may be heavier, but this in turn is in line with the demand for higher productivity that managers face nowadays. In fact, many times graduates of one-year MBAs meet their fellows of two-year programs during recruiting processes with equal chances of being hired by the same companies.

You may think that I defend a partisan view, given that my school offers one-year MBA programs, but I believe that a two-year option is a luxury most people simply cannot afford today. Moreover, many analysts estimate that after the implementation of the Bologna Accord in Europe, those students who have already completed the two cycles of bachelor (3 years) and master (1–2 years) would hardly enroll on a further two-year MBA program.

In the case of Executive MBAs things may be different, particularly if the program allows for modularity or is run on a blended methodology, i.e., combining face-to-face sessions with online sessions. In executive education, the basic principle is flexibility and those programs that better adapt to the circumstances of participants in terms of time and location will get the wider acceptance. For example, in the case of the just launched Global MBA at IE Business School, a program that runs mostly online, the preferred option by most candidates has been the 18-month format.

The "Experience" as a differential component of programs

Above and beyond the qualification to be gained by taking an MBA or Master in Management, one of the most important aspects of any program is the learning experience itself. Life on campus, meeting and forming friendships with other students, taking part in extracurricular activities, absorbing the values of the institution in question and sharing its ideals are just some of the more notable aspects of study, and that will allow future employers to identify graduates.

A school's location, along with the way that its students and teachers work within that environment, is a key defining characteristic. Some writers have looked at the relationship between a university and the city it is located in, and the influence each exercises over the other. For example, Greater Boston, where there are more than 100 colleges and universities, is an educational melting pot, with students attending courses in institutions other than their own, earning the city the title of the "Athens of America," and where academic life has played a key role in the identity and economy of the city.

Other colleges have made their home in smaller cities, preferring to highlight the benefits of a strong sense of belonging and exclusivity. Dartmouth College's magnificent campus in the small town of Hanover, New Hampshire, is a good example of a countryside campus where pupils have the opportunity to concentrate on their studies, college life, and sport, along with a range of extracurricular activities organized by the university. In this leafy environment, the elegant buildings of Tuck Business School, connected with each other by tunnels to allow easy access during the winter months, allow students to benefit from a close sense of community with teachers and other staff, a proximity that facilitates integration and strengthens a sense of belonging.

At the other end of the spectrum are those business schools that have decided to locate themselves in city centers, with an "embedded campus," perhaps believing that students need to be close to the heart of social life, to where business and political decisions are made, and that also offer a wealth of extracurricular activities. London Business School and Cass at City University, both in London, along with Columbia and Stern in New York are examples of urban campuses located in the center of major cities. Their location also allows them to offer executive education, to attract adjunct and practicing teaching staff, and to organize conferences with large corporations. At the same time, opting for a city center location limits the physical expansion of colleges, given the high cost of real estate or lack of available land or premises.

My school, IE Business School, is an urban campus, located in the center of Madrid, close to the financial and commercial districts. For several years we have been thinking about moving part or all of our activity to a suburban campus, where we would have access not only to new educational buildings, but also to sport and social facilities. In the end we reached the conclusion that our location in the center of a large city, with its cultural and leisure opportunities, is one of the things that our students most value. We may not have a restaurant for our students, but there is no shortage of competitively priced restaurants in the vicinity – which many other cities would be hard pressed to match. The city is our campus, and we have agreements with a wide range of service suppliers, foundations, and cultural organizations that allow our students to interact with the city and its inhabitants.

In recent years, some business schools have sought to set themselves apart from the competition by commissioning so-called starchitects. In some ways, business schools have taken on the role once filled by cathedrals or churches on traditional campuses, reflecting, perhaps, the position that they now hold in many universities. Examples of this trend include Frank Gehry's business school at Sydney's University of Technology, or Weatherhead School of Management, Norman Foster's plans for Yale School of Management, I. M. Pei's CEIBS in Shanghai, or Legorreta's at the different campuses of Monterrey's TEC in northern Mexico. Some newly established business schools have opted to install themselves in historic buildings of significant architectural interest, such as ESMT in Berlin, that is based in a building built to house the government of the former German Democratic Republic, close to the German capital's main museums, and whose entrance hall retains the Marxist-inspired murals depicting the workers' conquest of capital.

There is no denying that a business school's design and location are key factors within the experience of taking an MBA. That said, we should remember that a business school's investment priorities should be attracting the best teaching staff and the brightest students, along with developing new teaching methodologies. When all is said and done, these are the factors that give a school its true competitive edge.

Access to networks

One of the most frequent reasons cited by candidates applying to business school is access to a network of alumni, recruiters, company contacts, and other institutions. Most business schools have departments or teams that keep in touch with graduates over the course of their professional lives. In addition to strengthening the school's identity and boosting their prestige by associating themselves with successful men and women, such a policy bears two important fruit. In the first place, graduates are the best advertisement for a school, and the best way to attract new students. At the same time, they are often the source of considerable financial contributions towards endowments. US business schools have been particularly successful in developing these alumni networks, perhaps, because of the already-existing tradition of fund raising in the US, which is much more developed than in other countries. European schools, on the other hand, which are more focused on educational aspects, have tended to overlook maintaining links to their graduates.

Aside from the longstanding contribution that careers and alumni departments have made, in recent years, the Internet has played a growing role in developing networks. Looking at the main social networking sites such as Facebook, Twitter, LinkedIn, or MySpace, my impression is that there is a significant presence of business schools' alumni networks, but that at the same time it is also fragmented. This can probably in part be attributed to the fact that the top schools have their highly effective social networks, typically characterized by frequent social events and reunions.

Business schools as catalysts

Businesses are the most global institutions of our time. Their activities promote social and economic development, along with an improvement in our living conditions and rights. One of my favorite maxims, mentioned elsewhere, but worth repeating, is that *good business is the best antidote to bad international politics*. Business leaders generally understand each other and carry out their activities independent of their creed, political affiliation, ethnicity, culture, moral beliefs, or understanding of what constitutes the good life. There is no clash of civilizations in the business world. Good international business practices can be the means towards overcoming differences and misunderstanding between countries, and can also be the motor for regional and global integration.

A major challenge for international business schools nowadays is the transformation of their students into "cosmopolitan managers." By this I mean persons who consider themselves citizens of the world and who are able to manage their companies effectively in multicultural contexts for the creation of wealth of their stakeholders and society. Cosmopolitanism is thus opposed to nationalism, and its adherents consider their membership to a particular country as circumstantial, like the color of their skin or their height, but at the same time compatible with a sense of belonging to or being proud of one's community. The archetypal profile of a cosmopolitan manager prioritizes cross-cultural skills and understanding of diversity over traditional analytical capacities or technical knowledge.

How can business schools better prepare its students to become cosmopolitan managers? I will offer three recommendations that are, obviously, addressed to institutions that aim at becoming truly global, even though I respect those schools that have a domestic mission and serve their local management cadres – although every educational institution will face the same challenge at some stage.

The first recommendation is that international schools promote multiculturalism in the composition of the class and foster cross-cultural integration. I will deal with this more in detail in Chapter 9, but I truly believe that the more diverse a class is, in terms of cultural background and visions of the world and the good life, the more it potentially reflects the wide range of differences that global managers may encounter in real life. The key question, however, is not just how diverse the class is in terms of, for example, the number of nationalities represented, gender, age, religion, professional or academic background, and other vital criteria. Diversity should be also reflected in the composition of nuclear class units like, for example, working teams. In addition, and more importantly, diversity should be effectively managed by docents and program directors for participants' personal and professional development, as part of the learning process.

Some years ago, a German MBA student told me that, generally, he felt more satisfied working with his North American counterparts than with other fellow participants from Latin America. Let me put it bluntly, although his words were much more subtle: he believed that Latinos, in general, were lazier, did not contribute enough to teamwork, were always ready to start a fiesta, and mostly superficial. He admitted that Latinos, again in general, had some virtues such as passion and *joie de vivre*, but in the end he preferred Anglo-Saxons as workmates. As such, his views coincided with many clichés spread by cross-cultural studies on management. My response to him was counterintuitive: that he could learn more from Latinos – very divergent to his own cultural idiosyncrasies – than from similar people. Certainly, sameness is much less enriching for the learning process than diversity is. I believe I did not convince him, but I made a bet with him. He went into his exchange program at a US business school, with a much lesser diversity in its class profile, and I asked him to tell me when he returned whether the learning environment there or here was potentially richer. We made a bet, – you can guess what mine was – and I won it.

Constructive interpersonal relations among students from diverse cultures create the best context for the education of cosmopolitan managers. In addition, it helps participants to unmask prejudices that, very often, are obstacles to cross-cultural management. Contrary to what my German friend thought, Latinos are not genetically superficial; they are not more prone to cheating, and they may be as rigorous as the Anglo-Saxon exemplar, but the best way to learn this is by knowing them and dealing with them.

My second recommendation would be to incorporate into MBA and other degree programs subjects related to the main challenges facing the global society. The objective is to empower students with more and better information about how to address these challenges, as well as making them more aware of their responsibilities as managers of resources and activities that have an impact on the environment around them. For example, at IE Business School, we have introduced a module that takes place between the two periods of core studies called "Change in Action," which allows students the opportunity to talk to experts about such key issues as climate change, sustainability, poverty, population growth around the world, or the challenges facing the energy sector, among others. A deep-rooted understanding of these issues not only increases graduates' awareness, but also prompts some to look into the business opportunities related to them, for example renewable energy or recycling.

My third recommendation is to foster international internships and exchange programs. Ideally, each MBA graduate should work for at least a semester after graduation in a country where the culture is different from their native one.

The job of the business school dean

The role of the dean at a business school is tantamount to that of a CEO in a company, with the same responsibilities. Or so it is becoming, given the increasing expectations that different stakeholders of business schools have about their respective dean's performance. A significant fact is, for example, that the descriptions of the intended profile in recent dean's job vacancies emphasize managerial components over traditional academic qualities. But do business school deans actually organize their time in analogous ways to CEOs?

An interesting article ("Three-Year Forecast") published in Biz Ed[164] states what b-school deans consider their strategic challenges for the future along with their predictions about the future evolution of management education. The article includes intriguing data about what deans consider their three major pressures, which they are facing as heads of their business schools. The pressures that were mentioned most were: (i) Managing Faculty (74 percent); (ii) Identifying and Pursuing New Sources of Funding (45 percent); (iii) Distinguishing the Business School from Competitors (24 percent); (iv) Managing Enrolments and Program Emphases (21 percent); and (v) Managing Enrolments and Program Emphases (21 percent).

From this data it is clear that deans spend most of their time dealing with their faculty members. They also dedicate a significant slot of time to the search of new income for their schools: probably dealing with program managers, potential donors, and public institutions – in those cases where the school is a recipient of subsidies. What surprises me is the uneven distribution of the reviewed deans' time among the various internal and external stakeholders of the school. It is significant, for example, the importance given to the management of the external relations of the school. Would this be comparable to the priorities of CEOs?

Most of the opportunities for b-schools lie beyond their ivy-covered walls. This should have consequences in how deans deal with their pressures.

The role of the dean of a business school varies according to the role and the nature of the institution's mission. Traditionally, deans of business schools located within universities have tended to exercise what we might call delegated power, insomuch as their activities are limited by the university's board. This may prevent the dean of a university-affiliated business school from creating new programs, or recruiting more students and teaching staff, as well as limiting his or her scope for adopting new strategies. Deans of independent schools, or even those that are part of universities but that enjoy a particular status, such as London Business School or Harvard, can outline their own strategies, albeit with the approval of the school's board.

My experience is that more and more university-based business schools enjoy relative independence, largely as a result of the need for them to be able to respond to the needs of the market quickly and flexibly. The needs of business schools' stakeholders change more quickly than in other disciplines, such as the Liberal Arts, for example. Equally, the competition tends to move quickly, and schools bound by bureaucracy and lengthy internal negotiations with decision makers, all aimed at achieving a balance among the interests of different departments or schools are likely to lose the edge in a highly competitive market.

As mentioned earlier, perhaps the role of the dean of a business school is best compared to that of the CEO of a large company, with four main responsibilities:

1. to be the main architect behind the school's strategy, and to make sure that the strategy is properly implemented;
2. to be the person mainly responsible for managing the school's resources;
3. to capitalize on the school's talent, particularly in regard to teaching and research; and
4. to strengthen relations with stakeholders, and not just with those on the inside such as teaching staff, students, graduates, or corporate partners, but also with external players. As with large companies and other organizations, deans play a key role as a bridge with the outside world. In reality, deans are the public face of their institution, and this means playing an active part in public discussions, particularly bearing in mind the important mission that business schools are playing in creating an increasingly global society.

In this context, it is worth citing veteran dean Peter Lorange, who has carried out considerable research into management education. Peter outlined what he sees as the main tasks of a business school dean: "Being quick to identify new opportunities worth pursuing, whether in new academic areas or new geographies; mobilizing the business school's resources to create academic value...and creating an environment of trust and inspiration."[165]

At the same time, it is not easy to measure a dean's success in carrying out their role. As with a CEO, yardsticks are needed, among them obviously the school's financial results – an aspect all too often overlooked in education, particularly in state-funded institutions, along with stakeholder satisfaction, particularly that of students – best measured perhaps by their professional development after graduation, the school's contribution to academic research, which can be measured not only in terms of quantity, but quality, and the school's visibility, which can be measured in terms of how external stakeholders such as business, other academics, or recruiters assess it. Another criterion by which deans are assessed is whether their schools have risen in the key international rankings.

Clear and measurable criteria should be established that will allow us to compare deans' performance. It is only fair to point out that a business school's position in league tables does not necessarily depend on the initiatives that the dean has undertaken, but inevitably, for better or worse, they will be judged in this regard. It goes with the territory.

One final word of advice for my fellow deans who are about to take up their posts for the first time: as with the best CEOs, do not wait to put your strategy into effect. The first 100 days are essential to lay down your management approach and to chart the course you wish the school to follow; in this sense, business schools are no different from businesses.

The resilience of academic institutions

Regardless of what is often said, successful quality business schools are not dependent on the profile or the prominence of their deans. I recall an analogous idea expressed by Gary Hamel, when he affirmed that the performance of good companies is not essentially dependent on the actual competence of their CEOs and that companies can operate efficiently despite the lack of distinctive leadership at the top. Naturally, this line of reasoning can hardly be extended to small companies, particularly in their early stages of life, when the influence of the founder or CEO is key, but it can be applied to those organizations with a relatively large size and with sophisticated management systems, in which vacancy at leading positions does not cause substantial effects in its activities. "E la nave va," says an Italian proverb, meaning that a big ship can keep sailing without anyone at the helm. Good organizations – and consequently top business schools – are resilient; they can even overcome having bad managers at the top.

I do not mean that CEOs or business school's deans are just figureheads, but sometimes analysts overweigh their importance or their contributions to the schools where they serve. Furthermore, at long-standing institutions with deep commitment to tradition, the contribution of managers and staff is normally seen just as an additional link in the chain of its history. While studying as a PhD candidate at the University of Oxford, I remember how many managerial positions there were denominated related to the number of tenures in the line of its history (e.g., Mr. John Smith, XXV Curator of the Bodleian Library).

A study by Amanda H. Goodall, from Warwick Business School, analyzed the world's top 100 business schools, as listed by the *Financial Times*'s MBA ranking. According to this study, there is a close correlation between a school's position in the ranking and the standing of the dean, as determined by his or her own academic research record.[166] Certainly, this is not a major discovery, given the selection process of deans at most business schools. What I am not sure is whether these findings can be used for the actual practice of choosing deans. Do the results of the report indicate that the position of a dean is fundamentally academic and not managerial? Should candidates with the strongest academic profiles be appointed as deans regardless of their managerial aptitudes?

Indeed the results of the report are interesting but irrelevant in practice. Actually, recent appointments for positions of deans at leading business schools may indicate a change in the trends, for example, the nomination of young candidates – and normally with not so long research records – or outsiders to academia.

I have an academic background. However, I do not believe that my academic aptitudes metamorphosed into managerial skills when I was appointed dean of my school. The dean's job has more to do with management than academia.

If managing complex organizations is a challenging task, being at the helm of academic enterprises takes the biscuit. Several singular factors make managing educational institutions particularly hard. First, its objective, education – a common good – is subject to special scrutiny by governments; this can sometimes result in overregulation. Second, the number of stakeholders in education is larger than in other sectors, and many have representation in governance bodies. This requires outstanding diplomatic and negotiation skills from education managers to reconcile the concurrent interests of different groups. Third, academics, a core-stakeholder group, are less manageable than other mortals, partly due to the way they are trained, that develop inquisitorial and prompt-to-argue colleagues. To top this off, sources of income at academia are often more diversified and elusive than at other businesses, which sometimes demands a real juggling act.

However, if life is so stressful in the top echelons of those institutions, why do some people feel attracted to the job, even if they are remunerated worse than in business? The answer lies in the fact that business and management can have a hugely positive effect on the world.

CHAPTER 9

The students of tomorrow

An eternal debate within the business school community, and universities in general, is whether students should be regarded as customers. Technically speaking, says David Bejou, Dean of the School of Business and Economics at the Elizabeth City State University in North Carolina, the answer is obvious: "While some administrators find it difficult to accept the idea of students as consumers, in reality, that's what they are in today's competitive marketplace, schools are sellers offering courses, a degree, and a rich alumni life. Students are buyers who register for courses, apply for graduation, and make donations as alumni. The longer these ongoing transactions are satisfactory to both parties, the longer the relationship will endure, to the benefit of everyone."[167]

Seen in these terms, there seems little left to discuss. But it is worth pointing out that this somewhat reductionist, customer-supplier interpretation fails to see the student as a learner, who should trust the institution where he or she is studying, and who should be encouraged to see the learning experience as a personal transformation, and that at times will challenge the tastes, desires, and preconceived opinions they might have held till now. The term might have been misused, and certainly it has been criticized, but to a large degree, the student is raw material during the learning process, and progresses towards a finished product, but a product of their own choosing. It is precisely this voluntary immersion in a learning process that allows students to overcome short-term difficulties, and to understand, at least in retrospect, the importance of certain practices that they may not have understood at the time, as well as to value the ups and downs of personal development, but which will conclude with the satisfaction that comes from deep-rooted personal change.

A thoroughgoing learning process means being open to constant experimentation, to meeting challenges constantly, and to encouraging the spirit of personal development, while questioning previously held values that may have been less than thought through, or that may have lacked focus. Socrates was right to tell his new pupils "you know nothing."

In this context, Ted Snyder, Dean of Yale School of Management, succinctly noted: "The best students don't view themselves as customers, and they shouldn't be treated as such."[168]

My experience bears Snyder's opinion out: the brightest and best students tend to be modest, to respect the advice of their teachers, to be aware of the need to be open to new ideas, and thus tend to get the most out of the learning process.

This does not mean that business schools with an eye to the needs of the market are about to go under. As Stephen Joel Trachtenberg, Emeritus Professor at George Washington University, points out: "Students are not customers nor are they not customers. They are investing time and money with a purpose in mind. The school that does not serve that purpose will not survive. Students are looking for a quality education, and they want distinguished and accomplished professors on the faculty. But that alone is not sufficient."[169]

The most immediate mission of a business school is to train and educate its students so that they can become the best business leaders in their field after graduation, equipping them either to set up their own businesses, or to take up top posts in top companies. And feedback from the market would suggest that in the case of the better business schools, this is indeed the case. The *Financial Times'* business school ranking shows that in aggregate terms, investment in education brings returns at the professional and economic levels for MBA students.

At the same time, we should not lose sight of the fact that executive education is expensive. As Ted Snyder pointed out at the EFMD Deans and Director's conference in 2011, some US business schools have hiked the cost of their MBA programs, already far from cheap, by 6 percent over the past five years, an increase that is several percentage points above inflation. Europe's business schools have registered similar increases in tuition fees, at least in the top institutions. Nevertheless, a comparative analysis of income and costs at many schools, hard though it may be to believe, shows that they do not generate a net profit. The result is that for these schools to invest in improving standards, undertake research, take on new teachers, or extend their premises they must generate cash through executive education programs for senior management, or by fund-raising activities or by organizing conferences and seminars.

At the same time, business schools – particularly the top institutions – must also have the finances to provide for candidates who have shown the necessary talent, as well as having successfully undergone the admissions process, but who lack the funds to pay for their studies.

Most business schools either have some kind of loan scheme, offering low interest credit, or grant and scholarship programs for applicants from low-income families, poorer countries, or who belong to disadvantaged minorities. In some cases, particularly in the US, investing in an MBA is tax deductible.[170]

Are all business schools looking for the same students? Asked what type of student they are looking for, every dean or head of admissions that I have ever spoken to on the matter always produces the same answer: "The best." But are we necessarily talking about the same group of potential students, and as such competing to attract the same people? At first glance, it would seem so. The selection criteria are similar: GMAT or GRE tests – the most common filter[171] – along with similar types of exam; a candidate's academic record; their professional experience; and other achievements. Business schools that want to promote diversity apply other criteria such as diversity, gender, and even the fact that they come from a different academic or professional background. Seen from this perspective, the pool of candidates appears markedly similar; as a result, the objective is to attract the best within that group. It's a zero-sum game: the students can only go to one school.

Nevertheless, the pool of potential students grows bigger every year, says GMAC.

I believe that the pool of potential candidates, along with the criteria by which they are considered capable of undertaking an MBA should be convergent, complementary, but not identical. Some schools, for example mine, give priority to applicants with a strong entrepreneurial spirit, and who want to create their own businesses. Other schools are on the lookout for tomorrow's marketing experts, or who show the potential required to run a human resources department in a large organization. If candidates have different profiles based on their career paths, then different procedures should be applied in identifying their potential. I believe that one of the biggest challenges facing business schools in the future will be to come up with alternative ways of identifying talent, and of developing the means to bring out the best in them.

The most commonly used tests to pick out the "best" candidates, particularly in the case of GMAT and GRE, favor a particular type of intelligence, one that we might call analytical, and one that is also reflected in IQ tests. Studies show that there is a clear correlation between this type of intelligence and success in education, whether at the primary, secondary, or tertiary levels. It is also largely true to say that most of us consider people who perform well in these kinds of tests to be "intelligent."

But a growing number of academics and educationists have begun to question our traditional approach to assessing intelligence, among them Howard Gardner of Harvard University. His multiple intelligence theory argues that traditional measures of intelligence such as IQ tests fail to take into account cognitive and interpersonal abilities, which are equally important in learning and personal development, and of course for professional success. Gardner argues that there are at least nine forms of intelligence: spatial; linguistic; logical-mathematic; bodily-kinesthetic; musical; interpersonal; intrapersonal; naturalistic; and existential. Traditional education systems and measures of IQ have tended to emphasize linguistic and logical-mathematical intelligence, largely overlooking others.[172]

This may well explain why so many artistic talents and innovative thinkers have emerged from non-academic backgrounds, and why socially successful people tend not to pay much attention to conventional ways of learning. Might this not also explain why some of the most important entrepreneurs of our time, such as Steve Jobs or Bill Gates, have little formal academic training?

On the basis of studies about intelligence that precede Gardner's work, other scholars have contributed towards the theory of emotional intelligence, the ability to perceive, understand, and integrate intelligence in the way we behave, and thus increase our personal development. The concept of emotional intelligence has been a major influence in the work of Daniel Goleman in his book of the same name,[173] and among the most popular management books of our time. According to Goleman, emotional intelligence is not something that we are born with, but something that we learn along the way, and is reflected in a series of skills that can be developed through repeated practice, such as self-awareness, social awareness, or relationship management, all of them likely to improve one's management profile.

We all have come across students with a prodigious analytical ability, but who lack the emotional intelligence to be leaders, and it is easy to see that if they continue that way, they will never gain significant positions in any company or organization. Similarly, there is no shortage of CEOs or heads of state with average IQs, but who have learned to develop their emotional intelligence.

Current research into the links between intelligence and education provides business schools two major insights. The first is that despite earlier insistence that intelligence, as measured by IQ tests, was the result of genetics, according to Richard E. Nisbett, "it is now clear that intelligence is modifiable by the environment…educational environments have been changing in such a way as to make the population as a whole smarter – and smart in different ways than in the past."[174] The second is that teachers' input and interaction with students is key to the development of intelligence.[175] We all would hopefully have come across at least one teacher in our lifetime who demonstrated the ability to extract our maximum potential.

Finally, a contribution on the basis of my experience as a teacher and dean of a business school. There are myriad forms of intelligence that can be cultivated and strengthened in adulthood. At IE we have seen how people with a wide range of experience have increased their interpersonal skills, their ability to lead, or their ability to understand and analyze complex problems. Logically, developing these types of intelligence among senior executives and directors requires modesty, along with an openness and willingness to learn new things.

We need to develop new ways of identifying talent that go beyond conventional forms of intelligence. Success in the search for new categories of intelligence will expand the pool of potential applicants to business schools significantly, while at the same time allowing us to identify the candidates that are right for each institution and organization. At the same time, we need to develop new teaching methodologies and approaches to learning that bring out the entrepreneurial and innovation skills of management students, along with their relationship and leadership skills. This is without doubt the next frontier of teaching in business schools, and to get there we will have to work closely with educationists and psychologists. Such an approach will also have a tremendous impact on the content of future MBAs and on management in general. Once again, opening up our curriculum to the Humanities, while at the same time developing new teaching methods to identify individual aptitudes, offers promising horizons.

The MBA as the "Grand Tour" of the twenty-first century

The MBA is a generic denomination for a common category of programs, but not all MBAs are the same. In Chapter 8, I deconstructed what, in my opinion, are the four basic components of an MBA: content, modalities and formats, experience, and networking. These four elements are interwoven and differ depending on the culture, mission, and objectives of each business school's MBA. If we look at "content," for example, an MBA may include entrepreneurship as a core subject or not, or may emphasize the learning of "hard" over "soft" skills, or may be internationally reputed for its courses in finance or in marketing. What sort of experience are MBA applicants looking forward to?

The MBA represents a once-in-a-lifetime opportunity not only to acquire or update the basics of the major management disciplines but also to experiment and expose oneself to new and different things. It is a time of preparation and transformation for the future. The MBA experience conceived this way reminds me of the "Grand Tour," an expression used to designate the pattern of education that English noblemen and noblewomen underwent in the eighteenth and nineteenth centuries. Basically, it consisted of a voyage across Europe – principally France and Italy – during which young people learned about different cultures, arts, and traditions by learning first hand through visiting and sightseeing. It was an experience, in the truest sense of the word, which helped its participants to reflect, forge their character, and prepare to face their adult lives.

The MBA, properly conceived, should be a modern type of Grand Tour for its participants. The main advantage nowadays is that this Grand Tour has been democratized and is open to already and would-be managers and entrepreneurs from all continents. Whenever I am asked by future students who are thinking about taking an MBA, my first recommendation is that they should decide to do it abroad. It is an opportunity to learn a new culture, maybe a new language, a chance to think differently, and practice truly global citizenship. Of course, learners could eventually get all the knowledge of different cultures from books and become experts in a given field just by study. A doctor may know more about a given illness than her patient; despite she may not have suffered what she diagnoses. But I am sure you will agree with me that "knowing" is something different from "experiencing," and doing an MBA abroad provides the student with the opportunity to have both. Certainly, the word "expert" derives etymologically from "experience", and the fact is that many of the people who took the Grand Tour two centuries ago later became respected painters, writers, philosophers and business people.

Talent versus experience

Traditionally, the MBA has been regarded as a post work-experience program, meaning that its participants should have some relevant professional experience as an entry requirement. Since it is debatable what should be understood as "relevant experience," the easiest way to agree on a threshold is to take the length of the applicant's working years. For example, EQUAL (European Quality Link) Guidelines on MBA programs establish that the professional experience for MBA should normally be at least two years. AMBA (The Association of MBAs) has a more sophisticated system since, though it requires an average two-year professional experience in a given MBA class, it allows a significant percentage of participants with less or even no experience (up to 15 percent).

The requirement of working experience for those who apply to an MBA program is based on the supposition that, since MBA programs have very interactive methodologies – e.g., case studies, role-playing – a substantial part of the learning has as its main source, fellow participants. It is often said that, when using interactive learning methods, the role of the professor resembles even more that of an orchestra conductor or facilitator of sessions, rather than the lecturer role typical of traditional classes.

Recently, however, the requirement of previous professional experience is under question. Many b-schools – including some of those top ranked by the *Financial Times* – have wondered whether professional experience could be waived if the MBA candidate has some other significant talents or in order to increase the class' diversity, for example in terms of gender or international participants, or even more debatable, for keeping up the GMAT scores of the class given the less affluence of senior managers to full time MBA programs. However, a further vector of diversity is age itself: doesn't it enhance the learning experience to have participants with different levels of professional experience, even belonging to different generations, in order to replicate what actually happens at work in real life?

Indeed, the more diverse an MBA class is, the more enriching the learning experience is. True, sameness of participants – in terms of culture, business knowledge, experience, views of the world, and age – may provide a more homogenous setting that makes participants feel comfortable and achieve learning objectives in a very orderly way. However, allowing a small percentage (five to ten percent) of students who have less than two years of professional experience in a class, in order to foster gender diversity, or to have young highly talented candidates may enhance class diversity and contribute positively to the learning experience.

MBA programs are living educational offerings, and their entry requirements should change according to the evolution of circumstances.

The importance of student's diversity in the learning process

A large and decisive part of the learning at an MBA program is the interaction with fellow participants, inside and outside the class. This converts the composition of the student body into a vital element. What would be, in your opinion, the ideal profile of your future MBA classmates?

Your ideal class may align to one of two major perspectives. The first can be called the "one of us approach." You may be looking to share your program with people like you, with a similar cultural background, shared interests – even tastes, so that you could spend, for example, your leisure time together –, same language, and maybe the same academic preparation. This homogeneity would be good, for example, in order to make teaching more productive: all members of the class would have the same level, say, of finance, and this would avoid redundancies and help the general progression.

The "one of us approach" has been the pattern at many educational institutions for a long time. In some segments, such as management education, elitism was the prevalent culture supported by different mechanisms that guaranteed selectivity and exclusiveness. A quote from Peter L. Berger from the book *Many Globalizations: Cultural Diversity in the Contemporary World* is illustrative: "There is, for instance, a global network of ambitious young people in business and the professions ... a sort of yuppie internationale, whose members speak fluent English and dress alike and act alike, at work and at play, and up to a point think alike – and hope that one day they might reach the elite summits."[176]

Let me now turn to the second approach to the ideal composition of the MBA class that I will call "the diversity approach." Its rationale is that the wider the diversity in a class, the higher the potential of the learning experience. This view is supported by contemporary research in pedagogy and sociology, and it is a very intuitive view based on the principle-of-complementarities phenomenon in the learning process.

The elements that could be considered variables to get a diverse student body in a given MBA program are gender, nationality, academic background, and age. These four elements in different combinations may produce the blend sought by a school. For example, in my school we aim at having an MBA class more or less balanced in terms of gender. Interestingly, the first cohort of our Executive MBA in partnership with Brown University, which started in March 2011, had 40% of women participants, an unusually high percentage in this type of programs.

I would also value the presence of a wide array of academic backgrounds in a given group, i.e., not just a class composed of members whose major is in Economics or business. Imagine, for example, the great potential that a person with a major in dramatic art plus an MBA could have as a sales manager. In addition, having diversity in terms of age and years of experience seems very beneficial and portrays better what happens in real life than just meeting people of the same age. According to different sources, European business schools seem to have a more diverse student body than their American counterparts.

However, diversity confounds many people, and I would like to comment on its complexity in MBA groups. I highly recommend the book *Our Underachieving Colleges*, which has the subtitle *A Candid Look at How Much Students Learn and Why They Should Be Learning More.*[177] Its author is Harvard University's President Emeritus Derek Bok, holder of "the 300th Anniversary University" chair at the same university and also a prolific writer on educational issues.

Bok devotes an entire chapter to diversity in class and affirms that the developments in this field at American colleges "have added variety and intensity to campus debates, making the college environment at once more stimulating and more disputatious than it was throughout the first two-thirds of the twentieth century."[178] However, he explains that as the student body has become more diverse, colleges have encountered increasing difficulties and started to work "proactively to encourage students to be more understanding of the differences they meet among their fellow undergraduates" and that "officials have encountered a minefield of human emotions requiring exceptional sensitivity and skill in striving to create an environment in which everyone can feel welcome and respected."[179]

Bok's book covers mainly undergraduate programs and issues related to ethnic and gender diversity, but many of its ideas and findings could be applicable, *mutatis mutandis*, to graduate education and to the MBA in particular, despite the fact that participants at many MBA programs normally have professional experience, are more mature, and may have been exposed to multicultural situations.

Indeed, schools that have truly diverse student bodies and plan to implement diversity schemes face an interesting challenge. The objective of promoting diversity in the MBA is not an end in itself, but it is rather a means for providing a truly stimulating learning experience to participants. A diverse MBA class may be conceived as a little representation of the world, a little United Nations, if you like. Ideally, there should not be a clear dominant culture in class but rather a "working culture," a sort of artificial compound of amalgamated practices and routines, based on the principles of tolerance and respect for others, which allow for difference but at the same time promote teamwork. This working culture or "social contract" among class participants is realized, though normally in very broad terms, in ethics or behavior codes that MBA students accept when they join their schools. Some codes define, for example, the processes for solving difficult student cases and serve as guidelines to the committees and officials who are responsible for interpreting the code and adjudicating the pertinent sanctions.

Making the best of class diversity: Melting pots and mosaics

In my experience as a member of the board of several accreditation agencies, particularly EQUIS, I have often taken part in discussions about what it means for a business school to be international; that is to say, what requirements must it fulfill to attain such status. The most widely used criteria to measure internationalization are the number of foreign students and faculty, the existence of agreements and alliances with schools in other countries, and the availability of courses taught in English. The use of these criteria sometimes sparks argument, particularly in the case of schools in cities or countries that traditionally have not attracted foreign students, either because they are far from the main global business and education hubs, or for reasons to do with political stability. Until recently, emerging economies were not considered a good place to study business programs, mainly because of the lack of jobs in such economies that match the expectations of an MBA graduate. But things are changing, in large part due to the emergence of multinationals such as Tata in India, or AmBev in Brazil.[180] Other factors include the growth of cross-border operations, as well as the search for new careers related to social entrepreneurship, and the growing interest in cross-cultural careers.

The debate on the internationalization of business schools within the world of accreditation agencies also takes into account questions such as the extent to which national or regional diversity give a school a genuinely international outlook. Some see Western Europe as a single cultural space, and thus compare Europe's diversity of nations with the cultural and ethnic diversity of the US, along with the country's tradition of recognizing minorities. From this perspective, the presence of a wide range of ethnic groups in US business schools is comparable with the diversity of students from different European countries. This would justify the smaller percentage of foreign students attending US business schools: for example, 64 percent of Harvard Business School's class of 2011 is made up of Americans. Around 90 percent of students in the International MBA programs at INSEAD, LBS, or IE are from overseas.

It could be argued that comparing the presence of a large number of minorities with the presence of a large number of foreign students is myopic. Should diversity be measured in the simple mechanical terms of the number of different passports a business school can muster? Alternatively, should we come up with a different test to measure the diversity of an MBA course? Matters become more complicated if we take into account those countries with a large number of different ethnic groups within their borders. Should China or Brazil be considered markets in themselves, for example, when it comes to counting foreign students?

Looking at countries like China, it is clear why the concept of internationalization should not be reduced to simplistic measurements. Real internationalization comes about when there is no single dominant cultural or national group to reduce the wealth of learning to be found in a cross-cultural class. To illustrate this point to students, I suggest that business schools can adopt one of two cultural models in trying to attract greater numbers of foreign students.

On the one hand, there are schools that try to function as "melting pots," that is to say that they try to blend or bring together the different cultural backgrounds or perspectives of students into a uniform culture. The schools that cultivate this approach tend to give precedence to the most extended models of management and leadership skills, only looking at different models as external references, of interest purely from a comparative analysis perspective. In such a melting pot environment, it is not only logical, but also desirable to have a dominant nationality. That dominant nationality establishes an identity that the other students can aspire to. The best way to find out whether a school takes a melting pot approach is to look at the contents of its program, and to check whether the case studies analyzed as part of its MBA are mostly from one country or region, and whether analysis of other cultures and methods is marginal.

The other model is what I call the "mosaic of cultures" school. With this model, there is no dominant nationality. Students analyze a wide variety of different management and leadership models and use case studies from different countries. The mosaic of cultures sees multiculturalism as the best environment within which to understand a global environment. Sometimes this way of teaching is confused with cultural relativism, where, in the absence of a strong culture, there is a risk that students will not be given the tools they need to make adequate decisions. But this argument is mistaken. My experience of discussing case studies in such an environment, even when addressing culturally sensitive questions that raise ethical dilemmas, shows that in multicultural classes where there is a range of views, and where all management and leadership approaches are taught, solutions to problems can be found that are accepted by the majority.

This convergence, and the possibility of a solid learning base, compatible with the respect for different visions of the world, and what constitutes a good life, is also apparent in other educational environments beyond the business school. For example, Richard E. Nisbett, in his *The Geography of Thought*,[181] explains that,

> human cognition is not everywhere the same ... First, that members of different cultures differ in their 'metaphysics' or fundamental beliefs about the nature of the world. Second, that the characteristic thought processes of different groups differ greatly. Third, that the thought processes are of a piece with beliefs about the nature of the

world: People use the cognitive tools that seem to make sense – given the sense they make of the world.[182]

He also adds that the "differences in people's attitudes and beliefs, and even their values and preferences, might not be a matter merely of different inputs and teachings, but rather an inevitable consequence of using different tools to understand the world."[183] He then draws a conclusion that may prove problematic for educators: "If that's true, then efforts to improve international understanding may be less likely to pay off than one might hope."[184]

The reality of multicultural MBA classes at many internationally oriented business schools provides a more encouraging picture. In my experience with multicultural groups of students, MBA participants from diverse cultures engage in active debate about culturally sensitive issues – like corporate responsibility or ethics – and they use similar paradigms of thought in their analysis, and even reach similar conclusions. In the same way as musicians from different cultural backgrounds can play a piece of Mozart following the same standards, students with different views about the world can apply the same principles and pursue a common line of reasoning to take managerial decisions. Obviously, this does not entail uniformity, and the questions discussed in class do not have *a priori* solutions. But our experience suggests that the differing cultural views of students enrich the debate and do not preclude sharing the same understanding and reaching similar decisions.

Taking into account this tension between diversity and cognitive convergence in multicultural MBA classes, which methodology should business school managers and educators adopt? Should they suppose that world economic and political systems, and consequently values, are converging, in line with the thesis defended by Francis Fukuyama a decade ago? Or should they believe that the world is headed for a "clash of civilisations,"[185] according to the vision of Samuel Huntington,[186] who predicted continued differences of values across the board? I support the view of Shinobu Kitayama, quoted in Nisbett's book, that there is, "evidence that cognitive processes could be modified even after relatively limited amounts of time spent in another culture."[187] For example, my school's experience tells me that the multicultural exposure of participants in the MBA program facilitates respect and mutual understanding. At the same time, business is a subject that naturally promotes common understanding and convergence among practitioners. Its clinical character encourages management professionals to put pragmatism above cultural issues or the cognitive models they have acquired.

This pragmatic approach to business, coupled with the fact that well-run businesses generate growth and contribute to the social good, means that the understanding and collaborative spirit among people of different cultures is achieved quickly and almost intuitively. At this point, allow me to quote again one of my favorite maxims: "good business is the best antidote to bad international politics."

Convictions and conventions in managing programs

In the context of a multicultural MBA class, the cornerstone of coexistence is the respect for others. Each class member always shows a basic minimum of respect to each other, regardless of one's personal affinities. This is not so easy, since we all have natural preferences in choosing our friends or partners, and to enforce respect a business school community should engage in a set of principles and practices that embody the fundamental convictions about basic duties and rights of its members. These convictions may be substantiated in a code of ethics that comprises not only norms related to student's academic behavior – e.g., refusal to cheat or plagiarism – but also basic principles guiding interpersonal relations. Normally, codes of ethics contain prohibitions or duties – such as not insulting others – as well as aspirations formulated in the positive – e.g., assist fellow students in their basic needs, engage in constructive relationships with others.

The convictions that inspire most business school's codes of ethics tend to converge across the board, and they do not necessarily reflect a concrete ideology, religion, or morality, but they rather substantiate what could be called as cosmopolitan ethics. In fact, in a multicultural class composed of people who may have different views of the world or about personal morality, the adopted set of convictions should only cover the core rules. They should seek to guarantee a constructive coexistence among participants, a sort of minimum common denominator that balances diversity and respect for others with the adherence to common rules of behavior.

Besides convictions, conventions – customs shared throughout a community – also play an important part in facilitating the relations among business school's members, as in society at large. Indeed, the more diverse personal convictions are among the members of the class, the more important it becomes to respect the agreed conventions. In a book on the importance of conventions and etiquette, professor Salvador Cardús[188] develops the idea that conventions, although being the result of arbitrary choices by members of a given society – e.g., driving on a road's right or left side, are the basis of civism and fundamental for coexistence. Examples of conventions include dress codes, forms of salutation, or etiquette at the table. Cardús insists that conventions do not rely on values or moral principles – like convictions – and that being "a well mannered person" is not equivalent to being "a good person." It is plausible to think about someone with exquisite manners, but immoral in his actions. However, a person with bad manners – I am sure you will agree with me – will likely encounter the rejection of the group, in a different but analogous way to how immoral people experience the reproach of fellow citizens.

In recent decades, many educators have defended the idea that fostering spontaneity in students is desirable in order to cultivate creativity. A perverse understanding of this idea, however, entails the relaxing of conventions on the basis that they inhibit students from freely developing their personality. Like Cardús, I believe that the observance of conventions is, precisely, a requisite to nurture students' personalities, since it facilitates the integration of individuals in a community, thus opening multiple vital options not available for anchorites.

Cosmopolitan managers actively cultivate those conventions that make business relations with people from different cultures not only possible but also fruitful. A golden rule is to treat others like they want to be treated, which in multicultural situations might not be so obvious. This is a lesson that business schools' educators cannot omit. Indeed, it is an exciting challenge for those who aim at moulding cosmopolitan managers.

The importance of conventions affects even dress codes. According to a survey conducted by law firm Peninsula in the UK, four out of five companies found that a relaxed attitude to dress codes in the office increases productivity.[189] The survey was released at a time when the United Kingdom was experiencing one of the hottest summers in recent decades and when, consequently, workers wonder whether to dress in a cooler way and leave suits and formal shoes at home.

This piece of news reminds me of a comment made by Patrick Harker, former Dean of the Wharton School, where he announced the adoption of some measures at his school to strengthen etiquette and discipline, which included respecting a basic dress code and avoiding the use of cell phones, as well as avoiding eating in the classroom.[190]

For example, in July, temperatures in Madrid tend to be abnormally high – as in many other places – though the actual perception of heat here is lighter and more bearable than, for example, in London, given that humidity in Madrid is low. In summer, students tend to relax dress codes and some come to class in shorts and sandals. In those circumstances, I am approached by some professors who demand a stricter etiquette in class, since they explain that external appearance is an important part of convention and that a proper education at schools should include instruction on how a manager should look externally.

I remember reading in Herbert H. L. A. Hart's *The Concept of Law*,[191] a masterpiece on law, morals, and philosophy, that rules of etiquette were the younger sisters of moral norms. But does this mean that not observing the former entails a loose attitude towards the latter?

At many companies there is still a strict dress code, written or unwritten. Conventionally, formal dressing shows respect for the others. Should the findings of the abovementioned survey make us rethink and relax rules of etiquette for the sake of productivity? I guess that the answer to this question should take into consideration the local customs and traditions observed in each place. If we aim at developing cosmopolitan managers the popular maxim is especially indicated as regards conventions: "When in Rome..."

Beating cheating

In Part I, I dealt with the accusation that cheating is a malaise more widespread than what would be desired among management students. Business schools should not lay the entire blame for cheating on students, but rather involve other school stakeholders, particularly teachers. A wide range of measures should be deployed in order to make cheating difficult or risky, including the adoption of preventive measures such as publishing a rule list, backed by effective bodies that decide on sanctions and their implementation. A few of them are listed below.

- *Establish honor codes.* Surveys released by the Center for Academic Integrity (CAI) show that "cheating on campuses with honor codes is typically one third to a half lower than the level on campuses that do not have honor codes."[192]
- *Involve students in the ethical governance bodies.* At my school, for example, half of the ethics committee is made up of students, making the agreed-on sanctions more legitimate for their fellow students. It is essential that students know the technical means at our disposal to prevent cheating. The consequences of expelling a student are lasting. It should be the very last resort. Our approach is to dissuade rather than trying to catch and punish students after the act. All this creates an environment where honesty and endeavor are the guiding principles that produce fair play.

- *Empower and improve the conscientiousness of faculty.* According to the CAI, teaching staff are usually reluctant to take action against suspected cheaters. "In Assessment Project surveys involving almost 10,000 faculty in the last three years, 44 percent of those who were aware of student cheating in their course in the last three years have never reported a student for cheating to the appropriate campus authority. Students suggest that cheating is higher in courses where it is well known that faculty members are likely to ignore cheating".
- *Balance students' work assignments.* This may seem obvious, but in some schools, students regularly have to handle unrealistically large workloads. In some cases this creates the sense of desperation that drives some students to cross the line.
- *Deploy technical solutions.* Many schools use software to verify that students are not plagiarizing. Use of these tools sends a strong message that we take the protection of honest students seriously, with a spill-over effect in the way other tasks are approached, such as exams and presentations. It is in the interest of the top schools to use these tools to prevent inter-school plagiarism: the tools are constantly being improved through the many updates to the databases they reference, which include students' own assignments. On uploading a given assignment, the most popular academic databases are cross-checked, along with news and information sources, to assess the level of originality of the work. The results can be surprising and reveal the most sophisticated cheats, who use, for example, paraphrasing. Its effect as a deterrent can be enhanced by providing students with example reports on the originality of sample works.

If we aim at developing ethical managers, the first step is to implement effectively the principles and norms that guide the academic regime at our schools. The observance of these standards anticipates the later adherence to a professional deontology when exercising management.

CHAPTER 10

Faculty and knowledge creation: How does it work?

When the Ancient Greeks invented the Olympic Games, sometime during the eighth century BC, the king of sports was the Pentathlon. As its name suggests, competitors were required to show supreme skill in five areas: the long jump; javelin; discus throwing; the stadion, or 180-meter race; and wrestling.

Nobody is sure how the winner of the Pentathlon was established – perhaps by winning three events and doing well in two others. When the Olympics came along, the new heroes were the winners of the Pentathlon, and Aristotle, in his Rhetoric, explains that the participants in this sport were the most complete athletes, and were paid homage to, in the form of medals and commemorative urns. In fact, the Pentathlon became the basis for training recruits to join the militia.

When it was decided to revive the Olympic Games at the end of the nineteenth century, other combination events were devised, aimed at measuring the overall athletic ability of participants, and favoring in many ways the amateur spirit of the Games then: contestants were not professional athletes, nor were they usually specialists in a particular sport. Some of these multi-events have survived to this day, notably, the Triathlon, made up of swimming, cycling, and running, along with the Decathlon, an athletics-based series of 10 sports.

Translated to the world of business administration, today's academics might usefully be compared to the athletes of the past, insomuch as they must show excellence in a number of fields. The advantage they have over the Ancient Greeks is that the academic race is essentially a Triathlon, made up of three main activities: research, teaching, and involvement in the world of business – sometimes through consulting, or by holding a management or board post.

However, traditionally success as an academic has been tantamount to excellence in research, period. Universities have conventionally selected, promoted, tenured, and rewarded scholars who comply with certain requirements related to research activity and output. Other facets of academic life such as teaching, the spreading of knowledge, or interacting with the world outside universities have been considered as secondary activities for an academic career, sometimes even improper.

Nobody could reasonably deny the centripetal value that research should play in scholarly careers. It is probably the core activity of the Academic Triathlon, since it tests the capacity of the individual to assimilate the existing knowledge and to generate new ideas, concepts, and models, respecting methodological rigor. At the same time, considering research as an end in itself, or the only pure academic activity, entails a myopic and incomplete version of the academic vocation. Revealingly, an article in the *New York Times*[193] told that a Harvard team, formed by nine prominent professors of the university and supported by its former President, Derek Bok, was leading an effort to foster the culture of undergraduate teaching and learning. "The group has issued a report calling for sweeping institutional change, including continuing evaluation and assessment of teaching and learning, and a proposal that teaching be weighed equally with contributions to research in annual salary adjustments," says the article.

The need to complement research with teaching and practical work becomes particularly relevant for business school academics. Management education requires a special sort of scholar, a professional who can combine many different facets, from a solid research background, to the ability of performing effectively in class and to interface with top managers. Business schools need not only "Gurus" – wise sages who originate new thought, but also "Kangaroos" – academics able to jump from their research tasks to teaching, and from there to consultancy or an interview with a journalist. Kangaroos of this type are not born, but trained, and it normally requires a wide career span to exploit the necessary synergies between those different, apparently contradictory, but actually intertwined activities.

It is commonly believed that the career of a business academic has several natural cycles or stages. The first one, the "post-doc" (after obtaining the PhD degree), a time of creativity, is intended to boost and capitalize the research skills acquired during the doctoral years. A second period of maturity comes when the scholar develops teaching skills and becomes a master in class respected by the students, particularly by the participants of MBA or Executive MBA programs. The third stage, seniority, is achieved when the solid docent and researcher becomes the academic partner and advisor of managers, or even engages in management positions related to education. I believe that there are no time specifications for the fulfillment of each of those stages and the pace depends on the interests – personal and professional – of the individual.

That said, there is a widely held belief, and one particularly cherished by university insiders, that an academic career, particularly one based on research, must begin at an early age, preferably by completing a doctorate following graduation. This belief is based on the argument that it is during this time that our mental and critical faculties are at their peak, when we can best build the intellectual muscle we need to apply the analytical skills required in the academic quest. Some would go further and say that it is only while we are in the bloom of youth, typically during post-doctoral studies, that we combine the necessary creativity, imagination, and innovative spirit.

It will come as no surprise to the reader to learn that I do not share these beliefs. Doctorates, which require at least four years study, tend to be undertaken in the first years after finishing a degree program, as much as anything because in many people's lives, family and professional commitments come soon after, making it difficult to dedicate the necessary time and energy to study. But the recent appearance of DBA programs (Doctor in Business Administration), particularly those that can be studied part time, allow older professionals, who have a wealth of personal and professional experience, to undertake a doctorate and begin a career in research.

What's more, there is absolutely no scientific or empirical proof to suggest that we are more creative in our late twenties, other than statistical evidence showing that the majority of published research is produced during this period. This is largely due to the conventions of our university systems. More to the point, the major scientific discoveries and heavyweight contributions to thought over the centuries have tended to be produced by senior men and women. I never tire of reminding people that Kant published his *Critique of Pure Reason*, his masterwork, at the age of 57. There is no getting away from the fact that the key contributions to any field of academic or scientific research almost always come after years of analysis and experience, and are based on the ability to compare and contrast, from a cross-disciplinary vision combined with in-depth personal and professional development. The "learning curve" that lends its name to the title of this book is an appropriate metaphor when looking at an academic or research career in relation to business.

Right now, Kangaroos, – the type of multifaceted academics described above – are thin on the ground. When I talk to my colleagues at other schools, and ask them what worries them most about the future, the most common answer is the lack of teaching staff with the qualities that we are all looking for: that combination of proven investigative ability, sound teaching skills, and a profound knowledge of the world of business. The doctorate programs currently available in the world today are not sufficient to meet the demand, and on many occasions do not even produce the right stuff. One of business education's major challenges in the future is to meet that demand by designing programs to train consummate academic Triathlon champions. If we are able to do so, then the result will be a win-win for all, and one that will have made it worthwhile working together towards this common goal.

Developing well-rounded business academics

In Chapter 8, I argued that one of the main missions of business schools is to build bridges between Academia and the Agora: between the world of thinking and research and the practical world of business. Academic research makes a vital contribution to our body of knowledge on management. Academic methodologies bring the rigor and objectivity required for a clear analysis of reality, and allow us to come up with solutions on the basis of comparative studies. I would further argue that much of the blame for the recent financial crisis could be attributed to analyses and ideas from institutions that lacked the rigor that characterizes academic research.

The reputation of a business school is directly related to the research and knowledge that it produces, as has been shown by a number of studies[194] and is further evidenced by the leading business school rankings, such as that of the *Financial Times*. One of the criteria for inclusion in its league table is the amount of research a school has published in the top management journals. At the same time, from my experience with a range a stakeholders in the sector, and particularly in relation to corporate universities, a key criterion in choosing a school to provide a customized program for companies is its capacity for generating knowledge. The head of a corporate university with whom I shared a place on a recent panel on executive education told me that companies are attracted by business schools associated with new ideas and innovation, along with proposals that will allow them to better compete in an increasingly global environment.

To make business schools' research more relevant, I believe that it is necessary to come up with constructive proposals that will strengthen the ties between the academic and business worlds. In line with the arguments of Costas Markides, a widely respected professor at London Business School, who calls for "ambidextrous professors,"[195] I think that it is a mistake to underestimate both the value of academic research or seeing things in global terms. To do so will lead to the disappearance of a highly valuable and essential approach that has provided rigor to the management knowledge base we currently draw on.

I also agree with Markides that it is a mistake to foster the separation between academics who are only interested in academic research and practitioners. Markides' proposals to encourage younger scholars to publish not just in academic journals, but also in professional publications, are the way forward. In this way we will see the transfer of research to teaching, as well as encouraging cooperation between businesses and consultancies to identify new ideas and models for research.

On the basis of his tenure as President of IMD, Peter Lorange[196] also highlights the need for business schools to adopt an "interactive, two-way approach, where propositional knowledge meets prescriptive knowledge." This mutually beneficial virtuous cycle can be seen in executive education programs, or MBAs where participants have considerable experience, giving teachers the opportunity to benefit from feedback by professionals attending their classes.

Despite the constant criticism to the opposite, in reality the academic world is proactive when it comes to developing the mechanisms needed to change the systems that generate and distribute knowledge. This is shown by a concern for strengthening the clinical relevance of research, reflected in the significant number of articles on the subject published in recent years by the Academy of Management, the most influential forum on a global level for academic research in management. Some additional proposals that might contribute to strengthening the links between Academia and the Agora are:

- *Redesign PhD management programs* so that participants, aside from developing the skills of sound researchers, are also given the opportunity to practice the complementary skills that will allow them to teach, and also to take advantage of teaching to disseminate the results of their own research. What's more, doctoral programs should also facilitate contact between students and business leaders to give them first-hand experience of the real problems of management. This could also be achieved through internships.

- *Adapt tenure systems* to take into account not only teachers' published academic output, but also their teaching skills. Furthermore, it would be advisable to introduce procedures to evaluate to what extent teachers maintain links with the world of business, either through membership of boards, or through consulting work. Obviously, overall evaluation will still emphasize research output; the challenge is to find a balance that will allow teachers to incorporate these proposals over time. Once again, the Triathlon analogy comes to mind. The proposals mentioned above would probably require evaluation periods of at least one year, so as to provide sufficient perspective on the results and impact in each of the areas.

- *Work with business leaders* to identify the key issues affecting the business world. A growing number of business schools have already set up interdisciplinary centers aimed at going beyond the remit of traditional academic departments by setting up direct links with companies to develop specific projects. These centers not only encourage interdisciplinary research, but also develop training programs that address specific issues relating to business management. At the same time, it is important that business schools' boards and advisory councils understand the strengths and weaknesses of their respective institutions. These councils are generally made up of business people or alumni, and who can provide invaluable feedback on what the real world's knowledge needs are. I have always been struck by the proximity of the board members of France's *Grandes Ecoles* – who are often business people belonging to the Chambers of Commerce who finance the schools – to the research activity carried out there.

- *Encourage ties between research-oriented teachers and practitioners.* So far, this kind of cooperation has usually been restricted to developing teaching material for programs. But it can be extended to other areas. Responsibility for bringing together the two should be a key objective of department heads, who can advance joint research initiatives.

- *Develop procedures to assimilate knowledge produced outside the academic environment.* Business schools should be hubs, bringing in new ideas, concepts, and models generated outside their immediate sphere, for example, in consultancies, corporate universities, and other types of forums. The Internet offers limitless potential for exchanging ideas and information.

- *Appoint "embedded academics" in companies.* This would be another step towards setting up chairs financed by companies in business schools. The professors appointed to these Chairs would work on specific projects with the sponsoring companies. This approach is already in use among consultancies, who send consultants into a company for long-term or highly important projects. "Embedded academics" would have one foot in academia and another in the business world. At IE we have already put this approach into practice: we have a Human Resources Chair sponsored by leading Spanish fashion retailer group Inditex, or Accenture's Competitive Strategy Chair. The professors who hold the chairs spend a significant amount of their time working on specific projects with the companies involved, at the same time transferring relevant and up-to-the-minute academic research in their respective areas.

- *Develop ways to measure the impact of academic research on the real world.* This would mean going beyond the standard bibliometric indicators or article citation rates. We know that in management, as in the social sciences, the impact of ideas cannot just be measured by how often they are turned into patents or registered as inventions, the approach generally used in other scientific disciplines. I would suggest two approaches: (i) recognizing a piece of academic work on the basis of its inclusion in management programs taught around the world, for example, models or concepts such as the Balance Scorecard, Blue Ocean Strategies, or Non-market Strategies, which are now part of just about every MBA program; (ii) bringing together academics from business schools, corporate universities, development departments, consultancies, and even the publishers of management publications, to design systems that would allow for periodic analysis of research produced by schools and their use as management tools in the business world. The ideal would be come up with a range of measuring systems reflecting diverse cultural and business practices, and thus the heterogeneity of the research.

Research is one of the most valuable assets of the academic world, and should be encouraged and increased. Sadly, at times of crisis, Research, Development, and Innovation (R+D+I) spending tends to be the first to be axed, a policy that in the long term leads only to loss of competitiveness and innovative capacity. It is essential to raise awareness of the value of academic research for the business world, and this is something that business schools can play a key role in.

Revisiting the purpose of PhD Programs

PhD programs are essential to the whole education system. They are the pool of future university researchers and teachers. The Woodrow Wilson National Fellowship Foundation, a US-based non-profit organization dedicated to promote excellence in education, released the report "The Responsive PhD: Innovations in US Doctoral Education," an extremely interesting document on doctoral education in the US that calls for important reforms: "there have been too many words and too little action,"[197] it states. The report also comprises a series of successful initiatives developed in PhD programs at different US universities.

I want to focus on two recommendations of this report. First, that pedagogy should be an important part of doctoral preparation. For some time,

PhD programs have focused almost exclusively on training academic researchers. This has been essential, but not sufficient. In fact, the omission of some other important facets, such as preparing candidates to teach effectively and to link with the corporate world, has reduced the potential development and the opportunities of PhD graduates.

Another recommendation is the need for connecting doctoral programs with other major social stakeholders outside universities, mainly the organizations that may recruit or work with PhD graduates: "the doctorate in totality and in every discipline will benefit enormously by a continuing interchange with the worlds beyond academia," says the report.

This report should be very welcome, and it comes at a time when there is a growing market for DBA (Doctor in Business Administration) programs in Europe. Significantly, the Association of MBAs (AMBA) launched a new accreditation scheme aimed at DBA programs, to cope with the increasing demand from the market.

Some careers, such as medicine or education, are truly vocational. Many professionals who decide to dedicate themselves to education can root their calling back to feelings and experiences that happen sometimes very early in life. That is my case, since I learnt early on that I wanted to be a professor.

I am sharing this personal flashback because I believe that the call to Academia is sometimes felt genuinely very early and, in any case, it entails a disposition and frequently a passion, for both the development and the transmission of knowledge. Both facets, the generation and the diffusion of ideas, are valuable by themselves and inevitably interdependent. Indeed, research and teaching are both consubstantial to academic careers, and when I meet a scholar who disregards or abandons either of the two, I think I am in front of a lame academic.

Teaching and the interaction with students provide a unique opportunity to test the validity of knowledge. In addition, it can be one of the most self-fulfilling activities practiced by academics. As far as management education is concerned, the direct interface with managers is particularly important, since their behavior and their experiences are actually the object of management research. Is there really any other way to develop business research than by dealing with the major business stakeholders?

If research and teaching are two essential and fulfilling activities of academic careers, why do PhDs in management programs at most business schools focus mainly – if not solely – on the development of research skills? In fact, the reduction of PhD programs to the training of research skills is a malaise that has been criticized in different reports on both sides of the Atlantic. I hope that, if institutions do not react and solve this problem, PhD students will overcome their estrangement and demand a complete education. This sometimes makes me think about the popular call addressed to the working class but this time targeted to doctoral students: PhDs of The World, Unite!

The importance of teaching

The most dignifying and self-rewarding task that we, as educators, can engage in is dealing with the students in the learning process, particularly through teaching in class.

Teaching has been at the core of education and the essence of academic work since its origins, something reinforced by the etymology of the word "academia." Every time we read Plato's *Dialogues* we rejoice at learning his and Socrates' thoughts through the discussions between the master and his students. I do not mean that other scholarly activities are not necessary, even indispensable, for the correct performance of an academic job; I have discussed this before. But teaching seems pivotal to the others. It is then surprising, if not disheartening, that sometimes academics may lose this track.

I have found one of the most recent interesting pieces of analysis on American higher education in an article entitled "The Truth About the Colleges," written by Andrew Hacker.[198] The author comments on recent literature on university education and concludes that "all the books under review voice a similar lament: too many professors, perhaps most, are doing a mediocre job in the classroom."[199] One of the books covered by the article is the latest report produced by the *Princeton Review*: "The Best 357 Colleges: 2005 Edition." An interesting finding of this survey is that undergraduates show a higher degree of satisfaction, regarding teaching performance, in colleges that have small enrolments, that do not have graduate programs, and that do not enjoy a wide national reputation. Surprisingly, the lowest scores in the survey were obtained by undergraduate instruction at large, well-known research universities.

Another source mentioned in Hacker's article is the Carnegie Foundation for the Advancement of Teaching, according to which seven out of eight undergraduates study in campuses "where the work of devoted teachers is rarely rewarded, and prestige and high salaries are conferred on professors who concentrate on their research, graduate seminars, publications, and reputations."[200] Hacker further goes on and quotes Stanley Katz, a professor of public affairs at Princeton, who says that many universities "are dominated by faculties for whom thoughtful consideration of undergraduate education is simply not on the agenda."[201] The author concludes with the devastating statement: "As matters stand, one measure of a university's prestige is how little teaching is asked of its tenured professors. Although there are more endowed chairs at the top, more undergraduates are now taught by graduate assistants, adjuncts, and part-time faculty who will never be promoted."[202]

Teaching matters a lot. I believe that in management education we may be better prepared to avoid the undesirable syndrome described above. At most business schools I've visited, teaching performance is one of the key variables used in the selection and promotion of professors. It certainly becomes decisive for the assignment of docents in executive education programs. If we aim at achieving our mission, we need to enhance the teaching skills of our professors in order that they become true academics in class.

Contributing to knowledge

Some years ago, Umberto Eco[203], the prominent academic and writer, published an article in *L'Expresso*, the Italian weekly magazine, under the title: "The first duty of intellectuals: to remain silent when they cannot be of any use". The title is self-explanatory, but I extract a passage from the article that has been quoted often subsequently:

"Intellectuals are useful to society, but only in the long run. In the short term they can only be professional speakers or researchers, school administrators, communication managers at a political party or a company, or maybe blow the fife in a revolution, but they cannot perform a specific and distinctive task. To say that they are useful in the long run means that they work before and after the actual events, but never during those events. An economist or a geographer could have warned about the transformation of terrestrial transports when the steam machine came into scene and could analyse the future pros and cons of that transformation or develop a study one hundred years later to show how that invention revolutionised our lives. However, when stagecoach companies were becoming bankrupt and the first steam machines were taking the lead, [intellectuals] had noting to contribute or, in any case, much less than an engine driver. To ask intellectuals for something else is like reproaching Plato for not finding a remedy for the gastritis [...] The only meaningful thing an intellectual can do when his house is burning is to call the fire brigade"[204]

Indeed, it is an exemplary piece of irony. Let me anticipate that I do not agree with Eco's statement. I believe that intellectuals and academics can exercise their social task effectively and produce a direct impact on their societies, for the better. Countless examples could be used as evidence. However, Eco's scathing statement and the analogous ideas formulated by others are often used by critics of the "ivory tower" accusing academics of living in an unreal Arcadia, very detached from the real world. Suppose that Plato had been a professor at a business school in our days. Wouldn't we have asked him for concrete remedies to business problems?

Business schools need both academics and practitioners in their faculties, and deans look for those who represent the best symbiosis of the two. Most deans I have talked to agree with me on the need to have academics as well as practitioners, and they rightly believe that the challenge is to find the adequate blend of the two. Indeed, a real challenge for business schools' deans is how to manage diversity when the profile of faculty members is so complementary.

Traditionally, the reciprocal reaction between academics and practitioners has been to reject the other. It is time to overcome this mutual exclusion and explore the formidable synergies that could result from diversity. Again, this is one of the reasons I favor an attached view of business schools, i.e., that business schools should act as bridges between academic and the business world.

How can b-school deans foster valuable research and open new avenues that help young scholars to diffuse their academic contributions? Dennis Lapert, Director of Telecom Business School in France, raised, in an exchange in my blog,[205] the issue that the number of scholars and the volume of potential contributions have grown considerably in the past years whereas the number of academic journals has remained almost steady. This creates, in his opinion, a bottleneck "and many articles never see the light of day, even though they may be of great scholarly, and even public, interest." He suggests "that we work with organizations that represent faculty in the various management disciplines to make available the means that will enable young researchers (and even those who are not so young) to have their works published." I volunteer to support his initiative.

However, I believe that the pressing challenge mentioned should be also faced from a broader perspective. The key question is how business schools could more effectively foster the creation and the diffusion of relevant management research. This, in turn, is related to two issues: (i) what is relevant management research or knowledge, and (ii) what should be considered as valuable channels of diffusion of this research. The problem in distinguishing between these two questions is that, conventionally, the quality of a given piece of research is validated by its publication in some canonical vehicle of communication. For example, the quality of an article is supported by its publication in a refereed journal. Is there some way to escape this conceptual trap or, to put it differently, this Catch 22 situation?

Some years ago I was asked by EFMD (European Foundation for Management Development) to chair a commission on the definition of the concept of "research" for the EQUIS Accreditation standards. The aim of this commission was to develop some set of usable criteria that could help auditors in identifying when a school applying for accreditation had developed enough research, both in terms of quantity and quality. Our first challenge was to face the many meanings that "research" has for diverse institutions according to their respective missions. We decided to avoid the semantic trap of defining research in a univocal way (e.g., research is the output of contributions in academic journals) and opted instead for a wider conception that could cover different forms of production and diffusion of knowledge.

We stipulated a new concept imported from business: RDI (Research, Development, and Innovation) that could gather multifarious types of knowledge output, from articles in academic journals to brown books on industries, including teaching materials (case studies, technical notes), books, and articles in professional journals.

Consequently, the interpretation of RDI requirements for the accreditation of different institutions varies: an executive education center, for example, would be expected to develop practice-oriented materials, whereas a university-based business school offering PhD programs would naturally produce conventional academic research. Obviously, this new paradigm is not intended as a rule of thumb since it requires a deep analysis of the evaluated institution, its management processes, and its competitive standing, but RDI has proved to be a valuable instrument for the assessment of the academic contributions of an accredited school.

Going back to the question posed by Dean Lampert, I suggest we consider the enormous potential that the Web 2.0 brings for the diffusion of valuable knowledge. Take, for example, the Becker-Posner blog,[206] edited by two world-renowned scholars. Who would reasonably reject its value as a vehicle of relevant knowledge?

The nature of inventions in business research

Teppo Felin referred in Orgtheory,[207] one of my favorite academic blogs, to a list of the 100 world-changing discoveries and ideas that resulted from research projects developed at UK universities in the past 50 years. The list was published in a report produced by Universities UK. One of the objectives of the report was to show how basic research is linked to the improvement of society and well being, and it came at a time when the UK government was planning to change the system of funding university research, the Research Assessment Exercise (RAE).

Sadly, the report's list does not include any discoveries found at business schools. Nevertheless, it lists contributions originated at schools of social and political sciences: for example, the London School of Economics is credited with a significant number of new ideas that transformed society. The absence of business schools in the list of research innovators is not a consequence of their relative youth as compared with other academic institutions, since many b-schools were founded more than 50 years ago, the lifespan surveyed in the study. Is there any other reason justifying the lack of creativity at business schools?

A prestigious colleague from Europe told me that he believed there were very few ideas – if any – generated at business schools that have contributed to the transformation of real management practices. He sustained that the process of innovation in business knowledge works the other way round, that it starts with the analysis of real world practices and not in an academic vacuum. Management knowledge is made of human experiences, an amalgamation of "human devices." Since the only management facts to be discovered exist in the real world – and not in some other ideal, platonic, sphere – the development of management knowledge is distinctively clinical.

I agree with Teppo Felin that "Knowledge-building and research is about a systematic effort to explain, understand, and predict – driven by careful theory-building and data collection" but I am a little puzzled when he explained that "inherently choices need to be made as to which type of knowledge should be privileged, particularly in a b-school and university environment. Do we value scholarship (and teaching) that is theory-driven, or teaching (scholarship?) by executives that is experience-driven?"[208]

For a long time academia has strongly emphasized the excellence of "basic research," and the lesser value of the so-called applied research. It is probably time to reconcile the two, and it seems that the "attached view of business schools" defended in a previous post works in this direction.

Academic asepsis

Wilhelm Von Humboldt (1767–1835), founder of the eponymous Berlin-based university, is generally considered one of the fathers of modern university, and his ideas have inspired most higher education institutions in Europe and the Americas. One of the salient features of his legacy was the development of a sciences' taxonomy and the consequent organization of university departments according to a set of knowledge areas and disciplines.

The main aim of this was to advance the progress of knowledge through the specialization of academics. Since the compendium of human knowledge was, and still is, so vast, it was virtually impossible for academics to effectively develop research unless they focused on a given field of knowledge and dealt with their scientific peers. The specialization of academic knowledge and the consolidation of independent disciplines also resulted in the development of multiple degrees, according to the subjects studied by graduates at university. This changed the pattern existing before, when most university graduates shared a similar generalist degree, following common curricula, and most applied knowledge was learnt while practicing the profession.

Undoubtedly, the specialization of academic knowledge and the generation of research through university departments have produced an unprecedented progress across the sciences, the humanities, and the arts in the past two centuries. However, different factors affecting higher education in the past decades, including globalization and the impact of new technologies, have led some analysts – particularly in management education – to point out some of the negative consequences of the division and compartmentalization of knowledge. One of the more extended criticisms is encapsulated in the "silos syndrome," according to which university departments have become like silos where its academic members are detached from reality, partly because they are sharply separated from scholars of other disciplines. Putting it bluntly, finance professors relate only to other finance professors, they attend only finance congresses and publish only in finance journals, which are – obviously – read only by their finance colleagues; of course, they are authorized to teach and research only in their field of specialization, i.e., finance.

A further problem derived from this syndrome is what I refer sometimes to as "academic asepsis": only those academics with the right pedigree and who belong to an identifiable academic group – sometimes called "a school" – have the legitimacy of producing valuable research in their own field of knowledge. They are the authoritative sources of knowledge. Parvenus, such as practitioners lacking the conventional academic credentials, or those belonging to different disciplines, should be left out of the club, in order to guarantee the quality of the knowledge generated or taught. Certainly, I am drawing a caricature of what reality actually is and, I believe, even at very compartmentalized universities academics understand the value of interdisciplinary initiatives such as co-teaching or co-publishing by professors from different areas. However, department-driven universities face the challenge of articulating an integrated vision of the world to their stakeholders, mainly their students, and of avoiding a narrow and irrelevant concept of research. Certainly we need twenty-first century Von Humboldts.

Professors as mavens

When I ask my colleagues about the main challenges our schools face today, many of them point at the attraction, development, and retention of good faculty as few of the most serious. Indeed, today schools compete to attract those scholars who combine the best credentials in research with solid teaching skills and who also interface with the top management of respected companies. Let me now further elaborate on this multifaceted type of academics by opposing two models of faculty, which I will name "Humboldtian Faculty" and "Mavens."

"Humboldtian Faculty" was molded at the eponymous institution in Berlin in the early nineteenth century and has inspired the academic model prevalent at all Western universities in the past 200 years. Wilhelm Von Humboldt believed that, in order to make a significant leap in the sciences and in the humanities, the career of academics should become specialized – till then, university professors may teach a different discipline – and universities should be organized into schools and departments. A number of consequences for the academic profession followed over the decades, and I summarize some of these features in Table 10.1.

The Humboldtian Faculty model has rendered many positive results. Knowledge has experienced an unprecedented advance across the board. At the same time, a significant number of education analysts and scholars have warned about some undesirable effects of the model such as the "silos

Table 10.1   Different faculty models

Humboldtian faculty	Mavens
Specialized, academic pedigree	Mixed academic backgrounds
Masters of the learning process	Learning Orchestrators
Guardians of Knowledge	Catalysts of Knowledge

syndrome" derived from an extreme specialization and lack of integration of academics, teaching, and research at large.

In addition, the demands from stakeholders, the formidable impact of technologies in the learning process and the origination and distribution of knowledge are transforming the role and the ideal profile of scholars. I believe that the concept of "Maven," widely popularized by Malcolm Gladwell in his book *The Tipping Point*,[209] can adequately illustrate what is expected from business schools' professors today. Mavens are active gatherers of new trends, ideas, and data and have the key skills of identifying which of them may transform the world.

Furthermore, they exercise the necessary influence to have these ideas diffused through other major opinion makers in society – whom Gladwell calls "connectors" and "vendors." I include a number of characteristics of faculty as Mavens in Table 10.1. I hope this idea contributes to a constructive debate on how to better shape the academic profession and adapt it to current changes and demands. I do not believe that I am proposing a revolutionary change, but rather an evolutionary but significant adjustment of the role that faculty play in the modern learning process.

The rise of superstar professors

Let me recall a story read in the papers some years ago, and widely commentated in media and blogs. I refer to "Tom Cruise affair," related to the Chairman of Viacom's decision announced to terminate the company's contract with the mentioned celebrity. The recommendable article "A Big Star May Not a Profitable Movie Make,"[210] written by Porter and Fabrikant and published in *The New York Times*, explains the possible reasons behind this decision from a managerial perspective. According to the findings of the entertainment industry analysts collected in this article, "if a star-studded movie does well, it does not necessarily mean that the stars are causing higher ticket sales. In fact, it seems to move the other way around: stars select what they believe are promising projects. And studios prefer to put stars in movies that they expect to be a success [...] Movies with stars are successful not because of the star, but because the star chooses projects that people tend to like." Apparently, "stars, on average, were worth $3 million in theatrical revenue," which, in many of the cases, was much less of what they actually earn per movie.

The Tom Cruise story reminded me about the impact that superstar professors may have in the returns of business schools, and my intuition is that there are interesting analogies with the movie industry. By superstar professor I mean those academics that have gained an outstanding external recognition that results in high professional fees. As I have previously mentioned, they are sometimes referred to as "gurus." Superstar professors may be instrumental in some cases such as, for example, the international promotion of a business school that lacks exterior visibility, or for attracting large companies as clients of executive education offerings. Interestingly, however, business schools that may look for superstars in order to improve their own prestige may face a chicken-and-egg problem here since, according to my experience, the first reason professors select a school to work for is precisely the school's reputation. On the other hand, it seems that when a superstar leaves a school, the effects on the school's image are not relevant: business schools are resilient and their reputation is not affected, unless a substantial number of its faculty members leave.

Superstar professors tend to be more independent and detached from the school and they normally become less involved in the learning process – particularly in spending time out-of-class with students – than their faculty colleagues.

However, denying the value of superstar professors for business schools would be naïve, since stakeholders demand them. A major challenge for deans is how to create the necessary conditions in order to produce more academics of this sort and at the same time keep the balance in their faculties.

EPILOGUE

How will business schools look like when they are created on the surface of Mars some decades from now? What will have been the major advances in management science by then? How will management jobs and professional skills differ from the ones prevalent today?

I believe that these questions may be partly responded by analyzing what the most innovative business schools are implementing today. In earlier pages, I have identified the forces that, I believe, are shaping the present and the future of business education. The globalization of business and higher education, the impact of new technologies on the learning process and the role of teachers, the recognition of diversity, and new forms of intelligence in students, along with the development of multifarious sources and channels to distribute knowledge are some of the forces transforming education.

The new environment shaped by these forces provides many opportunities to business schools if they are open and adaptive to change. At the same time, those institutions that play "business as usual" risk losing relevance, market share, and even disappearing.

The recent crisis has represented an opportunity for business schools to revisit their basic mission of preparing the best possible managers and entrepreneurs and to implement some opportune changes that head towards this direction. Of course, we may not be able to avoid future crises just by changing the MBA curriculum or emphasizing professional deontology. Management is a complex phenomenon, deeply embedded in social practices and intricate as is any manifestation of human interpersonal behavior. We may still be in the infancy of our understanding of management, but the hopes are high for next big jumps in business knowledge if research is linked closer to real business challenges and connected to related advancements in the Humanities and the other Sciences.

In February 2011, almost during the completion of this book, I was invited by *BusinessWeek*'s Louis Lavelle to contribute a column summarizing my views on the relations between business education and the Humanities. I took that opportunity to write a piece that encapsulated some of the main ideas of "The Learning Curve," which I am now, with some variations, using as an Epilogue.[211]

Business schools face the challenge of preparing not just good financial engineers or accomplished management technicians, but also global citizens. Thus, education delivered at business schools can and should be a personal transformation process. My experience and the evidence provided by many business schools is that skills and traits can be learnt and developed in maturity, if the necessary attitudes are cultivated. In fact, business schools' success is based on the experience that education and training can transform the lives of managers throughout their careers and that this will in turn positively affect the performance of their companies and society at large.

Two of the most promising avenues for deepening this transformational nature of management education are: First, the systematic training of management students in what might be called the "managerial virtues"; and, second, integrating the study of management and the humanities.

Regarding the first, developing virtues – understood as habits or routines that form our character – has been a core aspect of teaching in all societies throughout the ages. Managerial virtues are operative good habits that are not innate, but achieved through constant exercise. It is never too late to start practicing or perfecting these good habits, and can make management education a transforming experience. The development of these core virtues has been central for "Positive Psychology" representatives like Christopher Peterson and Martin Seligman, and is starting to produce a beneficiary and influential impact in education.

In order to help students develop their managerial virtues, business schools should combine general teaching methods such as classes, with personalized attention to students through individual learning solutions: one-to-one sessions, tutorials, coaching, and mentorship, which may be run on a peer-to-peer basis. This personalized approach identifies weaknesses and builds strengths in students through a focus on the professional development of each person, bringing out their virtues where necessary. At the same time, this focused attention on the individual requires smaller size of classrooms – ideally around 50 – than what is currently the pattern – over 80. Interestingly, high quality blended methodologies that combine face-to-face methods with online ones have an enormous potential to foster student's skills and competencies.

My second proposal is to integrate the study of Humanities into business programs. The structure of contemporary programs has become sometimes extremely specialized, falling in what is commonly known as the "silo syndrome": academics dealing only with same-subject colleagues and students gaining only a narrow perspective on knowledge. Making Humanities a core part of all degrees will cement the learning experience and develop open-minded and well-rounded graduates. This spirit inspires our Executive MBA program recently launched by IE Business School and Brown University. We believe that by teaching Modern Art, for example, we nurture in participants skills such as perception and observation, typical of artists and architects, which may help managers, traditionally oriented towards action, to be more reflective while assessing risk. Courses on foreign cultures may help them better lead cross-cultural teams in their global companies. Modules on critical thinking may be of use to question unethical decisions imposed by their bosses in the future. Indeed, it is time to bring all the benefits of classical education to business schools.

At the same time, given that management is all-pervasive and that it affects all social and professional activities, I would suggest that it is taught transversally across all degrees at universities. In fact, we may be close to the time when management is included as a core subject at primary school, along with Mathematics or Literature. This may provide the opportunity to all to learn the basics of management knowledge and skills, a fundamental talent for many aspects in personal and professional life. Behind every good professional practice, there is good management, although we notice this only when things don't work. Doctors should be able to run hospitals efficiently and provide patients with quality care. Architects should be capable of completing projects on time and under budget. Indeed, good and sustainable management should permeate all new university offerings if we want our graduates, regardless of their degrees, to improve the world.

Management can be one of the noblest works if exercised with competency and honesty. We need more and better managers, and business schools have a formidable but fascinating challenge to respond to this global demand.

1 Why management matters

1. F. S. Fitzgerald, *The Love of The Last Tycoon*, (New York, NY: Scribner, 1993).
2. Ibid., p. 18.
3. Ibid., p. 16.
4. Ibid., p. 15.
5. Ibid., p. 24.
6. P. Drucker, "Management's New Paradigms," *Forbes*, December 5 1998, http://www.forbes.com/forbes/1998/1005/6207152a_4.html.
7. S. Ghoshal, C. Bartlett and P. Moran, "A New Manifesto for Management," in *Strategic Thinking for the Next Economy*, ed. Michael A. Cusumano and Constantinos C. Markides (San Francisco: Jossey-Bass, 2001), ch. 1, pp. 9–32.
8. "IBM Needs a New Boss: Who's Got the Right Stuff?" *Financial Times*, March 29, 1993.
9. R. Alonso: "México tendrá su primer museo del empresario." *El Universal*, Mexico, March 21, 2010, http://www.eluniversal.com.mx/articulos/61172.html
10. J. L. Cruikshank, *A Delicate Experiment: The Harvard Business School 1908–1945,* (Boston, MA: Harvard Business School Press, 1987), p. 8.
11. Ibid., p. 20.
12. http://www.pabook.libraries.psu.edu/palitmap/bios/Wharton__Joseph.html
13. R. Khurana, *From Higher Aims to Hired Hands: The Social Transformation of American Business Schools and the Unfulfilled Promise of Management as a Profession*, (Princeton, NJ: Princeton University Press, 2007), p. 7.
14. Ibid., p. 63.
15. Ibid., p. 3.
16. R. Khurana and N. Nohria, "It's Time to Make Management a True Profession," *Harvard Business Review* (October 2008), pp. 70–7.
17. http://www.ec.europa.eu/internal_market/services/services-dir/guides_en.htm. As a European Directive, it requires member states to achieve

a particular result without dictating the means and thus its full implementation depends on the actual development by said states.

18. New York State Bar Association, *New York Rules of Professional Conduct*, April 1, 2009, http://www.nysba.org/Content/Navigation Menu/ForAttorneys/ProfessionalStandardsforAttorneys/FinalNYRP CsWithComments(April12009).pdf

19. R. Baker, "No, Management Is *Not* a Profession," *Harvard Business Review* (July–August 2010), p. 6.

20. Drucker, Peter F., *The Ecological Vision* (New Jersey, Transaction Publishers, 1993), pp. 75–6.

21. John. F. Kennedy Presidential Library and Museum: "Remarks Prepared for Delivery at the Trade Mart in Dallas," November 22, 1963, http://www.jfklibrary.org/Historical+Resources/Archives/Reference+Desk/Speeches/JFK/003POF03TradeMart11221963.htm

22. Taken from the script of the movie "Shadowlands," by Richard Nicholson http://www.script-o-rama.com/movie_scripts/s/shadow-lands-script-transcript-winger-hopkins.html

2   Out of the crisis, confronting the critics

23. K. Holland, "Is It Time to Retrain B-Schools?" *The New York Times*, March 14, 2009.

24. B. Fryer, "How to Fix Business Schools," *Harvard Business Review Blogs*, May 5, 2009, http://www.blogs.hbr.org/how-to-fix-business-schools/

25. J. O. Light: "Change Is in the Offing," HBR Blog Network, May 7, 2009, http://blogs.hbr.org/how-to-fix-business-schools/2009/05/change-is-in-the-offing.html

26. The Debate Room, "Financial Crisis: Blame B-schools. Business Schools Are Largely Responsible for the U.S. Financial Crisis. Pro or Con?" *Businessweek*, November 24, 2008.

27. J. Lorsch, R. Khurana, "Pro: Failure to Promote a Higher Cause," in "Financial Crisis: Blame B-schools: Business schools Are Largely Responsible for the U.S. Financial Crisis. Pro or con?" *Businessweek*, November 24, 2008, http://www.businessweek.com/debateroom/archives/2008/11/us_financial_cr.html

28. Ibidem.

29. H. Mintzberg, *Managers Not MBAs: A Hard Look at the Soft Practice of Managing and Management Practice* (San Francisco, CA: Berret-Koehler Publishers Inc, 2004).

30. Ibid., p. 9.

31. Ibid., p. 74.

32. A. Wooldridge, "Global Heroes," *The Economist*, March 12, 2009.

33. P. Walker, "Who Taught Them Greed Is Good? To What Extent Are Business Schools' MBA Courses Responsible for the Global Financial Crash?" *The Observer*, March 8, 2009.

34. S. Ghoshal: "Bad Management Theories Are Destroying Good Management Practices," *Academy of Management Learning & Education IV* (2005), pp. 75–91.

35. Ibid., p. 79.

36. Ibid., p. 77.

37. Ibid., p. 75.

38. Ibid., p. 87.

39. C. Peterson and M. E. P. Seligman, *Character Strengths and Virtues: A Handbook and Classification* (New York, NY: Oxford University Press, 2004).

40. K. Starkey, "Business Schools – Look at History to Broaden Your Intellectual Horizons," *Financial Times*, October 20, 2008.

41. R. Sutton, "Do Economists Breed Greed and Guile?" in "How to Fix Business Schools," *Harvard Business Review Blogs*, April 5, 2009, http://www.blogs.hbr.org/how-to-fix-business-schools/2009/04/do-economists-breed-greed-and.html

42. S. Kaplan, "The Economists Have It Right," *Harvard Business Review Blogs*, April 7, 2009, http://www.blogs.hbr.org/how-to-fix-business-schools/2009/04/the-economists-have-it-right.html

43. S. Kaplan, "The System Isn't Broken But It Can be Improved," *Harvard Business Review Blogs*, April 22, 2009, http://blogs.hbr.org/how-to-fix-business-schools/2009/04/the-system-isnt-broken-but-it.html

44. F. Brown, "How Business Schools can Weather the Financial Crisis," *Chief Executive,* http://www.chiefexecutive.net/ME2/dirmod.asp?sid=&nm=&type=Publishing&mod=Publications%3A%3AArticle&mid=8F3A7027421841978F18BE895F87F791&tier=4&id=F69FD8FC46994537AC16E1524034610F

45. R. J. Hollingdale, *Nietzsche: The Man and His Philosophy* (Cambridge: Cambridge University Press, 1999), p. 143.

46. F. Nietzsche, *Thus Spoke Zarathustra*, trans. R. J. Hollingdale (London: Penguin, 1974), p. 18.

47. Taken from Berkshire Hathaway Inc., Code of Business Conduct and Ethics, quoted in Deanstalk.net, http://www.deanstalk.net/deanstalk/2009/01/warren-buffetts.html

48. Jim Collins, Level-5 Leadership, http://www.jimcollins.com/media_topics/level-5.html

49. R. E. Boyatzis and A. McKee, *Resonant Leadership: Renewing Yourself and Connecting with Others Through Mindfulness, Hope, and Compassion* (Boston, MA: Harvard Business School Press, 2005).

50. "Manager, not MBAs," op. cit., p. 74.

51. J. Chan, "The Top 10 MBA Program's Weakness," Money Economics website, October 26, 2010, http://www.moneyeconomics.com/Commentaries/The-top-10-MBA-Programs-Weakness

52. P. D. Broughton, *Ahead of the Curve: Two Years at Harvard Business School* (New York: The Penguin Press, 2008).

53. J. Pfeffer, "The Narcissistic World of the MBA Student," *Financial Times*, November 7, 2010.

54. Ibidem.

55. http://www.afponline.org/pub/cs/2010/compsurvey.html

56. http://www.chiefexecutive.net/ME2/Audiences/dirmod.asp?sid=&nm=&type=

57. K. Starkey, "Business Schools- Look at History to Broaden Your Intellectual Horizons," *Financial Times*, October 20, 2008.

58. http://www.money.cnn.com/magazines/fortune/bestcompanies/2010

59. Interview with Blair Sheppard, *McKinsey Quarterly*, January 2010, p. 2.

60. Blog *Musings on Markets*, December 31, 2008, http://aswathdamodaran.blogspot.com/2008/12/crisis-of-2008-lessons-learned.html

61. *The Economist*, December 1, 2009, http://www.deanstalk.net/deanstalk/2009/12/the-economist-deans-debate-santiago-iñiguez-de-ozoño-paul-danos.html

62. http://www.beyondgreypinstripes.org/

63. T. Piper, M. C. Gentile, and S. Daloz Parks, *Can Ethics Be Taught? Perspectives, Challenges and Approaches at Harvard Business School* (Cambridge, MA: Harvard Business School Press, 1993), p. 127.

64. Ibid., pp. 127–8.

65. A. Donovan, "Can Ethics Classes Cure Cheating?" *Harvard Business School Blogs*, April 14, 2009, http://www.blogs.hbr.org/how-to-fix-business-schools/2009/04/can-ethics-classes-cure-cheati.html

66. http://www.oxforddictionaries.com/view/entry/m_en_gb0140070#m_en_gb0140070

3   Developing better managers

67. A. Wooldridge, "Global Heroes," *The Economist*, March 12, 2009.

68. L. Kellaway, "The End of the Affair," The Economist: The World in 2010, November 18, 2009, http://www.economist.com/node/14742624

69. T. Piper, M. C. Gentile, and S. Daloz Parks, *Can Ethics Be Taught? Perspectives, Challenges and Approaches at Harvard Business School* (Cambridge, MA: Harvard Business School Press, 1993).

70. A. Goldsworthy, *Caesar: The Life of a Colossus* (London: Weidenfeld & Nicolson, 2006), chapter 2.

71. G. E. M. Anscombe, *Ethics, Religion and Politics* (London: Basil Blackwell, 1981), pp. 38–9.

72. A. McIntyre, *After Virtue: A Study in Moral Theory* (London: Duckworth, 1981), chapter 14.

73. C. Peterson and M. Seligman, *Character Strengths and Virtues: A Handbook and Classification* (Oxford & New York: Oxford University Press, 2004).

74. Carrington Crisp and EFMD, "Executive Education Futures," August 2010, http://www.deanstalk.net/files/execedfutures2010.pdf

75. F. Brown, "The Responsibility of Business Schools," paper circulated April 16, 2009.

76. P. Danos, "Paul Danos in wide-ranging interview for a French business publication," *Deanstalk*, January 25, 2008, http://www.deanstalk.net/deanstalk/2008/01/paul-danos-in-w.html

77. C. Baden-Fuller and J. Stopford, *Rejuvenating the Mature Business: The Competitive Challenge* (Boston, MA: Harvard Business School Press, 1994), p. 3.

78. The Graduate Management Admission Council. http://www.gmac.com/gmac

4 The changing landscape

79. G. Taber, *Judgment of Paris: California vs. France and the Historic 1976 Paris Tasting That Revolutionized Wine* (New York: Scribner, 2006).

80. D. Bradshaw, "US Schools See Their Powers Begin to Wane," Financial Times, July 25, 2010, http://www.ft.com/intl/cms/s/0/3a225134-966a-11df-96a2-00144feab49a.html#axzz1QTAf2FBG; http://rankings.ft.com /businessschoolrankings /global-mba-rankings-2011

81. R. Zoellick, "Current Multipolar World Requires a Multipolar Currency System," *Yaroslav Forum*, February 18, 2011, http://en.gpf-yaroslavl.ru/news/Robert-Zoellick-Current-multipolar-world-requires-a-multipolar-currency-system

82. Accenture, "From Global Connection to Global Orchestration: Future Business Models for High Performance Where Technology and the

Multi-Polar World Meet," 2010, https://microsite.accenture.com/NonSecureSiteCollectionDocuments/By_Subject/Management_Consulting/PDF/Accenture_Multipolar_World_Research_Report_2010.pdf

83. http://money.cnn.com/magazines/fortune/global500/2010/ç

84. http://rankings.ft.com/businessschoolrankings/rankings

85. M. Prest, "Timely Appointment for Warwick Business School," *Independent,* October 7, 2010.

86. *Securing a Sustainable Future for Higher Education. An Independent Review of Higher Education Funding and Student Finance*, October 12, 2010, http://www.hereview.independent.gov.uk/hereview/report/

87. Universities UK, "The Growth of Private and For-Profit Higher Education Providers in the UK," Research Report, 2010, http://www.universitiesuk.ac.uk/Publications/Documents/PrivateProvidersmar10.pdf

88. T. Lewin, "For-Profit Colleges Mislead Students, Report Finds," *The New York Times,* August 3, 2010, http://www.nytimes.com/2010/08/04/education/04education.html?_r=1&scp=1&sq=For-Profit%20Colleges%20Mislead%20Students,%20Report%20Finds&st=cse; Pell Grants, named after former Senator Claiborne Pell, are grants give by the Federal Government that don't need to be repaid, http://studentaid.ed.gov/PORTALSWebApp/students/english/PellGrants.jsp?tab=funding

89. J. Washburn, *University, Inc.: The Corporate Corruption of Higher Education*, (New York: Basic Books, 2005).

90. Laureate International Universities, http://www.laureate.net/en/AboutLaureate/Mission.aspx

91. J. Shiller, "For-Profit Colleges Will Be Next Bubble to Burst," Change.org, July 14, 2010, http://www.education.change.org/blog/view/for-profit_colleges_will_be_next_bubble_to_burst

92. http://www.personalmba.com/manifesto/

93. G. Gloeckler and J. Merritt, "An Ethics Lesson for MBA Wannabes," *Businessweek*, March 9, 2005, http://www.businessweek.com/bschools/content/mar2005/bs2005039_7827_bs001.htm

94. J. Kaufman, *The Personal MBA: A World Class Business Education in a Single Volume*, (New York: The Viking Press, 2011).

95. J. A. Byrne, "The Financials Behind the Harvard-Stanford Rivalry," *Poets & Quants*, December 4, 2010, http://www.poetsandquants.com/2010/12/04/the-financials-behind-the-harvard-stanford-rivalry/

96. P. Lorange, "Strategy Means Choice," *Deanstalk*, October 14, 2005, http://www.deanstalk.net/deanstalk/2005/10/management_educ_1.html

97. M. Porter, *Competitive Strategy: Techniques for Analyzing Industries and Competitors* (New York: The Free Press, 1980), p. 41.

5 E-Learning

98. D. Bradshaw, "Schools Drawn into New Webs," *Financial Times*, October 11, 1999.

99. H. Blustain and P. Goldstein, "Report on UNext and Cardean University," in *The E-University Compendium*, ed. P. Bacsich and S. Frank Bristow (The Higher Education Academy, 2004), ch. 11, http://www.virtualcampuses.eu/index.php/Report_on_UNext_and_Cardean_University

100. S. Carr, "Rich in Cash and Prestige, UNext Struggles in Its Search for Sales," *The Chronicle of Higher Education*, May 4, 2001.

101. *The Economist*, February 24, 2010, http://www.economist.com/node/15573278

102. "Old Mogul, New Media: Can Rupert Murdoch Adapt News Corporation to the Digital Age?" *The Economist*, January 19, 2006.

103. M. Gunther, "Iger's New Model: The Disney CEO's Embrace of Digital Technologies Means Big Change," *Fortune*, January 20, 2006, http://www.money.cnn.com/2006/01/10/magazines/fortune/disney_fortune/

104. *Financial Times*, March 20, 2006, http://www.deanstalk.net/deanstalk/2006/03/the_rich_experi.html

105. A. de Saint Exupéry, *The Little Prince*, trans. R. Howard (Boston: Harcourt, 2000), p. 63.

6 International stakeholders

106. M. McLuhan, *The Gutenberg Galaxy: The Making of Typographic Man* (Toronto: University of Toronto Press, 1962), p. 31.

107. A. Böhm, *Global Student Mobility 2025: Analysis of Global Competition and Market Share*, IDP Education Pty Ltd., November 2003, http://www.aiec.idp.com/PDF/Bohm_2025Media_p.pdf

108. Institute of International Education, "Atlas of Student Mobility," http://www.atlas.iienetwork.org/?p=54855

109. AACSB's Globalization of Management Education Task Force (Chair: R. F. Brunner), *Globalization of Management Education: Changing International Structures, Adaptive Strategies and the Impact on Institutions* (Bingley, UK: Emerald, 2011), p. 51.

110. D. Bradshaw, "The Stern School Drops GMAT requirement for EMBAs," *Financial Times*, March 3, 2011.

111. The Association to Advance Collegiate Schools of Business.

112. R. Loades (ed.), *The Future of Management Education in the Context of the Bologna Accord*, EFMD-GMAC, June 24, 2006, http://www.efmd.org/index.php/research-publications-a-awards/publications/other-publications/1174

113. M. A. Overland, "Australia Sees Big Jump in International Enrollments, Despite Downturn Fears," *The Chronicle of Higher Education*, May 6, 2009, http://www.chronicle.com/article/Australia-Sees-Big-Jump-in/42862

114. A. Sursock and H. Smidt, *Trends 2010: A Decade of Change in European Higher Education*, (Brussels: EUA Publications, 2010), http://www.eua.be/Libraries/Publications/Trends_2010.sflb.ashx

115. M. Kelo, *Support for International Students in Higher Education*, (Bonn: Lemmens and Academic Cooperation Association, 2006).

116. O. Wilde, *An Ideal Husband* (Mineola, NY: Dover Publications, 2000), p. 28.

117. C. A. Bartlett and S. Goshal, "Managing Across Borders: New Strategic Requirements," *Sloan Management Review* 28 (1997), pp. 7–17.

118. D. Mavin, "Harvard Business School Won't Open Asian Campus," *Wall Street Journal*, August 2, 2010, http://www.online.wsj.com/article/SB10001424052748704905004575404960728487290.html

119. K. Mangan, "Business Schools Worldwide Fall Short on Globalization, Report Says," *The Chronicle of Higher Education*, February 10, 2011, commenting the AACSB Report on Globalization of Business Schools 2011.

120. *Financial Times*, October 25, 2010, http://rankings.ft.com/businessschoolrankings/emba-rankings-2010

121. Y. L. Doz and G. Hamel, *Alliance Advantage: The Art of Creating Value through Partnering*, (Boston, MA: Harvard Business School Press, 1998).

122. http://www.efmd.org/index.php/conferences-learning-groups/upcoming-events/2011-efmd-meeting-for-deans-a-directors-general/1590-programme-27–25-january-2011

123. D. Bradshaw, M. Jacobs, J. Kwen Chan, "Hot Spots: The most popular cities in the world for Executive MBAs," *Financial Times*, October 25, 2010, http://www.ft.com/intl/cms/s/2/c206fc20-ddd3-11df-8354-00144feabdc0.html#axzz1T2bZqMyX

7 Melting pots of knowledge

124. http://www.dictionary.reference.com/browse/knowledge

125. J. Micklewait and A. Wooldridge, *The Witch Doctors: What the Management Gurus Are Saying, Why It Matters and How to Make Sense of It* (London: Heinemann, 1996), p. 247.

126. In the article titled "A Difference of Opinion," *The Economist* (September 3, 2002) stated that: "Another, more important difference is that Europe, where the state generally plays a larger regulatory role, believes more strongly than America in such notions as social justice and corporate social responsibility," http://www.economist.com/node/1312947?story_id=1312947

127. D. Antunes and H. Thomas, "The Competitive (Dis)Advantages of European Business Schools," *Long Range Planning* 40 (2007), pp. 382–404, at 387.

128. A. Sen, *The Argumentative Indian: Writings on Indian History, Culture and Identity* (London: Penguin Books, 2005).

129. A. Sen, *A Lecture on India: Large and Small*, http://www.planningcommission.gov.in/reports/articles/profsen.pdf

130. "China's B-School Boom: Meet the New Managerial Class in the Making," *Businessweek,* January 9, 2006.

131. S. Maple, "The Growth of On-line Education in China," Ezinearticles, http://www.ezinearticles.com/?The-Growth-of-Online-Education-in-China&id=2306070

132. A. Damast: "China: Why Western B-Schools Are Leaving Red Tape, Difficult Partners, and Weak Demand Have Western Universities Closing Executive MBA Programs," *Businessweek,* May 15, 2008, http://www.businessweek.com/magazine/content/08_21/b4085056706207.htm?chan=top+news_top+news+index_news+%2B+analysis

133. http://www.theregister.co.uk/2006/10/04/google_talks_tories/

134. D. Carvajal, "English as Language of Global Education," *The New York Times*, April 11, 2007, http://www.select.nytimes.com/gst/abstract.html?res=F20714F73E5B0C728DDDAD0894DF404482

135. G. Tuchman, "Wannabe U: Inside the Corporate University" (Chicago: University of Chicago Press, 2009), p. 12.

136. O. Tusquets Blanca, *Todo Es Comparable* (Barcelona: Anagrama, 2003).

137. F. T. Marinetti, "The Founding and Manifesto of Futurism," *Le Figaro*, February 20, 1909.

8 The purpose of business schools

138. G. Vidal, *Point to Point Navigation: A Memoir 1964 to 2006* (London: Little Brown, 2006).

139. Ibidem., p. 3.

140. I. Kant, *Teoría y Práctica* (Madrid: Tecnos, 1986). Further explanations of Kant's views on the nexus between Theory and Practice can be found in J. G. Murphy: "Kant on Theory and Practice," http://www.homepages.law.asu.edu/~jeffriem/kantarticlea.htm

141. P. J. H. Shoemaker, "The Future Challenges of Business: Rethinking Management Education and Research," *California Management Review*, vol. 50, no. 3 (Spring 2008), pp. 119–39, at 120.

142. Ibid.

143. Ibid.

144. W. C. Bennis and J. O'Toole, "How Business Schools Lost Their Way," *Harvard Business Review* (May 2005), p. 3.

145. Ibid., p. 6.

146. J. Pfeffer and C. T. Fong, "The End of Business Schools? Less Success Than Meets the Eye," *Academy of Management Learning and Education*, vol. 1, no. 1 (2002), pp. 8–85.

147. D. Rigby, "Management Theory and Techniques: A Survey," *California Management Review*, 43 (2001), 139–60.

148. S. R. Barley, G. W. Meyer and D. C. Gash, "Cultures of Culture: Academics, Practitioners, and the Pragmatics of Normative Control," *Administrative Science Quarterly*, 33 (1988), pp. 24–60.

149. R. Dworkin, "Pragmatism, Right Answers, and True Banality," in *Pragmatism in Law & Society: New Perspectives on Law, Culture, and Society*, ed. M. Brint and W. Weaver (Boulder: Westview Press, 1991), p. 359, affirmed: "For more than a decade American legal theory has been too occupied in metatheoretical debates about its own character and possibility."

150. T. Mayne, "Architecture and Education," presentation at the International Architectural Education Summit, June 30, 2011, http://news.university.ie.edu/tag/international-architectural-education-summit

151. http://www.mbaworld.com/templates/mba/images/accreditation/pdf/MBA_criteria_0807.pdf

152. S. M. Datar, D. A. Garvin, and P. G. Cullen, *Rethinking the MBA: Business Education at a Crossroads* (Boston, MA: Harvard Business Press, 2010), pp. 47–73.

153. Ibid., p. 47.

154. Ibid., p. 48.

155. M. C. Moldeveanu and R. L. Martin, *The Future of the MBA: Designing the Thinker of the Future*, (New York, NY: Oxford University Press, 2008).

156. Ibid., p. 93.

157. Datar, Garvin, and Cullen, *Rethinking the MBA*, p. 299.

158. D. Bradshaw, "Dean Profiles: Joel Podolny of Yale," *Financial Times*, January 29, 2007, http://www.ft.com/cms/s/2/3409e660-ad5a-11db-8709-0000779e2340.html#ixzz1ASmG17wu, "It is hard to imagine that a business school dean could change a school by sheer force of enthusiasm. But you get the impression that Joel Podolny might just do that."

159. D. G. Faust, "The Role of the Univeristy in a Changing World," http://www.president.harvard.edu/speeches/faust/100630_ireland.php

160. C. Christenson, M. Horn, and C. Johnson, *Disruptive Class: How Disruptive Innovation Will Change the Way the World Learns* (New York: McGraw Hill, 2008).

161. P. de L'Etraz, "What Can an On-line Program Do for You?" *Biz Ed*, November–December (2010), pp. 34–9.

162. http://www.mba.yale.edu/MBA/curriculum/cases.shtml

163. Yale SOM website, http://www.mba.yale.edu/MBA/curriculum/cases.shtml

164. J. F. Fairbank, G. Labianca, and D. LeClair, "Three Year Forecast?" *Biz Ed*, May–June (2005), pp. 46–51, http://www.aacsb.edu/publications/archives/mayjune05/p46-51.pdf

165. P. Lorange, *Thought Leadership Meets Business: How Business Schools Can Become More Successful* (Cambridge: Cambridge University Press, 2008), p. 182.

166. A. H. Goodall, *Socrates in the Boardroom: Why Research Universities Should Be Led by Top Scholars* (Princeton, NJ: Princeton University Press, 2009), http://edition.cnn.com/2006/BUSINESS/06/06/execed.deans/

9   The students of tomorrow

167. D. Bejou, "Treating Students Like Customers: Think of Them As Customers to Be Managed for a Very Long Time," www.aacsb.edu/publications/archives/marapr05/p44-47.pdf

168. *The New York Times*, January 3, 2010.

169. Ibid.

170. J. S. Schultz, "When You Can Deduct the Cost of Your M.B.A.," *The New York Times*, January 20, 2010: "Basically, the bottom line of all of this was that the court concluded that the M.B.A. improved her pre-existing skills. If you can connect the dots between the courses you are taking and your existing skill set or your job, you can deduct it. That's the basic gist."

171. D. Bradshaw, in *Financial Times* (December 2, 2010), comments that "A growing number of schools now accept the GRE as well as the GMAT: 39 per cent of the 288 schools surveyed by Kaplan, as opposed to 24 per cent last year. However, of the business schools that accept the GRE, 69 per cent report that fewer than 1 in 10 applicants actually submit a GRE score instead of a GMAT one."

172. H. Gardner, *Multiple Intelligences: The Theory in Practice* (New York: Basic Books, 1993).

173. D. Goleman, *Emotional Intelligence: Why It Can Matter More than IQ*, (New York: Bantam Books, 1995).

174. R. E. Nisbett, *Intelligence and How to Get It: Why Schools and Cultures Count* (New York: W. W. Norton & Company, 2009), p. 2.

175. Ibid., p. 73.

176. Peter L. Berger, *Many Globalizations: Cultural Diversity in the Contemporary World* (Oxford: Oxford University Press, 2002).

177. D. Bok, *Our Underachieving Colleges: A Candid Look at How Much Students Learn and Why They Should Be Learning More* (Priceton, NJ: Princeton University Press, 2005).

178. Ibid., p. 195.

179. Ibid., p. 196.

180. T. Khanna and K. G. Palepu, "Emerging Giants: Building World-Class Companies in Developing Countries," *Harvard Business Review* (October 2006), pp. 60–9.

181. R. E. Nisbett, *The Geography of Thought: How Asians and Westerners Think Differently... And Why* (New York: Free Press, 2003).

182. Ibid., p. xvii.

183. Ibidem.

184. Ibid., p. xviii.

185. F. Fukuyama, The End of History and the Last Man (Free Press, 2006).

186. S. P. Huntington: *The Clash of Civilizations and the Remaking of World Order* (New York: Simon & Schuster, 1996).

187. R. E. Nisbett, op. cit., p. 227.

188. S. Cardús, *Bien Educados: Una defensa útil de las convenciones, el civismo y la autoridad* (Barcelona: Paidós, 2010).

189. B. Clement, "Firms Find It Pays to Relax Dress Code," *The Independent*, July 26, 2006, http://www.independent.co.uk/news/uk/this-britain/firms-find-it-pays-to-relax-dress-code-409316.html

190. Presentation at EFMD/AACSB Annual Conference, Paris, April 23, 2006, http://www.deanstalk.net/deanstalk/2006/07/dess_codes.html

191. H. L. A. Hart, *The Concept of Law* (Oxford: Oxford University Press, 1961).
192. T. M. Dodd, "Honor Code 101: an Introduction to the Elements of Traditional Honor Codes, Modified Honor Codes and Academic Integrity Policies," CAI, http://www.academicintegrity.org/educational_resources/honor_code_101.php

10 Faculty and knowledge creation: How does it work?

193. S. Rimer, "Harvard Task Force Calls for New Focus on Teaching and Not Just Research," *The New York Times*, May 10, 2007, http://www.nytimes.com/2007/05/10/education/10harvard.html
194. D. Mitra and P. N. Golder, "Does Academic Research Help or Hurt MBA Programs," *Journal of Marketing,* 72, September 2008, pp. 31–49; P. L. Drnevich, C. Armstrong, T. A. Crook, and T. R. Crook, "Do Research and Education Matter to Business School Rankings?" *International Journal of Management in Education*, 5, 2011, pp. 169–87.
195. C. Markides, "In Search of Ambidextrous Professors," *Academy of Management Journal* vol. 50, no. 4 (2007), pp. 762–8.
196. P. Lorange, *Thought Leadership Meets Business*, p. 1.
197. The Woodrow Wilson National Fellowship Foundation, "The Responsive PhD: Innovations in US Doctoral Education," 2005, http://www.woodrow.org/images/pdf/resphd/ResponsivePhD_overview.pdf
198. A. Hacker, "The Truth About Colleges," *The New York Review of Books*, November 3, 2005, http://www.nybooks.com/articles/archives/2005/nov/03/the-truth-about-the-colleges/
199. Ibid., p. 2.
200. Ibidem.
201. Ibidem.
202. Ibid., p. 3.
203. Taken from A. Tabucchi, "La gastritis de Platón," trans. Carlos Gumpert (Barcelona: Anagrama, 1988), p. 31.
204. *L'Expresso*, April 24, 1997.
205. D. Lapert, "Do Not Be Discouraged, Young Researchers in Management!" *Deanstalk,* April 4, 2006, http://www.deanstalk.net/deanstalk/2006/04/do_not_be_disco.html
206. http://www.becker-posner-blog.com/

207. http://orgtheory.wordpress.com/2006/07/10/benefits-of-basic-research/#more-302

208. http://orgtheory.wordpress.com/2006/07/06/knowledge-knowledge-and-veriphobia/

209. M. Gladwell, *The Tipping Point: How Little Things Can Make a Big Difference* (New York: Little Brown & Co., 2000).

210. E. Porter & G. Fabrikant, "A Big Star May Not a Profitable Movie Make," *The New York Times*, August 28, 2006, http://www.nytimes.com/2006/08/28/business/media/28cast.html?pagewanted=1&_r=1&th&adxnnl=1&emc=th&adxnnlx=1156764452-SpOp5MnnRPzbNeU/nKHbpQ

Epilogue

211. S. Iñiguez, "Business school RX: Humanities," February 14, 2011, http://www.businessweek.com/bschools/content/feb2011/bs20110210_718571.htm

Index